NOT GUILTY!

THE STORY OF
SAMUEL·S·LEIBOWITZ

FRED·D·PASLEY

GW00729127

1933

G. P. PUTNAM'S SONS

NEW YORK

SAMUEL S. LEIBOWITZ

CONTENTS

NOT GUILTY!

CHAPTER ONE

HAPPY ENDING

"SO help me God!"

The spring sunshine, slanting obliquely through the glazed and steel barred windows had laid a latticed pattern upon the courtroom floor. Like a tired chantey man the clerk droned the ritual of the oath. As the witness stood there, midway between judge and jury, parroting him, his upraised hand was silhouetted momentarily against the pattern.

His voice was flat, his face expressionless, his bearing mechanical. Only his eyes seemed alive. They were burningly intense—jet black pupils centered in preternaturally large whites and they seemed to be peering into remote distances.

He sagged into the witness chair and the hand vanished. The bars remained. He gazed across them as he had gazed through them for three years at Sing Sing as convict No. 75990. They symbolized for him not only the shadow of prison but the shadow of the electric chair.

Muted to faint echoes by the thick masonry of the courtroom walls, came the city sounds, the rumble of elevated trains, the clangor of trolley cars, the honking horns of automobiles and the whistles of traffic policemen.

Alien echoes they were in the decorous atmosphere of this august tribunal, where the People of the State of New York were prosecuting Harry L. Hoffman for murder in the first degree.

"So help me God!"

No aura of sanctity attached to the archaic formula for No. 75990; no sense of probity; nor honor; only guile, deceit and equivocation.

"Go split up your rewards with your bunch of lying witnesses. You know I'm as innocent as you are," he had screamed at District Attorney Albert C. Fach of Richmond County when they led him away to prison in May of 1924.

It was the month of May again now—May of 1929— and the place was Brooklyn.

Aloof, impersonal, Supreme Court Justice Burt Jay Humphrey turned in his high back swivel chair. Foreman Reginald C. Thomas and his peers in the jury box hunched forward. Spectators craned their necks.

They were looking not at the witness but at a man in a blue sack suit sitting at counsel for defense table, who was engrossed in the study of a paper of pins, a fence post, a needle and a spool of thread, a saw, a can opener, a fountain pen, a screw driver, hammer and nails.

Such commonplace articles would have gone unnoticed in a shop window or home but here they assumed dramatic qualities by reason of their very triviality. They were fraught with life and death implications. They represented the unknown quantity X.

Fingering the spool of thread as one might a chess

piece, the man moved it over by the can opener, rose tc his feet and walked around the table to stand before the witness. His voice was the only sound audible in the room as he began his examination:

Q. What is your name? A. Harry L. Hoffman.

Q. How old are you? A. Thirty-seven.

Q. Will you please speak loudly so we can all hear you? A. Yes, Mr. Leibowitz.

Q. Where were you born? A. In New York City.

Q. Just sit right back. Where were you educated? A. Boston.

Deftly the interrogator guided the witness through the routine preliminaries and the factual details. It was ten o'clock in the morning when he started; it was midafternoon when:

Q. Have you always maintained your innocence, Harry, from the start? A. I always have and I always shall, yes, sir.

Q. Harry, I am going to ask you to do some little things here to show whether you are a right handed man or a left handed man. I have brought a post here, with some nails and a hammer. I am going to ask you to show the jury later how you strike the nail with both your right and your left hand.

Q. When you were a child, Harry, you used to write with your left hand? A. I started to write with my left hand.

Q. How were you broken of that? A. By being rapped across the knuckles by my teacher.

Q. Aside from writing with your right hand, which hand do you always use? A. The left.

Q. For all normal purposes? A. Always.

Q. Recount some normal purposes. A. I shave with

my left hand. I lather my face. I use a knife, throw ball, sew, thread a needle, use a hammer, a screw driver, and tools like that.

Q. Do you deal cards? A. I deal cards with my left.

Q. Do you light a match? A. Yes, and fill my pipe and count money.

Q. Are you prepared now, Harry, to let these men give you any test they wish? A. Certainly.

NEVER in the history of the venerable courtroom had a man threaded a needle in the witness chair. Never had its high paneled walls resounded to the blows of a hammer driving home a nail. It was superb showmanship. It was Samuel Simon Leibowitz in action.

Leibowitz in action in his seventy-fifth first degree murder case. Leibowitz with seventy-four acquittals to his credit. Leibowitz, the immigrant Jewish boy, son of a pushcart peddler, now at thirty-six the most talked of criminal lawyer in New York City.

Which explained the packed courtroom, the tense attitude of spectators and jurors, the rapt attention to every gesture of the Leibowitz hand, to every inflection of the Leibowitz voice. For on this trial depended not only the ultimate fate of Hoffman but the prestige of the Leibowitz name and the political career of District Attorney Fach. He aspired to the Supreme Court bench and this was his *cause célèbre*.

The two adversaries were juxtaposed as the courtroom drama moved toward its climax. Fach, thick jowled, a man of massive presence, sat comfortably in the No. 1 chair at the prosecution table, benignly complacent. The case was a thrice told tale for him. He had come to court with his sixty experienced witnesses, his fifteen assistants, his one hundred and fifty cardboard cases of evidence, his exhibits from A to Z and 3,600 pages of previous testimony.

Fach had been associated with the case for five years. Leibowitz but three months. Fach had back of him the New York City Police Department, the chief medical examiner's office and his own detectives to prove Hoffman's guilt. Leibowitz had only Hoffman's word that he was innocent.

Ten thousand dollars was Leibowitz' minimum fee and he could hand pick his clients. Within a year, in fact, he was to be offered one hundred thousand dollars to defend Al Capone in the gang leader's income tax evasion trial at Chicago. Yet he had taken this case without fee.

Why? Because of a penny post card from the Raymond Street jail in Brooklyn. Laboriously scrawled with a lead pencil it read:

"Dear Mr. Leibowitz, I am writing this as a last desperate appeal. I do not know you personally and of course you don't know me. I am accused of murder but I am an innocent man. I was sentenced to from twenty years to life in Sing Sing. I have fought for five years to win my freedom. My friends raised a fund for my defense but that is gone. Will you help me?"

It challenged Leibowitz' interest and inherent sympathy for the underdog. He visited the jail and met the writer, Hoffman.

Leibowitz is an uncompromising skeptic. He has seen everything and heard everything. But the story he heard that day in the Raymond Street Jail so impressed him, so took possession of his heart and mind that he said to convict No. 75990:

"I'll defend you and I'll free you," and his only retainer was the penny post card.

HARRY L. HOFFMAN played the slide trombone in the Tall Cedars band and the first violin in the Grace M.E. Church orchestra of Port Richmond, Staten Island.

It was a treat to watch Harry nursing his fiddle, its flat belly tucked snugly under his double chin, and a sight for sore eyes to behold him tootling his trombone. He was only five feet, six, and weighed 190 pounds. Rotund as a billiken and chubby faced, his cheeks would distend as he put soul and feeling into the music until it seemed as if they would burst like a toy balloon if he exerted another ounce of lung power.

The band and orchestra, however, were but avocations for him. He earned his livelihood in an eight by ten booth high up in the rear of the gallery of the Palace Theater, the community's main stem movie house. He was a motion picture machine operator.

Life had given Harry a swell break if you asked him. Here he was at thirty-two with a wife he adored, two children he idolized, one-year-old Dorothy and five-year-old Mildred (Beanie)—and a bank account of almost five hundred dollars, the savings of nine years.

He owned a car, a second hand model T flivver sedan, which he had equipped with a $2.50 combination motometer and radiator cap with nickel plated mercury wings. Tuesday afternoons, his day off, he generally would take the family motoring.

Next to his slide trombone Harry was proudest of his deputy sheriff's badge, emblematic of his civic standing. He wore it pinned to the underside of his coat lapel. It had been given to him in 1916 by Sheriff Spiro Pitou.

In between reels at the Palace Harry might be met passing the time of day with Pete Marino, the barber, or chewing the fat with the boys in Symons Drug Store, across the street, the town pump and forum. His favorite tipple was chocolate ice cream soda and occasionally he would ride the ferry to Manhattan for a debauch of chow mein and green peppers.

In the big little world that was Port Richmond, fat, good natured, bespectacled Harry was a popular figure, moving contentedly about his circumscribed orbit.

He was transparently simple, of a susceptible imagination, something of a dreamer, and when in the solitude of his eight by ten coop, he lived in the melodrama, the romance and the mystery plots his machine projected on the screen. The characters became real; often he would step into their shoes. The hare and hounds action of detective drama thrilled him to the marrow.

A day in the life of Hoffman was a round of commonplaces. As, for example, Tuesday, March 25, 1924. He arose at 10:30, slipped into his bathrobe and slippers, padded downstairs to the basement, cleaned out the furnace and refueled it, opened the chimney damper and then went upstairs to shave and bathe.

Five-year-old Beanie was already outside playing with her chums. He called her in, brushed her teeth, washed her face and scrubbed her ears, as was his daily custom, while Agnes, his wife, got breakfast.

It was his day off and wouldn't Agnes go to Manhattan with him for a Chinese dinner? No, Agnes must stay home. One-year-old Dorothy was teething and very restless.

Harry probably didn't give a second thought to Agnes' decision as he stepped into his Ford sedan and drove to the St. George ferry. He was to remember it later as he was to remember every trifling incident of the day. Luck and chance were stacking the cards against him and Agnes' decision was card number one. He parked the sedan, bought a newspaper and took the 1:10 boat for New York, arriving there at 1:45.

It was a fine sunshiny day. Harry strolled leisurely up the Battery, dropping in at the stock brokerage offices of Hutton and Company, 60 Broadway, for a look at the board. He had a couple of shares of Stewart-Warner. The stock wasn't doing so well, and he left without even pausing for a word with his market adviser, Francis X. McCabe, in charge of the customers' room.

Turning off Broadway at Park Row, he started for the Oriental Restaurant in Pell Street, his favorite Chinese eating place. He suddenly remembered, however, that he had read in a Sunday newspaper of a shooting and killing there. Maybe it was another tong war. He would go instead to a place in Sixth Avenue near 28th Street. So retracing his steps to the Battery he took an elevated train and soon was wielding a pair of chopsticks over a bowl of chicken chow mein and green peppers.

His inner man at peace he rode back to the Battery and took the boat for Staten Island, arriving there at 4:30. He got in his car and drove directly home. Beanie's chums, Edith Goldenberg, 15, and Alice her sister, 10, were playing in the front yard, but Beanie wasn't there. He asked where she was.

"Beanie and baby sister and mother," said little Alice, "all went down to Aunt Lizzie's."

Aunt Lizzie was Mrs. Elizabeth Rowan, his wife's sister.

It was five o'clock. Harry drove down to the Rowans',

but his family had already left for home so he returned there to find them. Dorothy was crying.

Harry trotted her on his knee and sang to her until finally her eyes closed in slumber. He put her in her crib. His wife was opening a can of soup.

"Are you hungry?" she asked.

"No, I filled up on chow mein," said Harry.

She looked disappointed, so he joined her in a plate of soup just to be sociable.

Then he removed his trombone from its case and gave it a thorough cleaning and polishing. He and a few of the boys from the Tall Cedars Band were playing that night for the B. and O. dance. Harry left the house at seven o'clock and picked up three of them. The dance started at eight and finished at midnight. He was home and asleep by two o'clock.

Harry performed his usual household duties the next morning, Wednesday, practicing a while on his trombone while awaiting a tardy breakfast. Mrs. Hoffman had been reading a story in the local paper. She called Harry's attention to it. It told of the murder of a Mrs. Maude C. Bauer in the lonely Chelsea section of Staten Island.

"Gee," said Harry, as he scanned the details, "she only lived a few blocks from us."

"I never heard of her," said Mrs. Hoffman.

"Neither did I," replied Harry, and, helping himself to another cup of coffee, "You want to be careful where you go when I'm not along. We've had two other murders like that around here."

The newspaper account read in part:

"Mrs. Maude Bauer, 35 years old, was murdered on Staten Island yesterday afternoon, apparently by a fiend, who had enticed her into his automobile, a Ford sedan.

She was shot twice when she resisted his attempt to attack her. The crime was committed within 1,500 feet of where Mrs. Bauer's mother and three-year-old daughter sat waiting in a stalled automobile but they heard no sounds. The body was left by the roadside.

"Late last night all the police machinery of New York, working at high pressure, had failed to get the slayer or even a hopeful start on the trail that would lead to him.

"Satisfied that he was on Staten Island, the police closed every exit, including the ferries to Manhattan, to Brooklyn, and to New Jersey, and subjected all persons to searching examination. Uniformed men and men in plain clothes, afoot, on horseback, in police automobiles and on motorcycles, swept back and forth and criss-cross over the Island.

"Mrs. Bauer, wife of Walter Bauer, an electrical engineer, was waiting for a lift to a garage to get a tow for her car. She lived in Port Richmond with her husband, her two children, Maud, 7 years old, and Helen, 3; her father, George E. Pero, a retired postal clerk, and Mrs. Pero."

Finished with the story Harry kissed Agnes and the children good-by and left for his movie house five blocks away.

He stopped en route to buy a package of chewing gum in the candy store of Mr. and Mrs. Otto Jaeger. Mrs. Jaeger emerged from the living quarters in the rear as a bell attached to the front door tinkled.

"Good morning, Mama Jaeger," smiled Harry.

The usually beaming countenance of Mrs. Jaeger was wan and haggard; her eyes were red from weeping.

"Did you hear about the murder yesterday?" she asked.

"Yes, I just read about it."

"What do you think happened last night?"

"What?"

"Oscar was standing behind the counter and a half dozen detectives walked in and they said, 'Come on, Oscar, we want you.' Oscar thought they were kidding and laughed and said, 'What do you want me for?' They didn't say a single word. They grabbed him and yanked him over the counter and smashed the counter to splinters and took him down to the morgue or police headquarters and gave him the third degree and beat him and he came back only a little while ago hysterical, running around and shouting and breaking dishes. I had to call a doctor for him."

"How did they come to pick on Oscar?" asked Harry.

"Well, there were some children up there where this woman was murdered and they said the man had a Ford car. So that's why they picked Oscar up."

Harry bought his chewing gum and continued on to the theater. He passed the Masonic lodge hall and observed on a telegraph pole notice of a reward of one thousand dollars for the arrest and conviction of the murderer.

It contained a random description of a heavy set man wearing a brown hat, a brown overcoat and tortoise-shell glasses, driving a flivver sedan. Harry hurried into the theater and up to his coop where he changed his nose pincers for the thick-lensed tortoise-shell spectacles he wore at work.

Everybody was discussing the murder and the main stem wags were wise cracking to those who owned brown overcoats or wore glasses, "Where were you Tuesday?" and "You'd better change your benny."

They were kidding a clerk at the stamp window of the post office while Harry was there during the luncheon hour, and in the afternoon Otto Zeitz, Palace Theater orchestra leader, was joshed by the boys in Symons Drug Store because he had a brown hat, wore glasses and owned a Ford sedan.

Harry left home early Thursday morning. The theater was changing its program and he had to prepare the cues and get ·the spotlights ready.

In front of the public school at Heberton Avenue and Vreeland Street he encountered his old friend, Policeman Joseph Venditto, guiding the children across the avenue.

"Hello, Joe," he called.

"Hello, Harry," and, when Hoffman had gone on a few steps, "Hey, you know," laughing, "you answer that description pretty good."

"What description?"

"Why, the description of that fellow they're looking for for the murder."

"I'll get a false mustache," was Harry's comeback, but a vague uneasiness stirred within him.

The telegraph pole in front of the Masonic Hall had burgeoned with a new placard. The rewards now totaled $8,500 and citizens were urged to read the local newspaper for a full description of the murderer. Harry bought one, took it up to his coop. There it was staring at him in glaring black type—the description.

He went over it line by line. The man the police wanted was heavy set. So was he. Dark complexioned with thick black hair. So was he. A brown hat, a brown overcoat, tortoise-shell spectacles, a Ford sedan. Harry's overcoat was gray but otherwise the description fitted; although he hadn't worn his brown hat Tuesday.

With his working specs on he went down to get the cues for the new vaudeville acts. The city fireman, on duty in the wings, and the stage hands bantered him about the tortoise shell frame. The property man offered to sell him a brown overcoat to go with his brown hat.

The evening papers came out with official announcements that every Ford sedan owner would be questioned and made to furnish an alibi for his movements on the afternoon of March 25.

The authorities appealed to "all citizens who have any suspicions whatsoever, no matter how slight they may be, as to the identity of the murderer to communicate with us by mail or telephone, anonymously or otherwise. Detectives will investigate each bit of information."

Mrs. Bauer had been killed with a foreign make of firearm—a Spanish pistol, said the police. Consoling statement! Harry had no such gun. His home arsenal consisted of a .32 caliber American Bulldog; a .38 navy revolver and a .25 Colt automatic pistol.

Dr. George Mord, assistant medical examiner, had completed his autopsy. Of the two bullet wounds, one was in the neck and one in the abdomen. He had recovered but one bullet—the one fired into the abdomen—although both shells were found. The police had been studying the bullets and shells and in the Friday morning newspapers their finding was announced. Harry read it at the breakfast table.

Mrs. Bauer had been killed with a .25 Colt automatic pistol.

He read it and went to the telephone. He called McCabe, his market advisor with Hutton and Company, the stock brokerage firm.

"Do you recall," he asked, "seeing me in your office about two o'clock Tuesday afternoon?"

"I'm sorry," came the answer, "but I didn't see you."

It dawned on Hoffman, then, that he had no alibi. The Chinese waiters in the Sixth Avenue restaurant wouldn't remember him. He hadn't met a soul he knew on the ferry trips between Staten Island and New York. He had seen nobody, so far as accounting for his movements went on that day, until he arrived home at five o'clock and talked to the little Goldenberg girls. Mrs. Bauer had been murdered about four o'clock.

Man is a bundle of inherited emotions transmitted from the dim past when the imagination of his superstitious ancestors peopled the jungle wastes with unseen forces and malevolent gods. Blind fate and circumstance had cornered Hoffman and he succumbed to the primal instinct of fear.

That day he wore a cap to work, had Pete Marino trim his hair and had a confidential talk with Racey Parker, his buddy and a motion picture operator at the Liberty Theater, nearby. Racey had dropped in on him at the Palace. He had passed Mrs. Bauer's funeral procession and remarked he had never "seen such crowds and so much excitement in all my life."

"You know, Racey," said Hoffman, "that thing has got on my mind. Don't look so scared. I didn't kill her, but it's got me worried."

"How?"

"Well, for instance, you are here with me now. Where were you last Friday on your day off?"

"I don't know."

"Let me put it this way. Have you ever gone to the city and come back and not meet a single solitary soul that you knew?"

"Yes, sure. Often."

"Well, I'm in the same boat. I went to the city that day

and I didn't see anybody. So far as I know, nobody saw me. And now all owners of Ford sedans are to be questioned. I haven't got a soul to turn to. If you would say that I was in your booth Tuesday afternoon it would save all this unpleasantness. You know what they did to Oscar Jaeger."

Racey was eager and willing to help his friend and they framed an alibi that Hoffman was in his coop at the Liberty from 3:30 until around 4:30.

Hoffman that night burned in the furnace a revolver holster he had bought the previous December from the sporting goods store of Abercrombie and Fitch. And next day he mailed to his brother, Albert Hoffman, in the Bronx, the .25 Colt automatic pistol, with a note, reading:

"Hold this. Keep it in a safe place. If you hear of my being in trouble give it to my attorney."

Hoffman for nine years had been grinding out movie plots—eight and ten thousand feet of them three times a day six days a week; living a dream life in his isolated coop, viewing the world as a detached spectator. And now he, himself, was involved in a situation as inconceivably fantastic as any he had ever projected on the screen.

In the movies virtue was ever triumphant. The scenario writer inevitably extricated the innocent victim in the last five hundred feet of film. There was always a happy ending.

Instinctively Hoffman viewed his plight from the movie standpoint—clung desperately to the hope he would be vindicated and all the while in his frenzy to escape the unseen forces he felt closing in on him he was committing acts of damning import. Fear had hypnotized him. Plunged from his dream world into the hard realities, life had become a nightmare to him. He moved about like a somnambulist.

He sent for Harry Bartell, the painter. Could Bartell paint the sedan right away? No, he couldn't. He was pretty busy. The job would have to wait a few weeks. He removed the fancy radiator cap and motometer and offered to sell the car to Thomas Marron, manager of the neighborhood tea store, for one hundred and sixty-five dollars with a five dollar down payment. Marron didn't buy it.

The dread thing Hoffman had anticipated for days came to pass Sunday evening, March 30, while he was grinding out a two-reel comedy at the Palace. His wife telephoned him, "The police are here." They wanted to see the car which was locked in the garage. They examined its interior with a spotlight. Then: Did Harry have any guns? Yes, two. They took the American Bulldog and the navy .38 to the precinct station.

Hoffman followed them next morning when he was summoned into the presence of Captain Ernest L. Van Wagner of the local detective bureau. Was Hoffman the owner of a brown overcoat? No. Did he have a brown hat? Yes. It was old though, and he seldom wore it. How many pairs of glasses did he have? Two, the nose pincers he was wearing and tortoise-shell spectacles used at work.

Did he own a .25 Colt Automatic? No, and he never had. What did he do the afternoon of Tuesday the 25th? He went to Manhattan, visited his stock broker's office, rode the L to Chatham Square and back to the Battery, then returned to Staten Island where he dropped in at the Liberty Theater for a chinfest with his friend Racey Parker.

That was all for Hoffman that day but he must return

for further questioning on the morrow. He did and this time Parker was present. The interrogation was substantially the same as on Monday except that Captain Van Wagner asked Parker if Hoffman had visited him and Parker said he had.

Hoffman was allowed to go home. Weeks passed and it seemed as if the police had forgotten him. They hadn't. They were occupied with a choice morsel of information supplied to them by one John P. Schaefer, a clerk employed by Abercrombie and Fitch. He had been reading the newspapers and studying the pictures they published of Hoffman. He was sure he had sold Hoffman a revolver holster and he so stated in a letter written to Captain Van Wagner.

It was April 17 when Hoffman was again escorted into Van Wagner's presence. The captain's manner was abrupt and his voice harsh as he shot at the unsuspecting Hoffman:

"We've learned you had a holster for a .25 caliber Colt automatic."

"Well—well—yes, I had one."

"What did you do with it?"

"I burned it up."

"Why did you burn it up?"

"I didn't want to leave it lying around the house."

"Well, then, you had a gun for it, too, didn't you?"

Hoffman was dazed. How had they learned about that holster? How much more had they uncovered? They probably had questioned his brother, Albert, and knew all about the gun. They were just playing cat and mouse with him. He was trapped.

"Yes, Captain," he blurted, "I had a .25 Colt. I mailed it to my brother, Al. He's still got it."

Hoffman didn't return home that day to Agnes and the children. He was put under arrest charged with first degree murder. He tossed the night through on an iron bunk in a police station cell with but one thought to comfort him—that the alibi framed with Racey Parker was still intact. He had slipped a message out to his old buddy to "stand firm."

The police brought Parker to confront him the next afternoon.

"What have they been doing, Racey," asked Hoffman, "bulldozing you?"

"No," Parker's face was flint. "You told me you didn't have a .25 caliber Colt. You lied to me. I'm through."

He stalked away and with him went Hoffman's last hope. The structure of falsehood he had so painstakingly fabricated for his exoneration lay in ruins. His little world had collapsed.

Staten Island, lying like an inverted pear five miles south of the tip of Manhattan, is essentially rural, a collection of little hamlets, each with its Main Street and its intensive small town life. The murder of Mrs. Bauer had stirred the island to its depths. Talk of lynching was common.

Hoffman was a Jew in a community essentially Gentile. The Jews comprised less than three per cent of the total population of 140,000. Arrested on Thursday, he was arraigned Monday, April 21, pleading not guilty, and as he was bustled away manacled to a detective, "a howling mob of men, women and children spat upon him and shrieked 'murderer.' "

The populace was clamoring for a victim. And the authorities took their cue. Hoffman was indicted April 25 and went to trial May 19 before County Judge J. Harry Tiernan in the Richmond County Courthouse, St. George, Staten Island.

He had no money to retain a lawyer. The five hundred dollars he had saved was needed by Agnes and the two children. It was all they had. The court appointed attorney Alfred V. Norton as his counsel. Four days was consumed in selecting a jury, five hundred talesmen being examined. And six days in the taking of testimony.

Hoffman's acts returned to confound him like multiple shades of Banquo's ghost. The haircut, the false alibi, the burned holster, the effort to sell the Ford sedan, the sending of the .25 Colt automatic pistol to his brother, Albert—District Attorney Fach made the most of each of them.

"The consciousness of guilt," he thundered, "continued to pursue this defendant!"

Detective Sergeant Harry F. Butts, ballistics expert of the New York City police department, testified Hoffman's pistol had been fired when he examined it. Also that the fatal bullet "could have been discharged from the two shells found beside the body," and that the "two shells could have been fired from the Hoffman pistol."

And Professor Frank N. Whittier, bacteriologist, pathologist and photomicrographist, traveled from Brunswick, Maine, to Staten Island to testify that "the firing pin of Hoffman's pistol discharged the shells."

Barbara Fahs, thirteen-year-old school girl, and Matthew McCormack, a patrolman, identified Hoffman as the driver of the Ford sedan.

The jury retired the evening of May 28 and returned with its verdict at seven o'clock the morning of May 29. Hoffman was guilty of murder in the second degree.

Within ten minutes Judge Tiernan had sentenced him
from twenty years to life in Sing Sing at hard labor.
Three deputy sheriffs were leading him out of the courtroom when he turned and screamed at District Attorney
Fach:

"Go split up your rewards with your bunch of lying
witnesses. You know I'm as innocent as you are."

Handcuffed to a couple of guards Hoffman made the
trip to Sing Sing the morning of May 31 in the comfortable seven-passenger sedan of Sheriff Harry Rudolph
of Richmond County. He was received at the prison by
Chief Clerk Edward Hickey who inventoried his worldly
wealth. It consisted of $3.03 in cash, a pocket mirror, a
comb, a toothbrush and a ninety-eight cent watch.

"You know I won't be in Sing Sing long," was his farewell to Sheriff Rudolph. "I am going to appeal right away,
and I am confident that I will be acquitted at my new
trial."

He had much to learn about the high cost of justice.
Three hundred thousand words of testimony had been
pothooked by court stenographers during the trial and
would have to be transcribed in book form before an
appeal could be taken. The least estimate for the job
would be $1,500. Beside, there would be an attorney's
fee—another $1,500, as well as incidental expenses. Hoff-
man might be as innocent of crime as a new-born babe
but it would avail him nothing without the cash in hand.

Meanwhile the Sing Sing routine was functioning with
the celerity and mathematical precision of a Ford as-
sembly plant conveyor system to process the raw product
that was the easy going, hail-fellow-well-met slide trom-
bonist of the Tall Cedars Band into the finished felon.

It began at the south gate, where new prisoners are

received. The armor-plated steel door opened, Sheriff Rudolph drove in, the door closed, and Hoffman, handcuffs and manacles removed, was delivered into the custody of a guard. Up a narrow sidewalk to a one-story brick building, the guard marched him. In a room filled with desks and filing cabinets, a stolid robot with a scratchy pen jotted down his meager who's who, asking him some sixty form questions. He was photographed, Bertilloned, refingerprinted and given his prison number.

The routine, in the person of the guard, shunted him along to another building where he was stripped of his civilian clothes and searched for drugs. An expert in anatomical hideaways peered into his mouth, investigated his gums, explored his ears and pried beneath the nails of his toes and fingers. Followed a shower and the issuance of an outfit of coarse underwear, a hickory shirt, brogan shoes, gray coat and pants and cap. The suit was three times too large and flapped ridiculously when he walked. It seemed somehow to swallow up his identity. His best friend would not have recognized him. It completed the processing routine. Harry L. Hoffman had disappeared. In his place stood convict No. 75990.

Next, the hospital for examination by the physician, the surgeon, the psychiatrist and the physiologist. The prison chaplain inquired into the state of his soul.

Then to the bucket rack, in a corner of the yard, for an iron slop pail, and finally to the cell block of the No. 13 gallery, oldest building at Sing Sing, a rock structure built one hundred years ago, where newcomers undergo their reception period, in what amounts practically to solitary confinement, to impress upon them the harsh reality of their status.

They led Hoffman through a narrow corridor to his cell.

It was seven feet long, three feet three inches wide, and six feet seven inches high. Its walls, floor and ceiling were of rock. It was in effect an above-ground dungeon, for no sunlight ever reached it and it was almost without ventilation. Its furnishings consisted of an iron cot, a straw mattress, pillow, blankets, an electric light, a tin drinking cup and the iron slop pail.

On that May day in 1924, when Hoffman's identity was merged into the anonymity of two thousand other Sing Sing inmates, he was also deprived of all personal volition regarding habits and conduct. He was strait-jacketed into a daily program of existence that prescribed for his every movement. His life was regulated by bells and whistles. A bell rang at 6:00 A.M. to awaken him; a second bell at 6:30 for him to be up and dressed, and to shuffle out to the open sewer to empty his iron slop pail; a third bell at seven o'clock for breakfast—prison hash or cereal; a whistle at 7:50 for work on the coal pile; a whistle at 12:00 noon for mess; another at 12:50 for "back to work," and on through the day until sunset and the return to his cell with lights out at 9:30.

So it went with Hoffman behind the high gray walls of Sing Sing, watching empty time creep by, waiting for letters that never arrived, for visitors that never came—forgotten by the world and apparently by his friends and relatives. Still he hoped.

The days lengthened into weeks, May became June and July was just around the corner when a bit of news seeped in to him. The Motion Picture Machine Operators Union, Local 306, of which he was a member, was raising a fund to finance an appeal and a new trial. Hoffman couldn't believe it—it was too good to be true—but a few days later a letter which he opened with a pounding heart confirmed it. The Union had raised $25,000 and retained in Hoffman's behalf a fighting attorney, Leonard A. Snitkin, former municipal judge of New York City.

Drama of a kind Hoffman had never unreeled for the screen preceded the Union's action. Its one thousand members had first sat as a jury to deliberate on his guilt or innocence. The verdict, returned by unanimous vote, was that he was innocent.

"A factor in the vote," explained Harry Macklin, president of the Union, "was our inherent belief in Hoffman, born of long acquaintanceship and familiarity with the character of the man."

The significance of the action was that Hoffman might have a new trial if he were willing to take a chance with another jury that might send him to the electric chair.

Would he do that?

Gladly.

Attorney Snitkin went to work with zealous promptitude and on July 7, 1924, filed his appeal with the Appellate Division of the New York State Supreme Court for a reversal of Hoffman's conviction, and the new trial.

The indictment upon which Hoffman was tried for murder in the first degree, it should be explained, read that he committed the crime in an attempt to commit a felony "without a design to effect the death" of Mrs. Bauer. The seven words in the quotation marks represent the crux of the appeal and demonstrate likewise the niceties, if not the preciosities, of legal phraseology. Snitkin cited them and stressed the fact that while Hoffman was indicted for murder in the first degree he was convicted for murder in the second degree.

The Appellate Division, upholding Snitkin in a unanimous opinion, handed down a decision reading in part that in County Judge J. Harry Tiernan's charge to the jury he erred in listing "all degrees of homicide, on the theory that the homicide may have been committed with premeditation and 'with a design' to effect death, when the indictment charged a felony killing 'without a design to effect death.' " The decision then went on to state that the jury had found Hoffman guilty of murder in the second degree and therefore had found "an intent to kill" when the indictment expressly charged there was an absence of intent.

In other and plainer words, as expressed by Justice Walter H. Jaycox, who wrote the opinion, "There is no second degree of the crime as charged in this indictment. The jurors were permitted to find a fact denied in the indictment and to base their verdict thereon."

We are getting ahead of our story. When District Attorney Albert C. Fach, Hoffman's nemesis, was apprised of Snitkin's entry into the case and that he intended to file an appeal, he issued a statement that, "No errors were made by the trial judge. If the verdict is reversed, however, the people of the state of New York will have no complaint. If there should be a retrial I am confident that the verdict will not be for second degree but for first degree murder"—with death in the electric chair.

Hoffman, deluding himself with visions of speedy vindication, learned more about the inexplicabilities of the law. Whereas, in Judge Tiernan's court, but ten days had been consumed in finding him guilty and putting him in Sing Sing, two and a half years passed from the time Snitkin filed his appeal until the Appellate Division handed down its decision.

It was February 4 of 1927 when Justice Jaycox' opinion was announced. District Attorney Fach immediately petitioned the Court of Appeals for a review of the decision. The petition was granted and more delay ensued, but in midsummer the Court of Appeals sustained the Appellate Division and Hoffman, after more than three years in Sing Sing, journeyed back to the Richmond County Jail to await his second trial, under a new foolproof indictment for first degree murder.

It was early the next spring—March 4 of 1928—when Hoffman launched his second fight for freedom. It ended abruptly two weeks later when Attorney Snitkin collapsed of a heart attack while cross-examining a state witness and was unable to proceed. A mistrial was declared. Snitkin recovered sufficiently to argue for a change of venue, which was granted.

And Hoffman, caged in his cell, saw spring pass into summer and summer into fall. It was November 7 when the third trial started in Brooklyn. It lasted three weeks. The jury after deliberating twenty hours reported it could not reach an agreement and was dismissed. Snitkin made a motion for bail, which was denied. Hoffman, in so far as freedom was concerned, was no better off than in 1924 when the gates of Sing Sing closed behind him.

He had been transferred from Staten Island to the Raymond Street jail in Brooklyn. His hope now centered in Snitkin's promise to continue his fight at a fourth trial. Snitkin never fulfilled the promise. He died of heart disease January 19, 1929, and Hoffman was left not only without an attorney but without funds to retain new counsel. The $25,000 raised by the Motion Picture Machine Operators had been exhausted.

An idea born of desperation came to him. He would write to the criminal lawyer whose name was a byword in every prison. Thus Hoffman made his penny postcard plea because "I am an innocent man," and "I have fought for five years to win my freedom." He concluded with the direct appeal, "Will you help me?"

It was a fortuitous if not a happy ending.

CHAPTER TWO

SAMUEL SHOWMAN LEIBOWITZ

"DO any of you gentlemen know Horatio J. Sharrett . . . ?"

The Leibowitz manner was frank and guileless—oh, so ingenuously frank and guileless!—as the sonorous syllables of the name rolled unctuously from the Leibowitz tongue to surge in ear-filling volume through the courtroom. He was addressing the twelve talesmen in the jury box, but it was from none of them that the answer came.

A strident voice cut in almost before he had finished the question. District Attorney Albert C. Fach had leaped to his feet with incredible agility for one of his ponderous bulk. His face was livid with rage. He waggled a quivering forefinger at the bland and smiling Leibowitz, and:

"I object."

"He is a brother," continued Leibowitz, "of Clinton J. Sharrett, chairman of the Republican County Central Committee of Richmond County, Staten Island."

Fach was pirouetting like a dancing bear, and roaring:

"I object."

Justice Burt Jay Humphrey, imperturbably judicial in

his flowing black robes, cast an interrogative glance at Leibowitz' adversary. It had a soothing effect.

"I object to the characterization, your Honor," he said.

"Sustained," murmured his Honor, and Fach out of the corner of his mouth snarled at Leibowitz, "Don't play politics."

"We'll get along nicely," purred Leibowitz, "if counsel will address his objections to the court but not if he makes them *sotto voce* to me and the jury."

With which Leibowitz, elated, resumed his task of jury picking. Fach was worried. Three times he had prosecuted Harry L. Hoffman and his familiarity with the case had instilled in him a definite sense of self-confidence and of his complete mastery of its finest details. His clashes with Snitkin had only served to enhance the feeling, for they had enabled him to strengthen the case's vulnerable points. He was like an army general in the field already occupying an advantageous position, who has had abundant leisure to entrench himself securely and refortify.

This fourth trial, however, was developing problems in strategy and artifices of attack with which he had never had to reckon. Leibowitz was a new kind of tactician. Only a few days before the trial he had broadcast that a person as yet unnamed would be revealed as the murderer of Mrs. Maude C. Bauer, and that:

"I will produce two new witnesses who saw him and know that he committed the crime. These women have lived in fear of their lives that the fiendish slayer of Mrs. Bauer would attack them if he learned of their knowledge."

It seemed to Fach too absurd to consider.

"Just bluffing," he snorted, "talking for the effect on prospective jurors."

Fach apparently was mistaken. Leibowitz continued talking right into the courtroom, hammering away at the talesmen with such questions as:

"If you find the evidence shows a really guilty man was whitewashed, would you hesitate to acquit this defendant, regardless of whom your verdict might hit?"

And again:

"It is not the part, ordinarily, of the defense to produce a criminal before the bar of justice—that is up to the district attorney—but before this trial is over we will produce the real murderer."

It frayed Fach's nerves. In his opening address, after saying he would prove Hoffman was the driver of the Ford sedan in which Mrs. Bauer rode to her death and that it was Hoffman's pistol that killed her, he thundered at the jury:

"And we will show you conclusively that Horatio J. Sharrett had nothing at all to do with this murder, as has been inferentially said here."

"Your Honor," interjected Leibowitz mildly, "I did not inferentially say that Mr. Sharrett was connected with this murder. I made no such remark."

There had indeed been nothing of inference in Leibowitz' blunt opening address. He had related cold facts. Mrs. Bauer's body was discovered by two schoolboys alongside an old tote road—popularly known as Lovers' Lane.

"Motorcycle Policeman Thomas Cosgrove was summoned by the boys," recounted Leibowitz, "and he sped to the nearest telephone to give the alarm. On his return trip he saw a Ford sedan coming out of the lane, and, lo and behold, as large as life in that car was Horatio J. Sharrett."

Leibowitz explained that Sharrett, a realty developer and building contractor, had a construction job in the neighborhood and thus had a legitimate right to be there. It was also obvious that he would have a rope readily available.

Motorcycle Policeman Cosgrove accosted Sharrett and Leibowitz quoted the conversation:

"Do you know, Mr. Sharrett, that a woman has been murdered?"

"Oh yeah? Is that so?"

Whereupon Mr. Sharrett drove away without inquiring as to the woman's identity and the circumstances of her death.

Leibowitz carried his attack on past the jury box and into the examination of the prosecution's witnesses. Robert Ferguson, grocer's delivery boy, was on the stand. The day of the murder he had stopped his truck near the spot where Mrs. Bauer's body was found. A motorist drove up alongside.

Q. Did you not tell your boss and maintain for weeks afterwards that it was Mr. Sharrett you saw? A. I thought it was.

Q. Did you tell Detective Lewis on the night after the murder that it was Mr. Sharrett? A. Yes.

Likewise with Motorcycle Policeman Cosgrove:

Q. Did you examine Mr. Sharrett or his car? A. No.

Q. Did you search him to see if he had a pistol? A. No.

Also with Police Inspector Ernest L. Van Wagner, captain of detectives on Staten Island:

Q. On the Thursday and Friday after the murder, did

you send detectives to ask Horatio J. Sharrett to come to your office? A. Yes.

Q. Did he come up? A. No.

Q. Did not Mr. Fach ask you to lay off Mr. Sharrett and give him a clean bill of health? (Fach was on his feet with an objection which was sustained. Leibowitz reframed the question.)

Q. Did Mr. Fach tell you he had interrogated Mr. Sharrett and that Mr. Sharrett was O.K.? A. Yes.

Nor was the striking resemblance between Sharrett and Hoffman—so far as concerned general description—overlooked. Both were heavy set; both dark complexioned; both wore or owned tortoise-shell glasses; both drove Ford sedans.

Thus, relentlessly, Leibowitz bludgeoned away at Sharrett, shifting attention from his client and putting Fach on the defensive for the first time since the inception of the case. The full glare of the trial spotlight was turned on the wealthy and politically influential Staten Islander. The common topic of conversation was, "What will Leibowitz do to him when he gets him in the witness chair?"

The harassed Sharrett steeled himself for the verbal rack. He was called to the stand the ninth day of the trial, and the *dénouement* was startling. His examination was so cursory as to be scarcely even a formality. He was questioned merely as to his movements on the day of the murder. Leibowitz was a revelation of urbane graciousness and courtesy. He was sweetness and light personified.

Sharrett stepped from the stand mystified, the courtroom fans leaned back in chagrined bewilderment and the wily Leibowitz shook hands with himself. His maneuver had succeeded. He had outflanked the enemy, as it were, in the preliminary skirmish of the campaign. Sharrett was the means to that end. Through him he had shown it would have been circumstantially possible for another man to have become involved in Hoffman's predicament. He had established incontrovertibly in the jurors' minds the portentous element of "reasonable doubt," and to that extent had weakened Fach's case, and strengthened his own.

AN old military axiom has it that the test of generalship is not the number of victories gained but the use to which each is put in relation to the whole scheme of the campaign. Leibowitz, judged by this standard, is a master strategist who conceives his every move with painstaking deliberation and blocks it into the pattern of his case with the meticulous care of an architect's draftsman penciling a scale drawing.

Before Leibowitz entered Justice Humphrey's courtroom in Brooklyn the morning of May 6, 1929, he had read 3,600 pages, or 750,000 words of testimony, poring over it until he knew its salient details by heart and the part played by each of the state's sixty witnesses as well as by the fourteen for the defense. He had gone into the laboratory of the New York City morgue for clinical observation of gunshot wounds; he had spent three months studying the science of ballistics, and the cryptic hieroglyphics imprinted upon the caps of shells and surfaces of bullets when fired from pistols; he had checked weather charts to determine the visibility on March 25 of 1924 and whether the sun was shining brightly.

His analysis of Fach's case revealed three structural bases, or three main props. They were (1) Barbara Fahs, thirteen-year-old schoolgirl and star witness, whose testimony was that Hoffman was the driver of the Ford sedan in which Mrs. Bauer obtained a lift and rode to her death; (2) Patrolman Matthew J. McCormack, who identified Hoffman as driving away from the vicinity of the murder a few minutes after its commission, and (3) the state's ballistics experts, Detective Sergeant Harry F. Butts of the New York police department, Professor Frank N. Whittier, photomicrographist of Brunswick, Maine; and Colonel Roy D. Jones, U. S. A., retired, formerly of the Smith and Wesson Company, all of whom testified that the bullet found in Mrs. Bauer's body and the two shells beside it came from Hoffman's .25 caliber automatic Colt pistol.

The remaining witnesses, needless to say, had their value, too, but it was secondary. They were the trimmings, the decorative ensemble, so to speak, of the Fach structure. They would be demolished in the general crash if Leibowitz could only knock the three main props from under it.

Having utilized Sharrett to his advantage, Leibowitz, the master strategist, stepped aside to permit Leibowitz, the showman extraordinary, to interrogate an obscure witness named Edward Schneider, who was employed as a woodchopper near the spot where Mrs. Bauer was murdered. His testimony was perfunctory—merely fixing the time of the killing, he having heard the two revolver shots —and neither Attorney Alfred V. Norton, Hoffman's counsel in the first trial, nor Snitkin, in the second and third trials, had bothered to cross-examine him. But Leibowitz—ah!

Fach had concluded a humdrum examination—the story had been staled for him through repetition—and he had dismissed Schneider with a curt, "That is all," when

Leibowitz arose as the woodchopper was leaving the chair, halted him, walked over to him and:

"You say the shots were how far apart?"

"About a minute."

"A minute is a long time. Suppose you clap your hands to indicate the interval," and Leibowitz brought the palms of his hands together in a resounding smack. A brief wait, then another smack.

"That fast?" he asked.

"Faster."

"Like that?" and Leibowitz clapped again.

"No, more like this," and Schneider essayed a timid clap.

"Louder," said Leibowitz.

Schneider clapped again.

"Now the next bullet," said Leibowitz.

A long pause and another clap.

Leibowitz frowned and pursed his lips as if in deep perplexity. He pulled out his watch and noted the time aloud as he had Schneider clap again. Fach produced a watch, one by one the jurors produced their watches, and finally Justice Humphrey himself produced his. Leibowitz suggested His Honor's watch be used as the official timepiece, and instructed Schneider:

"Now when I say 'Go,' you clap your hands once. Clap your hands a second time when you think a sufficient interval had elapsed for the firing of the second bullet. His Honor will time you."

Schneider, who by now had become skilled in his impromptu skit, obliged with alacrity, and His Honor ruled that three seconds had elapsed between the shots.

Leibowitz beamed upon the court and the twelve good men and true.

"Thank you, Your Honor," he bowed, and turning, with another bow, "Thank you, gentlemen of the jury."

How had this benefited Leibowitz? Let him tell it as he did to the biographer in expounding his philosophy of courtroom procedure:

"I try to make the testimony vital; I try to make it animate; dramatic; I try to make it live. That is only a beginning. I avail myself of every opportunity to advance my cause. If I don't find an opportunity I make one. That's what I did with Schneider, an inconsequential witness. Do you know what I accomplished through him? No? I excited the jury's interest and induced it to go to work for me—I mean the timing with the watches. Experience has taught me that whenever I can contrive to do that I have stimulated a responsive attitude, a receptive mood, a subconscious tendency to favor my side of the case. I have used the Schneider expedient with variations scores of times and have yet to see it fail."

Tongue in cheek at credulous humanity, behind the bland mask of Leibowitz, the showman, peeps Leibowitz, the crafty fox of courtroom psychologists. He it was who seated in the jury box a shipyard superintendent, a cotton converter, a factory manager, a civil engineer, a railroad engineer, a bridge contractor, a building construction foreman, among others. He wanted a preponderance of technical brains. He wanted men with forthright understanding and appreciation of things mechanical, who would react sympathetically to an audacious project he had evolved to annihilate at one stroke the bulwark of the prosecution's case.

Fach was unsuspecting. Patiently Leibowitz bided his time; methodically he developed his plan of attack as the Hoffman drama moved toward its unanticipated climax.

Aged Mrs. Catherine Pero, a frail, drooping figure in black, mother of Mrs. Bauer, told her story for the fourth time. She detailed the incidents leading up to the murder and the discovery of the body in the recitative tone of one speaking set lines. Her testimony was like a prologue. It keyed the drama.

The story was a simple one, its essence was of the home, the common things of life; the everyday existence of people in humble circumstances.

Mrs. Bauer, a comely brunette of thirty-five, finishing her housework early on March 25, 1924, took her three-year-old daughter, Helen, and with Mrs. Pero set out from Port Richmond in Mrs. Pero's car to visit a married sister in the village of Bloomfield, five miles away.

They drove south and west, Mrs. Bauer at the wheel, and were within less than a mile of their destination when an untoward accident occurred. A speeding motor truck, hogging the road, bore down upon them, and to avoid a collision Mrs. Bauer swerved off the concrete onto a dirt shoulder. It was snow and rain soaked and the car was hopelessly mired.

They were headed west in Merrill Avenue and within 150 feet of an intersecting highway known as South Avenue. The section was sparsely settled and heavily wooded.

The time was 3:30 P.M. Mrs. Bauer, after futile attempts to extricate the car under its own power, got out and walked down the Avenue in search of a tow or a telephone to notify a garage. A Ford sedan, bound north in South Avenue, halted as Mrs. Bauer reached the corner. There was a short conversation and the driver opened the door. Mrs. Bauer called back to Mrs. Pero, "Mother, I am going with this man to get a rope." She got into the sedan and it turned around to go south in South Avenue. The time was about 3:40.

"That was the last time I saw her alive," recited Mrs. Pero. "I remained in the car for maybe fifteen minutes, playing with little Helen to keep her from crying. A motorist came along then, put a rope on the car and pulled it out of the mud onto the concrete.

"The only thing for me to do was to continue to wait for my daughter. I guess I sat there twenty-five minutes longer before Patrolman Thomas Cosgrove of the New Dorp police station drove up and asked me who I was and what I was doing. I told him. He then said, 'There is a young woman lying injured down the road around the corner and I would like to have you go with me and see if you know her.' "

Mrs. Bauer's body lay beside a ditch just off the concrete in South Avenue, a third of a mile from Merrill Avenue and near the entrance of the tote road known as Lovers' Lane. She was on her back. She evidently had struggled with her assailant. Her clothing was disarranged and torn and there were lacerations about the face. She had been shot twice—in the neck and in the abdomen.

"You say, Mrs. Pero," asked Leibowitz gently, "that the sedan in which your daughter obtained a lift was 150 feet away when she stepped into it?"

"Yes."

"Did you observe the driver?"

"Yes, I saw his full face when he turned to open the door."

"Do you recognize the man in this courtroom?"

"No."

"Did you ever identify him at all?"

"No."

"Did you ever identify the Ford sedan?"

"No."

"Visibility was good March 25 of 1924, wasn't it? I mean it was a beautiful day, a beautiful afternoon?"

"Yes."

"Indicative of the advent of spring?"

"Yes."

"A sunshiny, balmy day?"

"Yes."

"That is all. Thank you."

As gently as he had questioned her he assisted her from the stand and so completed the gesture of chivalrous deference. He resumed his seat to await the state's next move. It came as a surprise. It was only an innocent looking fragment of striped velour upholstery eighteen inches square, mounted on heavy cardboard and taken from the side of the rear seat of Hoffman's car.

Fach, while examining Detective James F. Boylan who had identified photographs of the car's interior, paced slowly up and down before the jurors holding the fragment at such an angle that they could see a hole supposedly made by a bullet. He stressed its significance repeatedly and when he had concluded his questioning he approached the court stenographer, laid the fragment before him and announced:

"I offer this for identification."

Leibowitz catapulted to his feet, demanding:

"Let me see it."

"You can't," retorted Fach.

By all the rules governing the legal game Fach was right. His opponent could neither touch nor utilize in any way the exhibit so long as its status was that of identification. It must be offered in evidence. Leibowitz was stalemated.

The ugly implication of the upholstery is, of course, obvious to the reader. A shot had been fired in Hoffman's car at a height corresponding to that of Mrs. Bauer's throat. The state's new exhibit served to account for this neck wound and also to explain away a mystery that had baffled the police since the murder. Only one bullet had ever been recovered, that in the abdomen. A most intensive search of the vicinity where the body was found had failed to yield the bullet which had pierced the neck.

If Leibowitz was stalemated it was only temporarily. He knew his book of rules as well as did Fach, and hardly had the latter finished speaking when Leibowitz, seizing the upholstery, bellowed:

"I offer it in evidence."

Reversing it quickly he subjected the cardboard backing to close scrutiny. Then going over to the jury box he handed it to the foreman, requesting him to pass it on so that each juror might see for himself what he had discovered.

There was no hole in the cardboard backing!

"As to the hole in the upholstery," said Leibowitz, "I will leave it to you gentlemen whether it has not been made by a cigarette."

Boylan was still in the witness chair. Under Leibowitz' cross examination he admitted no blood stains had been found in the Hoffman car, and likewise that the upholstery had not been introduced at any of the previous trials.

Undeterred by the spectacular setback, Fach, now in mid career of his case, renewed the attack with still another surprise move, this time a new witness, William S. Whittet, former reelboy at the Palace Theater. The purpose was immediately disclosed. Hoffman had asked him, Whittet testified, "Where is a nice dark road to go out on with a girl in the night?" And Whittet recommended South Avenue to him. They drove there, Whittet continued, and Hoffman made a personal inspection of the woodland adjoining Lovers' Lane.

A major contention of the defense, it should be interpolated, was that Hoffman not only was far from the scene the day of the murder, but that he had never been near it in his life.

The testimony, as it stood at the conclusion of Fach's direct examination, was a damning indictment of Hoffman's character.

Leibowitz took the witness.

Q. Have you ever been convicted of a crime? Yes or no. A. I have.

Q. About how many times? A. Twice.

Q. The first time you were convicted for being a Peeping Tom, weren't you? A. I wasn't.

Q. What? A. I wasn't.

Q. Speak loud, please. A. I wasn't.

Q. What was the first conviction for? A. Grand larceny.

Q. Being a thief, is that it? A. That is it, yes.

Q. What was the second time you were in trouble? A. Disorderly conduct.

Q. Was that for being a Peeping Tom? A. That was, yes.

Q. You did what? A. What do you mean? Did what?

Q. What did you do there? What were you convicted of? What were the facts? A. You just said it.

Q. What was it? A. Peeping Tom.

Q. What were you doing? What was the nature of the offense that you were convicted of? A. Watching a lady disrobe.

Q. In her home? A. Yes.

Q. You were in the street? A. Yes.

Q. You were caught? A. Yes.

Q. What happened to the case? A. Probation for one year.

Cracking his Q and A whip, Leibowitz forced the admission that Whittet had never mentioned the supposed conversation and trip until after his Peeping Tom conviction, when he was seeking probation. The surprise witness left the stand discredited.

Fach nodded to one of his fifteen assistants, who arose and tiptoed into an anteroom. He was gone only a minute. A flurry of whispers, swelling into a concerted murmur, greeted his return. He was escorting a young woman, who seemed to shrink from the curious stares. She walked between the tables of opposing counsel, and within arm's length of Hoffman as she made her way to the witness stand. The court stenographer, perched in front of the stand, picked up a newly sharpened pencil and, lifting a lack-luster eye, asked her name.

"Barbara Fahs," she said.

Fach had produced his star witness. She was thirteen years old when she gave the testimony at the first trial that sent Hoffman to Sing Sing. She was eighteen now.

Fach put the routine questions, eliciting that on the afternoon of the murder Barbara, then a schoolgirl, was running an errand for her mother. She arrived at South and Merrill Avenues, and:

"I saw this automobile [Hoffman's] stop, and this lady [Mrs. Bauer] asked him if he had a rope and he said no; and he said 'I will take you to get a rope,' and she got in and they drove away."

Yes, she recognized the defendant. He was driving the car, and when Fach showed her a picture of the Hoffman sedan, she said:

"That's it."

"All Fords," observed Leibowitz in a philosophical aside audible to the jury, "look alike."

"When did you next see the defendant?" continued Fach.

"At the police station."

"What was the condition of the defendant's hair?"

"He had a haircut."

"Did the defendant have glasses?"

"Yes, big tortoise shell glasses with side bars."

Leibowitz' cross-examination of Barbara was amiable, even fatherly. He displayed solicitous interest in her identification of Hoffman.

"Let's see; it was at the police station, wasn't it?"

"Yes."

"What officers were present when you got there?"

"I didn't take notice."

"Do you know Police Inspector Ernest Van Wagner, Captain of Detectives?"

"Yes."

"Wasn't he there?"

"Yes."

"After you had viewed Hoffman the first time at the police station didn't you say to Captain Van Wagner, 'No, sir, that is not the man'?"

"Yes."

"And then didn't you view Hoffman a second time and say to Captain Van Wagner, 'That isn't the man'?"

"Yes."

Barbara's identification, Leibowitz' questioning finally developed, wasn't made at first hand but through a picture in a newspaper, published almost a month after the murder and shown to her by her parents. It was a full front view.

"You saw only one side of the man's face, didn't you?"

"Yes."

"And you really don't remember which side you saw?"

"No."

Barbara was fidgeting and twisting her hands. Leibowitz abruptly shifted his line of questioning.

"Did you ever live in Mersereau Avenue?"

"Yes."

"Do you remember the number?"

"No."

"Do you remember how many rooms there were in the apartment?"

"No."

Leibowitz was giving her the I.Q. test to register her mentality with the jury.

"You lived in Bloomfield Avenue five years ago?"

"Yes."

"Do you remember the number?"

"No."

"Did you attend Public School No. 6 in Manhattan?"

"Yes."

"What was the location?"

"I don't remember."

"You testified at Hoffman's third trial in 1928?"

"Yes."

"In what month was it held?"

"April or May."

Leibowitz read from the court records to show the trial was held in November. On that note closed the cross-examination.

Patrolman Matthew McCormack, whose testimony was second in importance only to that of the star witness and supplemented it, followed Barbara on the stand.

He was waiting for a lift home at an intersection a mile and a half from Lovers' Lane on the afternoon of March 25.

"Did you," asked Fach, "observe any car pass?"

"Yes, sir, the defendant's."

McCormack wigwagged the driver as it approached but it kept on going. The driver's face was "very white and his right eye was crooked," and he looked neither to the right nor left. He was going twenty miles an hour.

Besides identifying Hoffman, McCormack's testimony served to complete the time cycle of the crime. Barbara Fahs had seen Mrs. Bauer step into the car at 3:30; woodchoppers heard the two shots around 4:15 and McCormick saw the sedan drive away between 4:25 and 4:30.

Leibowitz' strategy with McCormack was a two-point attack on his testimony, based on motive and credibility.

McCormack did not identify Hoffman until a month after the crime, when rewards totaling $8,000 had been posted.

"Because a murder happened on that day," began Leibowitz, "did you come to the conclusion that the man you saw in the car might be the guilty person?"

"Yes."

The answer was the signal for the launching of the Leibowitz attack.

Q. Did you talk to Captain Van Wagner, your superior, the following day about what you had seen? A. No, sir.

Q. That would be March 26? A. Yes.

Q. Did you tell him anything on March 27? A. No, sir.

Q. Did you get in touch with Captain Van Wagner on the 28th of March? A. No.

Q. The 29th? A. No, sir.

Q. The 30th? A. No, sir.

Q. The 31st? A. No, sir.

Q. April 1st? A. No, sir.

Q. April 2nd? A. No, sir. At no time did I get in touch with him.

Q. The 3rd, 4th, 5th, 6th, 7th, 8th, 9th? A. Right.

Q. I am going to start to count in the twenties now. The 21st? A. No, sir.

Q. At no time? A. At no time at all.

Q. You know where the rogues' gallery is located, don't you? A. Yes, sir.

Q. Did you at any time during that whole month beginning with the 25th of March and running all the way to the 25th of April, go to the rogues' gallery and take out all the folders and look at the pictures to see if, possibly, this man whom you suspected might be an ex-convict, and he might be located in that fashion? Did you? Yes or no. A. No.

Q. When was the first time that you told any official that you had seen this defendant? Give us the date. A. What do you mean by an official? Any policeman?

Q. Any official, I say. Any official—the District Attorney, Captain Van Wagner, or Detective McGann, who was in charge of the detectives. When for the first time

did you breathe this to any official? A. The day that
I saw him in court.

Q. What date? A. April 25, 1924.

Q. One month after Mrs. Bauer's body was found. Do
you mean to tell these twelve men in the box that you
carried the image of that man for an entire month?
A. Yes.

Leibowitz then bore down on McCormack's credibility.
McCormack had testified he saw Hoffman in the Sheriff's
office April 25.

Q. Did the District Attorney send you to the Sheriff's
office? A. No, sir, I went there myself.

Q. Do you want to change that statement? A. No, I
won't change it.

Q. Let me see if I can refresh your memory. At page
750 of the minutes of the second trial.

> "Question: Now, then, who told you to go to the
>   Sheriff's office?
> "Answer: Mr. Fach."

Did you say that? A. I don't remember saying it. No, I
don't.

Q. Then the question immediately after that:

> "Question: Are you sure about that?
> "Answer: Positive."

Did you testify to that? A. No, I didn't.

Q. Is your memory poor about that? A. No, my
memory is good about that.

Q. Which is the truth? Did Mr. Fach send you or did
he not send you? A. He didn't send me.

Said Leibowitz to Fach:

"Is it conceded that that is what he said or must I bring the court reporter here?"

Said Fach to Leibowitz:

"You need not bring him here; that is the testimony."

And the state rested its case. It was 2:55 o'clock the afternoon of Friday, May 17, 1929.

GRIMLY entertaining and diverse is the collection of courtroom memorabilia attesting the Leibowitz prowess, mileposting the high road of the Leibowitz career, each item with its story of a climacteric moment in a murder trial. It stirs disquieting thoughts.

The collection is Leibowitz' hobby. He discusses it with the passionate zest of a connoisseur of rare *objets d'art*. He lingers over each piece with an eye to detailed minutiæ. He exhibits an article resembling a pipe cleaner except that it has a handle and the bristles on the five-inch length of twisted wire are stiffer.

"A man's life depended on whether or not there was oil on that brush," he says.

He lifts a .25 caliber automatic Colt pistol from a cardboard box.

"Hoffman's gun," he explains, and chuckling, "Say, I didn't know a pistol from a derringer when I took that case."

He fingers two discharged shells:

"Our star witnesses. Found beside Mrs. Bauer's body."

The box next yields a lead pellet:

"The fatal bullet, and, you might say, our 'surprise' witness."

Leibowitz refills his stubby, briar pipe and applies a contemplative match. Idly he watches the blue smoke spiraling lazily ceilingward. The reminiscent mood grows upon him. He becomes volubly expansive:

"Hoffman bought the gun new and our contention was that after taking it apart he put it away and forgot about it. But the prosecution through its experts claimed he had fired it and then cleaned it, because 'there was oil on the brush.'

"The crux of the case, however, pivoted on the breech-block, which does the 'fingerprinting' on the cap of the cartridge or, to use a commoner phrase, the face of the shell. Breechblocks are hand-finished by filing and no two are alike in surface markings—because it is impossible to make the same stroke twice with a file.

"When a gun is fired there is a repercussive pressure of about 14,000 pounds to the square inch, and the breechblock imprints its markings inversely on the shell face.

"There are also two other identification markings—the indentation made by the firing pin on the soft copper primer in the center of the cap; and the impressions engraved on the bullet itself by the rifling in the pistol barrel—the grooves and the raised surfaces known as land marks.

"Experts prefer the breechblock markings to the others, considering them the most nearly infallible. The difficulty is that they are not often available because the empty shells are seldom left at the scene of a crime. We were fortunate in that respect in the Hoffman case."

EVEN Justice Humphrey, inured by fifteen years' experience to the devices of criminal lawyers, was frankly curious as he ascended the bench the morning of Monday, May 20. The railed off enclosure used by opposing counsel had been transformed into something between a laboratory and a classroom. A wheeled table supported a mysterious contrivance mounted on a mahogany base, a thing of shining brass and gleaming silver, with levers, wheels, screws, columnar uprights and a crossbar with a tubular eyepiece. It was a comparison microscope, the first ever brought into a courtroom. Near it was a battery of easels with charts, pictures and diagrams, conveniently placed for inspection by judge and jury.

Leibowitz was toying with a riding crop.

The states' three ballistics experts, led by Captain Harry F. Butts, of the New York Police Department, had unanimously identified Hoffman's pistol as the fatal weapon, Butts testifying that after firing a half hundred bullets from the gun, he found that the markings on them corresponded to those on the bullet extracted from Mrs. Bauer's body. He said further that the breechblock markings on the caps of the test shells were similarly identical.

Their testimony constituted the bulwark of the state's case, which Leibowitz had set himself to smash at one stroke. Success meant acquittal; failure the chair. For Leibowitz was under an unusual handicap. Hoffman not only had no alibi but was on the record as having tried to fake one. His admission, not made until after the police had trapped him, had prejudiced the entire jury in the first trial and a part of it in the second trial. Leibowitz could discredit—could almost disqualify—the state's chief witnesses, but he couldn't achieve his grand objective by such means. He must convince the jury beyond all doubt that Hoffman's gun did not kill Mrs. Bauer.

Leibowitz, the showman, collaborated with Leibowitz, the psychologist, in picking the defense experts. They were chosen as much for the impression their names and prestige as ballistics engineers would make upon the mechanically minded jury as for the value of their opinions. They were:

Captain William A. Jones, for thirty-two years a member of the New York Police Department, and its official firearms expert, appointed in 1895 by the late Theodore Roosevelt, then police commissioner; Merton Robinson, for twenty-five years chief ballistics engineer for the Winchester Repeating Arms Company, and commissioned by the United States Government during the war to inspect the small arms factories of England, France, and Italy; and Albert Foster, general manager of the Colt Company, which made the Hoffman pistol.

Captain Jones was the first witness and Leibowitz, after a brief demonstration of pistol mechanics, proposed that he fire the Hoffman weapon before the jury to demonstrate the dissimilarity between breechblock and firing pin markings on the caps of the two shells found beside Mrs. Bauer's body and a test shell from the Hoffman gun.

"Can you not demonstrate with those that have already been fired?" demurred Justice Humphrey.

"Your Honor," replied Leibowitz, "I would rather have it done here so that there will be no question about it."

"Are there no shells in evidence," mildly insisted His Honor, "that are not disputed?"

"I would rather," pressed Leibowitz, "have one fired right here in front of the jury so there will be no question about it."

"I am not entirely in accord with counsel's idea of firing the pistol in the courtroom," observed the judge and there the matter rested.

Leibowitz steered his wheeled table to a position directly in front of the jury box. He was bringing the comparison microscope into play. Captain Jones put a test shell and one of the fatal shells on the twin stages of the instrument.

"I suppose," interjected Justice Humphrey, "the jurors will have to come around and have a look?"

"If Your Honor please," murmured Leibowitz.

And the judge, who had left the bench to join the sightseers, announced:

"Now, gentlemen, form a line on the right, in the order in which your numbers are called."

The unique parade was quickly under way. One by one the jurors peered through the single eyepiece at the shell caps, magnified one hundred times; and what to the unaided eye had seemed smooth surface assumed the rugged physiognomy of a relief map modeled to large scale with ridges, furrows and serrations, crisscrossed with inequalities and eccentricities of contour.

Leibowitz was plying Captain Jones with questions. Had he compared the two fatal shells and the test shell? He had.

"As a result of your examination and comparison, captain, do you say that the breechblock markings on the test shells compare in any shape, form, or manner with the breechblock markings on the fatal shells?"

"They do not compare at all, sir."

Using his riding crops as a schoolmaster does his pointer, Leibowitz indicated the chart on which had been superimposed photographs of what appeared to be the bottoms of ten-inch pie pans. They were enlargements of pistol shell caps—two of them those of the shells found beside Mrs. Bauer's body, and four others, those of test shells fired from Hoffman's gun. They supplemented the microscopic demonstration.

The pointer hovered over distinctive markings plainly visible across the courtroom on each of the fatal shells.

"Captain," said Leibowitz, "please explain to the jury what these markings mean."

"They form the Roman numerals VI. They were imprinted by the breechblock."

"Did you find any such markings on any of the test shells?"

"No, sir."

Leibowitz handed him the bullet recovered from Mrs. Bauer's body:

"What does your examination disclose as to the kind of barrel that came from, and why?"

"It was fired from a barrel that was rusty because rust marks show on the bullet."

"Did the barrel of Hoffman's pistol show any evidence of rust?"

"No, sir."

It was the high moment of Captain Jones' testimony, and Leibowitz capitalized it by letting the jurors view the fatal bullet and a test bullet side by side through the comparison microscope and determine for themselves the dissimilarity in markings.

The state, building its case around Hoffman's gun, admittedly purchased but a short time before the murder, was irrevocably committed to the theory that the bullet had been fired from a new pistol. Butts and its other experts had so testified.

The wire brush, on which "a man's life depended," entered the picture here. The prosecution contended Hoffman had immersed it in oil and swabbed the barrel with it to eliminate any evidence of the pistol's use. Leibowitz countered with a chemical analysis which showed that no oil had ever been present on the brush; that it was, in fact, in the same condition as when it left the factory.

Robinson, following Captain Jones, testified Butts called on him at the Winchester factory in New Haven, Connecticut, early in 1924, for tests to establish whether or not the two shells found beside Mrs. Bauer's body were fired from Hoffman's gun. Fifty shells were used but none revealed breechblock markings corresponding to those on the Bauer shells.

Robinson had also examined under a microscope for comparison purposes the fatal bullet and test bullets, and his finding was that "the fatal bullet was fired through a barrel either rough or rusty. All the land and groove impressions were badly scored." The test bullets fired from the Hoffman gun, on the other hand, were in "good condition," and "the land and groove impressions didn't show any well defined scratches or marks."

So Leibowitz, caught in reminiscent mood, tells the story in between puffs of his stubby briar pipe:

"My job was to popularize my side of the case with the jurors; to make the technical issues actually live before their eyes. I had to sell unwilling customers a bill of goods they didn't want. All the prosecution's experts had done was to talk of their merchandise; what we did was to open up our sample case, hand ours over to the jurors and let them finger it. Seeing is believing."

Step by step he reviews the trial, describing Fach's discomfiture at Jones' and Robinson's testimony; how "he got so flabbergasted he began talking about a No. 2 gun."

He confides that his threat to reveal "the real murderer" was a bluff, but that he did produce two new witnesses—housewives living in the vicinity of Lovers' Lane—who testified to seeing an excited stranger driving away the afternoon of the murder. And he was "heavy set, dark-complexioned, with tortoiseshell glasses, and was wearing a dark brown overcoat and fedora to match." He was headed in an opposite direction from that of the suspect Patrolman McCormack saw.

Again Leibowitz puts Hoffman on the witness stand. Not the Hoffman the little world of Port Richmond knew before March 25 of 1924. Not the rotund, chubby-faced billiken who played the slide trombone in the Tall Cedars Band. Not the good-natured village fat boy who was wont to pass the time of day with Pete Marino, the barber, and wisecrack over chocolate ice cream sodas with the gang in Symons Drug Store.

A beaten creature faced the jury in Justice Humphrey's courtroom; a creature with a famished look; sharp, gaunt, haggard features; sunken cheeks, deep parenthesis lines from nostrils to lip corners. Seventy pounds had sloughed away from his five-foot six-inch frame in the five years of his ordeal. He had gone to prison weighing 190 and was now down to 120.

His home was broken up. His wife, Agnes, had deserted him during his first year in Sing Sing; quietly divorced him and remarried, putting their baby daughter, Dorothy, in an orphanage.

Leibowitz goes into action. He hands Hoffman the .25 caliber Colt automatic.

"Did you ever fire that pistol?" he asks.

"I never fired a shot out of that gun in my life, Mr. Leibowitz; so help me God I never did."

"Why?"

"I didn't know how to handle it."

"What was the trouble with it?"

"It had a right-handed safety catch. That was on the wrong side for me. It would be very awkward for me to manipulate, I being left-handed. So I was sorry I had bought it. I said to myself, 'I have picked up another lemon,' and thrust it in a buffet drawer and forgot about it."

Leibowitz knew the answer before Hoffman gave it. It was the cue for him to play a trump card. The bullet recovered from Mrs. Bauer's body had entered the abdomen two and a half inches to the left of the median line, and had lodged in the spinal region directly on that line. Therefore, it had traveled two and a half inches to the right. Leibowitz, after a series of tests on animal carcasses, had satisfied himself that the bullet could only have been fired by a right-handed man.

Hoffman's left-handedness had not been disclosed at any of his previous trials. Leibowitz exploited it with questions as well as demonstrations, and the prosecution was so concerned as to its effect on the jury that it interviewed the prison chef at Sing Sing with a view to subpœnaing him as a witness—Hoffman having worked in the kitchen there. However, he didn't remember anything.

"In my summation," reminisces Leibowitz, forgetting this time to light his pipe, "I told the jury:

" 'This man was plucked from his home and has been caged like a wild animal for five years merely because he told a lie—a lie born of an overweening fear that in no sense sprang from a sense of guilt.

" 'It is not only conscience that makes cowards of us all, it is also environment. Thus a man may be courageous with his fists, but afraid of lightning and afraid to be in the woods at night. It almost looks as if there has been a curse on this man, as though an act of the devil entangled him.

" 'I do not believe any jury would convict a dog on such evidence as has been presented here. I leave the verdict in your hands.' "

Leibowitz refills and relights his pipe. Silently he watches the blue smoke spiraling ceilingward. A half smile is on his lips and in his eyes a look of beatific peace. The roar of the crowd is in his ears and the sweet music of clicking cameras. Hoffman stands beside him, so do his two daughters, Mildred and Dorothy, now respectively ten and six years of age. There will be screaming headlines on the morrow, and pictures and captions:

"Harry Hoffman shakes hands with his attorney, Samuel S. Leibowitz."

Or:

"Little Mildred and Dorothy Hoffman thank Samuel S. Leibowitz for 'Bringing Our Daddy Back To Us.' "

Et cetera.

For Leibowitz had done it again. The verdict had been: "Not Guilty!"

CHAPTER THREE

SIDEWALKS OF NEW YORK

PEERING now ahead, now astern, Captain W. J. Roberts paced the bridge of the steamship *Kensington,* pausing only momentarily when the steward handed him a cup of black coffee. He had been there twenty-four hours. His oilskins were streaming and his beard was rimed with mist.

Suddenly he signaled to the senior officer of the watch and the ship's telegraph, which had stood at "Full Speed Ahead," was shifted to half speed, then to slow, then stop. As the gong in the engine room clanged the final message the rhythmic thudding of the propellers ceased, along with the vibrations pulsating through the frame. It was as if a mighty steel heart had stopped beating. A strange hush pervaded the ship, broken only by the mournful blast of her warning siren.

The *Kensington* was marooned in a pea soup fog and her wise old master, who had learned his trade in the days of sail, knew the only thing to do was to wait for it to lift. Fortunately the sea was calm. But he was not deceived. The Atlantic was noted for its treacherous weather, especially in midwinter.

Leaving Antwerp the morning of February 27, the going had been perfect down the Scheldt River to Flushing and into the North Sea past Ostend and Dunkirk. It was off the Isle of Wight in the English Channel, under a mackerel sky, that a slapping nor'easter developed into a hurricane and the plucky little ship, after rounding the Scilly Islands, rolled and pitched in the trough of crosswise waves and pushed her sharp nose through huge walls of water that crashed down upon her fore and aft, wrenching deck chairs from their fastenings, sluicing through companionways and flooding cabins, and threatening once to disable her steering gear.

She was a day overdue when the pea soup fog halted her twenty-five miles from her goal, pier 14 of the Red Star Line, North River, Manhattan. She was off Sandy Hook and it was 6:38 o'clock the afternoon of Tuesday, March 9, 1897. A night and two days she lay there, resuming her journey Thursday. She steamed through the Narrows, into the Upper Bay. The city's skyline loomed ahead with Bartholdi's Statue of Liberty off the port bow when a barge hove alongside and she again slowed down and stopped.

Her cabin passengers, leaning over the rail of the promenade deck, saw a curious sight. A gangplank had been let down from steerage quarters amidships, and across it to the barge shuffled a motley procession, a half thousand men and women, young and old, boys and girls and toddling children, ludicrously appareled. They moved awkwardly, hampered by unwieldy bundles of clothing, bedding and cooking utensils. Most of the women, who wore kerchiefs about their heads and brightly colored shawls about their shoulders, clasped nursing babies to their breasts.

Doubtless, herded thus together indiscriminately, they all looked alike to the cabin passengers. It was essentially a crowd picture and individuals, even family groups such as the three Lebeaus, were scarcely more than indistinguishable details in the mass composition.

The transfer completed, the *Kensington* proceeded to her berth, the barge to Ellis Island where, in the shadow of the Bartholdi statue, one more batch of immigrants set foot for the first time on American soil. The ordeal of inquisition and the detention pen confronted them, but that they would gladly endure for the privilege of ultimate citizenship in this new land of their choice.

Trifles have a way of obtruding at the wrong time in human affairs and stealing the show. Here were Papa and Mamma Lebeau on the threshold of the supreme adventure of their lives, and miserably unhappy. They had boarded the *Kensington* at Antwerp only to learn after she was under way that there was no kosher food aboard. They were strictly orthodox Jews, as were a hundred and fifty other steerage passengers. With them they subsisted for thirteen days of the voyage entirely on tea and biscuits, eagerly anticipating their arrival here with its prospect of a bounteous meal. Ellis Island, however, in that respect proved to be as bare as Mother Hubbard's cupboard. A committee was organized. It appealed to the Hebrew Sheltering and Guardian Society and a messenger was dispatched forthwith to Manhattan for emergency rations. He returned with kosher frankfurters, which not only did not allay the pangs of hunger but were conducive to indigestion.

Young Mr. Lebeau, going on four years old, was as unhappy as his parents. He had been so seasick all the way across that he had not once risen from his cot in the ship's hospital. The enforced diet of hot dogs annoyed him exceedingly and he vented his feelings long and lustily.

Contributing to his querulousness was homesickness for the playmates and familiar associations of the Rumanian town where he had been born and reared—Jassy, with its vineyards and gardens, in the uplands of Northern Moldavia, on the River Bahlui.

The Lebeaus lived near the railroad station in a two-room house of native timber and plaster, with an earthen floor. Cooking was done on an open air charcoal stove and the water supply came from the roof, collected in barrels under the eaves after rains. There was an intimate neighborliness because the houses were arranged in semicircles. Young Mr. Lebeau was prone to park himself beside a knothole in the fence, through which he would peek at a Turk next door who manufactured candy—all-day suckers in the form of chanticleers. He liked to watch the chanticleers emerging from the molds. He liked, too, to listen to the railroad station master across the street ringing his big brass bell every time a train departed.

Papa Lebeau kept a drygoods shop in Jassy. The family would have remained there, perhaps, had it not been for the unremitting persecution of the Jews by the Rumanian government. They had been deprived of voting and other civil rights and were unable to own rural land, although they were subject to military service and the payment of taxes. An Anti-Semitic League, organized in 1895, so aggravated conditions already well nigh unbearable that a general hegira to America was begun.

The morning of March 17, St. Patrick's Day, a wheezy tug sidled up to the Battery wharf, at the tip of Manhattan, and the Lebeaus stepped ashore. The landing excited no attention. Momentous events were in the making both for the city and the nation. The 69th Regiment, New York National Guard, the Hibernian Rifles, the Society of the Friendly Sons of St. Patrick, the Fire and Police Departments, the Street Cleaners' Band and the braves of Tammany Hall were planning that day the greatest parade Fifth Avenue had ever seen. Out in Carson City, Nevada, a lanky Australian named Robert Fitzsimmons was to fight one James J. Corbett for the heavyweight championship of the world. Down in Washington, D. C., a new President, William B. McKinley, was thrilling a hopeful electorate with rosy visions of revenue to be derived from a strong, protective tariff, and thus lessen the tax burden and lift the country out of the depression trenches.

The Lebeaus settled on the fourth floor of a tenement at 66 Essex Street, near Rivington Street and the Williamsburg Bridge, in the heart of the lower East Side Ghetto, and Papa Lebeau, investing fifty dollars, began his career as a pushcart peddler. Mamma Lebeau had brought with her a pair of diamond earrings, heirlooms. She carried them sewed into the side pocket of her skirt. The fourth day in the new home she returned with her son from a marketing tour. Her purchase of meat and vegetables was in a large paper bag which she hugged with both arms as she climbed the dark, narrow stairway of the tenement. Arrived at the door of the flat she set the bag down and reached in the skirt pocket for the key. It and the earrings were gone. The pocket had been cleanly slashed as with a razor. Mamma Lebeau remembered having seen a youth dart into the stairway ahead of her.

It was Sam's first contact with the fraternity that was to supply many of his future clients.

There were urchins in the tenement rookeries that hemmed him round about who were destined to write assorted local history. Some would become social climbers, some porch climbers; some bankers, some safe crackers; some Wall Street brokers, some stick-ups; some would jimmy their way into politics, some into Sing Sing, and a few would live to achieve the eminence of Public Enemies in the golden age of gangsterism, ushered in by Volstead.

Essex Street and its environs, hiving Irish, Jew and Italian, were his melting pot kindergarten. Life was raw, savage. Youngsters, emulating their big brothers, roamed the streets in kid gangs and fought like hell. The Bowery, rendezvous of Monk Eastman, the gorilla who walked like a man, was the racial deadline. Swashbuckling Monk, the Paul Bunyan of the sidewalks of New York, was their bedtime story hero.

They played street games like Pussy Cat. A block of wood was teed on a manhole cover and the batsman walloped it with a broomstick handle. The idea was for the fielders to catch the block and toss it back. Often they wouldn't have a chance because the block would sail through a window pane. The crash of broken glass was always a signal for the gamins to beat it. They swam in the East River, diving off Grand Street dock near the outlet of the sewer. They disported in the altogether and therefore had to be wary of the neighborhood cop.

Essex Market Court and Ludlow Street jail were near the Lebeau home and the patrol wagons with their loads of prisoners were common sights. Sam liked to watch the fire department gallop past. He admired the splendid red apparatus. He had a retentive ear for music and would follow for blocks the hurdy-gurdy man and the accordion player with the dancing bear, when spring came round to Essex Street. The accordion fascinated him.

Around the corner on the Bowery was Miner's Burlesque Theater, a forbidden place for youngsters because of its plump femininity in tights. Hips were fashionable then. One day some of the older boys took him there and when he arrived home he wore such a guilty look that his mother took him to task. He confessed he had been to Miner's and she turned him over her knee for a sound spanking.

Slowly the breadwinner of the family, the elder Lebeau, adjusted himself to the new environment with its strange language and customs, its bewildering complexities and hurly-burly. In his eagerness to speed the adjustment process he sought the advice of a fellow pushcart peddler, who warned him with eloquent upturned palms:

"You will get nowhere, Isaac, with that last name of yours. They will always take you for a foreigner. You must Americanize it."

And so Isaac Americanized it by changing Lebeau to Leibowitz.

What between his business acumen and Mamma Leibowitz's thrift he soon saved one hundred and fifty dollars. He said farewell to Essex Street and the pushcart and opened a small drygoods store at 2081 Second Avenue, near 107th Street, in Harlem's Little Italy. The family lived in the rear in two rooms overlooking a Hungarian beer garden, and Sam learned "Ach du Lieber Augustine" by heart. He was attending the 110th Street public school. His classmates included Negroes, Italians, Poles, Swedes, Germans, Norwegians, Jews and a few

Chinese. In this polyglot atmosphere he was to spend his boyhood until he turned thirteen.

Sam preferred outdoor sports to classroom work. His aversion to study was so marked that his teacher in history said to him one day during the course of an oral examination: "You don't know whether Bull Run was a battle or a cow pasture."

Declamation was his forte. He memorized prose and poetry with equal facility and could recite impromptu such classics as "Curfew Shall Not Ring Tonight," "The Charge of the Light Brigade," "Thanatopsis," "The Wreck of the Hesperus," "Barbara Frietchie" and "Old Ironsides." He could rattle off the preamble to the Constitution, The Declaration of Independence, Lincoln's Gettysburg Address, and for an encore give Hamlet's soliloquy.

A bizarre contraption appearing on the streets in the early nineteen hundreds provided gleeful divertissement for the youngster. It was a two-cylinder, four-wheel vehicle with a belching exhaust, and its drivers wore goggles, gauntlets and linen dusters. It hurtled along at ten miles an hour and the kids would run after it yelling:

"Get a horse, get a horse!"

Sam developed a sudden flair for scholastic research, which overjoyed his parents. At last the boy was getting interested. He devoted hours of his spare time to the onerous work. It kept him out late Saturday nights. He was studying with fellow students, he explained. If Papa and Mamma Leibowitz had followed him their way would have led to the gallery of the Star Theater at 107th Street and Lexington Avenue; admission, 10, 20 and 30 cents.

The research included "Nellie, the Beautiful Coat Model," "The Curse of Drink," "The Burglar's Daughter," "Bertha, the Sewing Machine Girl," "Bowery After Dark," "Young Buffalo, King of the Wild West," "Why Girls Leave Home." In between acts the gallery patrons would munch peanuts until the special police officer rapped on the floor with his nightstick. It signaled the rise of the curtain and meant that the cracking of peanut shells must stop.

Papa Leibowitz was prospering. The Second Avenue store had proved a money maker. Still he was not satisfied. He wanted to expand. His ambition had a vital bearing on his son's future for it caused the family to remove to Brooklyn. The new enterprise was located at 839 Fulton Street. It enhanced the Leibowitz fortunes materially and they ended their peregrinations to settle in their own home in the Cypress Hills section of Brooklyn. Sam was graduated from the Jamaica high school in the Spring of 1911. It was the occasion for a solemn conference between the elder Leibowitzes. The boy should go to college. It would entail a sacrifice but he must go. He was called in and told of the decision.

"Good," he said, "I will be a civil engineer."

He had seen the spans of two great bridges rise above the East River, and they had caught his imagination.

"You will be a lawyer," corrected his father, "or you will not go to college."

His psychology was typical of that of the first generation of Jewish immigrant. He was in trade, he was a merchant. The law was a patent of social and professional distinction.

Sam matriculated at Cornell in the Fall of 1911 and, to lessen the financial burden for his father, waited on tables and washed dishes at the Cascadilla School, the University's preparatory institution. He also sold novelties and subscriptions to magazines to supplement his tuition fee. He entered with gusto into the extra-curricular activities—track, baseball, basketball, soccer, and became a member of the Cornell Station, United States Volunteer Life Saving Corps.

The first Jew to belong to the Dramatic Club at Cornell, in his Freshman year he played the part of the second butler in Pinero's "Rogue's Comedy," carrying a tray and wearing a gray, double breasted, swallowtail coat with a brigadier general's epaulets and gold braid festooned across the chest. For three weeks he rehearsed before a mirror. He had but one appearance to make and a single line to speak. It was:

"The lady is without, sir."

His declamatory talents sent him into the arena of forensics. So successful was he that he qualified as a member of the Cornell intercollegiate debating team. He was also one of six selected from the entire student body to compete in the '94 Memorial prize contest, annual oratorical event.

In his Senior year he was president of the Cornell Congress. Yet with all these activities he found time to carry on the research begun in his public school days in Manhattan. In the 1915 *Cornellian*, his class book, it is written:

> *"In Boardman is Lee*
> *Works like a bee*
> *Till night falls there he's seen*
> *Then at Lyceum or Star*
> *From a stage he's not far*
> *For a view of the lovely chorine."*

He had become "Lee" in the undergraduate tradition for abbreviated surnames.

Sam wasn't sure what kind of a lawyer he wanted to be when he entered the University. He was simply a dutiful son obeying his father's dictates, but as time passed and he became more interested he arrived at a decision. He announced it at the beginning of his senior year to Edwin Hamlin Woodruff, Dean of the College of Law.

"Dean," he said, "I am going to specialize in criminal law."

Woodruff threw up his hands in horror.

"No, no, Sam," he pleaded, "anything but that."

"But, Dean," protested Sam, "somebody has to do it. We have to have criminal lawyers. I might as well be one. Anyway I have made up my mind."

Twenty-two years old, Sam, after his graduation in 1915, went to Rochester for his bar examinations and passed both parts at the first test. He and his sheepskin represented an investment of approximately $5,000, but the legalistic world of New York City seemed unimpressed.

His first job was in the office of Attorney James A. Farrell, 27 Williams Street, at five dollars a week; his second with Cohen Brothers, 64 Wall Street, at fifteen dollars. He asked for a dollar a week raise. The Cohens wanted to compromise at fifty cents and he quit, going to Brooklyn.

It was early in 1916 when he associated himself with Michael F. McGoldrick, an Irish lawyer with an extensive practice among the Roman Catholics. The window of his office overlooked a downtown business street and when the name, Samuel S. Leibowitz, was lettered in under his there was a general arching of eyebrows. Sam got along so famously with the clients, however, that it wasn't long before people were calling him the Roman Jew. Working for McGoldrick was pleasant and thirty-five dollars a week not a bad salary for a fledgling lawyer. The difficulty was that the ambitious Sam wanted to work for himself; wanted to develop his own practice. He was obscure and without influence. He had no connections, no in, as the saying went. How to go about it then? It was a sockdolager of a question. He appealed to a friend, a veteran of the Brooklyn bar.

"I'll fix that; I'll get you an indigent case," said the friend and took Sam to the Kings County Court, introducing him to Judge Howard P. Nash, who assigned him to defend one Harry Patterson, a bleary-eyed, booze-crazed bum accused of burglary.

The specific charge was that by means of a skeleton key Patterson had gained entrance to a saloon in the early morning hours and rifled the till of seven dollars. The police produced the key, which had been found on Patterson, and claimed he had made a confession.

Experienced lawyers advised Sam to enter a plea of guilty. He hadn't a chance of winning. The evidence was overwhelming and, besides, a jury had only to look at Patterson to convict him.

Sam listened respectfully and decided otherwise. It was his first case, his first appearance in court as Leibowitz, the criminal attorney with Leibowitz's own personal client. He spent three weeks preparing his defense and devising strategy. His knees were wobbly the day the case was called for trial. Assistant District Attorney Louis Goldstein was the prosecutor and until they met in court he had never heard of this fellow Leibowitz.

The initial surprise came when Sam announced his

client would plead not guilty. Goldstein put his police witnesses on the stand and quickly concluded the state's case. Sam countered with testimony by Patterson that the police had obtained the purported confession only after beating him with a hose. As for the skeleton key, yes, it was the property of his client, but:

"If your Honor please, I request that you permit the jury to go to the scene of the robbery and try it for themselves in the door of that saloon. I will stake my case on the demonstration. We contend the key will not open it."

The proposition caught Goldstein off guard. He had no idea what doors the key would or would not unlock. He hadn't experimented with it. He could only reply with a grandiloquent protest that:

"I oppose wasting the time of these twelve busy citizens on such a fool's errand."

The court sustained him. The twelve busy citizens marched into the jury room, deliberated three minutes and marched out with a verdict of not guilty.

Sam had won on a bluff. He had privately tried the key on every door in the courthouse and it had unlocked them all. He figured, though, and rightly, that Goldstein, having made no preparation or investigation, would not dare to call the bluff. In later years he was to philosophize:

"Sometimes you have to do it. It was really a pot shot or, say, what they call in the prize ring a haymaker. They start from the floor and hope against hope it will hit the button. Mine hit the mark for Patterson."

The victory emboldened him. He went to the bank, drew his entire savings of $260 and toured the second-hand stores, buying a desk, a four-unit sectional book-case, a filing cabinet, a typewriter, three chairs, a handsome brass cuspidor and an elegant red rug. He had them delivered to the side room of a suite occupied by a realty broker at 50 Court Street, Brooklyn; rent, thirty dollars a month. He called in a sign painter and on the door an inscription burgeoned:

SAMUEL S. LEIBOWITZ
ATTORNEY-AT-LAW

It was May of 1919. Sam at twenty-six had opened his own office.

All he had to do now was to sit and wait for clients. Of the $260 but $25 remained. He had invested in a sartorial outfit to conform with his new professional dignity. It consisted of three suits of clothes of collegiate cut, a dark gray fedora, pearl gray spats, and a blond Malacca walking stick. A fresh boutonnière daily and pinch nose glasses completed the Beau Brummell picture.

In the devising of his sitting campaign he foreshadowed something of the crafty genius of the future. Incoming calls for the realty broker were answered by his steno, whose desk was midway between Sam's office and the main entrance of the suite. Sam arranged with her that if and when a client materialized she was to tap on his door, open it just wide enough to poke her head in; close it, inform the client "Mr. Leibowitz is busy," and keep him waiting five minutes. She was then to admit him. Sam would be talking into his extension telephone. The client was to cool his heels for another five minutes before he was ready for him.

They rehearsed the act until both were perfect. A week passed. Two weeks passed. Still no clients. The steno had stepped out for noonday lunch on a warm Monday in June, and Sam, coat removed and shirt sleeves rolled up, was lolling in his chair, his back to the desk and his feet on the sill of the office's one window. A voice aroused him. A stranger with a furtive eye and an ugly mug was addressing him from the doorway:

"Are you Leibowitz, the mouthpiece?"

"Yes," replied Sam.

"You ain't such a bad mouthpiece. I watched you with that bum Patterson. I just got a rap but it wasn't a right fall."

(He was saying in underworld patois that he had been arrested but that the evidence against him was not legitimate.)

"I was standing outside the freak sideshow in Dreamland at Coney Island Sunday afternoon when a sucker squawked he felt my mit in his kick. Can you beat it? And me a cannon for twenty years!"

(Meaning that the complainant alleged that while the defendant was robbing him, he felt the defendant's hand in his pocket. A cannon is a pickpocket.)

"You gotta spring me, see? I gotta hit the air. June, July, August and September are our heavy months and if you spring me we'll keep you plenty busy."

Sam didn't know that the underworld scouts courtrooms as the major leagues scout the minors, for promising talent; that when it retains an unknown lawyer it has "made a find."

"What's your fee?" asked the cannon and Sam, screwing up his courage, blurted:

"One hundred dollars."

The client peeled off five twenty-dollar bills from a fat roll and tossed them on the desk. Sam put them in the right lower pocket of his vest.

"You'll sure be at the Coney Island Magistrate's Court tomorrow morning?" asked the cannon.

"Yes," replied Sam, "and we will do the best we can."
The steno came in as the cannon left.

"Look!" shouted Sam, "the ice is broken. Look!"

He reached into the vest pocket. His face went blank.
The $100 was gone. He searched his other pockets and
ransacked the drawers of the desk. He was on his hands
and knees going over the rug when the cannon returned.

"Say, young fellow," earnestly, "I just want you to
understand I've been twenty years in the racket and no
sucker ever felt my hand in his pocket. See? Here's your
$100."

Sam won an acquittal but it was the last cannon case
he ever handled. The client was Izzy the Goniff, indexed
in the Rogues' Gallery as the "Millionaire Pickpocket,"
and the Leibowitz of today laments, "If I had known
what the standard fee was then, I would have charged
him $2,500 and he would have paid it and thanked me."

Sam resumed his sitting campaign, wondering when the
next cash customer would turn up. It was a telephone call
this time and it sent him into action in his first murder
case. The genesis of the call is interesting as illustrative
of the variety of circumstances entering into the upbuild-
ing of a budding lawyer's practice.

Sam, during the World War, tried to join the United
States Marines. He went to the Brooklyn Navy Yard for
his physical examination and was rejected because of
deafness in his left ear, caused by scarlet fever. He then
enlisted as a four-minute man with Edward J. Meade,
chairman of the Liberty Loan drive, speaking nightly in
Brooklyn theaters.

It was Meade who telephoned him on a fall evening in
1919 that Angelino Clementi, bartender in a saloon.at
100 Flatbush Avenue, had shot and killed a patron

known as Big Bill Rooney. Meade had recommended Sam to Clementi's friends.

Rooney, who had just finished a term in Sing Sing, was a bad man when in his cups. He had staggered into the saloon brandishing a gun. Clementi was quicker on the trigger. At the trial Sam produced business men who testified as character witnesses for Clementi. He had never before been in trouble. The plea was self-defense and the jury, after brief deliberation, returned a verdict of not guilty. The historical value of the case is that it marked the first of the eighty-five Leibowitz acquittals—obtained consecutively—in murder cases.

It yielded the magnificent fee of three hundred dollars. Sam bought himself an accordion.

CHAPTER FOUR

MOTLEY AND MYSTERY

JOTTINGS from a young lawyer's notebook, A.D. 1920:
April 30: No clients today. Practiced on accordion.

May 4: To vaudeville show last night. Enjoyed Phil Baker, also the feature act, the "Great Gallando," the sculptor who models in clay.

May 7: Defended George Washington Jackson, colored, accused of stealing a dressed chicken from a ›meat market. The proprietor stepped from a rear room, he testified, and surprised Jackson, who beat it so fast his derby blew off. It was brought to court and introduced in evidence by the state. I proved an alibi for Jackson and got an acquittal. As we were leaving the courtroom he whispered to me, "Now that the case is over can I have my hat?"

May 10: Heard of a new third degree stunt today. At the ———— police station they were giving the works to a robber suspect. They took him into the squad room where another supposed prisoner, really a plant, was refusing to answer questions. He was in shirt sleeves with his back to a screen. A uniformed policeman with drawn revolver was facing him.

The boss dick was saying:

"We'll give you one more chance and if you don't talk we'll let you have it."

The plant of course remained silent.

"Count three and fire," said the dick to the policeman.

The gun wasn't loaded. A copper with a jumbo fire cracker was concealed behind the screen. The fuse had been timed. At the count of three it exploded. The plant fell and the dicks surrounded him. One emptied a bottle of mercurochrome over his shirt front and it was stained crimson.

"Shot through the heart," announced a phoney doctor. "He's dead."

They carried him from the room and turned to the robber suspect, standing him against the screen. The uniformed policeman leveled his gun at him and the boss dick asked, "Are you ready to talk?" The suspect was so scared he fainted. They revived him with a drink of whisky and he babbled out a confession.

May 11: Practiced on accordion.

May 12: Ditto.

May 14: Appeared in Federal Court for Wing Hai, cook on an English vessel, the *Castle*, which had sailed away while he was sightseeing. He had been seized by immigration inspectors, who claimed he had been smuggled into this country, although he carried a shore leave permit signed by the *Castle's* captain.

I obtained a writ of habeas corpus on the grounds that he had been framed by the interpreter at the Ellis Island hearing. The interpreter had handed Wing Hai a bag of peanuts, of which Chinese are very fond.

"You like them?" he would ask each time Wing Hai

would crunch one. Wing Hai would nod and the stenographer would make notes.

He had "answered yes" to such questions as "Weren't you smuggled in?" "Didn't you forge the captain's signature?"

It was a new use for peanuts.

May 18: Retained today by Kate Farris, a shoplifter and a five time offender. She lived under an assumed name in a quiet residential section of Brownsville in Brooklyn and was highly esteemed by her neighbors who thought her a widow in comfortable circumstances. She was devoted to her thirteen-year-old daughter, Mildred, a blue-eyed, golden-haired child, who was to be graduated in June in the public school and was, of course, as unsuspecting as the neighbors of her mother's profession. The police had been hunting Mrs. Farris for two years for jumping bail while awaiting trial on a shoplifting charge. Yesterday, while she was sewing on a birthday party dress for Mildred, two detectives walked in and arrested her.

May 20: A small world. The "Great Gallando" sent for me today. He broke down and cried as he talked. It's different from any case I've ever handled; damnedest story I've ever heard.

PATROLMAN EDWARD SHERIDAN of the Richmond Hill precinct, Brooklyn, traveling his beat in the early morning hours of May 19, 1918, overtook a sixteen-year-old girl wandering aimlessly about at Benedict and Atlantic Avenues. She was faint from hunger and slightly incoherent.

Her name was Florence Smith and she lived in Hempstead, Long Island, but she could remember neither the

street address nor the telephone number. She swooned as
Patrolman Sheridan pressed the questioning. He called
a police ambulance and sent her to St. Mary's Hospital,
Jamaica. She remained there until June 15, when she was
discharged into the custody of the Protestant Big Sisters
of Manhattan.

They treated her kindly and educated her and she developed mentally and physically. Her weight increased
from seventy pounds to one hundred and twenty. She was
paroled to Dr. Helen Montague, a psychologist interested
in child welfare.

In late April of 1920 the Big Sisters decided it was time
for her to receive confirmation and first communion in the
Episcopal Church. On the eve of the ceremonies she told
Dr. Montague she could not receive the sacrament until
she had revealed some things about her life. Dr. Montague
summoned Charles Harstadt and Miss Mary Ginnanie of
the Children's Society, and the girl told her story.

Her name wasn't Florence Smith and she didn't live in
Hempstead. She was Minnie Gallender and her father
was the "Great Gallando." He was now married to his
third wife, known on the stage as Mabel Delamere.

The father and stepmother utilized their spare time in
drinking beer and practicing systematic torture upon her,
she said. She had been beaten, stabbed, branded, starved
and imprisoned. She had never gone to school until the
Big Sisters befriended her. She had but one dress, a slip,
at home, and when she washed it she had to go nude.

The day before she ran away, she continued:

"I was in the kitchen when I heard my father's voice.
He threw a piece of wood with a nail in it at me, and it
hit me on the left side of the head. It stuck there and my

stepmother pulled it out and hit me again with it. My father threw a saucepan at me, then threw a knife, a fork, and a small flatiron at me.

"I screamed and crouched in a corner and my stepmother heated a knife in the stove and jabbed me with it."

Other acts recited by her were:

They told her she was going to die soon and they had dug her grave in the cellar.

A half brother, Albert, was instructed by the stepmother to pull out the girl's teeth with a pair of pliers. He broke off four at the roots before she fainted.

She was forced to stand undressed in the middle of the kitchen while her half brothers and sisters hurled knives, forks and dishes at her.

A bottle of water and a bun were her only sustenance at night. She skulked through alleys in the daytime searching garbage cans for stale bread and meat, drinking out of water troughs.

They stuck safety pins and hat pins into her. Dr. Ernest M. Vaughan, medical examiner for the District Attorney's Office, found fifty-one scars.

Her father was arrested, charged with felonious assault and his bail fixed at $2,500. It was then that he retained Leibowitz.

The "Great Gallando," commonly described as the Rodin of the stage, was an international celebrity, as much at home in the capitals of Europe as in the larger cities of America. He had modeled kings and queens, presidents and first ladies. He had entrée into the swankiest circles. It seemed unthinkable that he could be so accused.

Speaking through Leibowitz he denied everything and, "defied anybody to prove I have at any time ever abused my children." However, the girl persisted in her story, and the "Great Gallando" was indicted and brought to trial. District Attorney Harry Lewis took personal charge of the prosecution. He said that if the charges were true it was "the most terrible case in my experience as a lawyer."

A girlish picture in a straw sailor, white middy blouse and duck skirt, black curls falling to her shoulders, the daughter faced her father in court and calmly repeated her story. A searching two-hour cross-examination by Leibowitz failed to shake her. Dr. Vaughan testified as to the fifty-one scars. The "Great Gallando" could only enter a general denial and his testimony, therefore, was of no value, being negative.

The sympathy of the jury was naturally with the daughter.

Leibowitz, in this first critical test of his ability, had been doing some intensive thinking—and scientific reading. He had observed that all the fifty-one scars were on the left side of the girl's body. He consulted a neurologist, and when the latter confirmed what was in Leibowitz' mind, he subpœnaed him as a witness. The neurologist followed the "Great Gallando" on the stand, and his testimony stripped of technical phraseology, was that:

Minnie Gallender was suffering from hysterical amnesia, a comparatively rare ailment, involving physical as well as mental phenomena. That is to say, a benumbing of certain parts of the body and a splitting-off of the normal cerebral processes. The outward symptoms were insensible patches developing on the skin.

They may "not infrequently affect an entire lateral half

from head to foot; and the insensible skin of, say, the left side will then be found separated from the naturally sensitive skin of the right side by a perfectly sharp line of demarcation down the middle of the front and back."

The victims experience hallucinations, losses of memory and a species of self-hypnosis, due to the fact that the splitting off process results in two personalities, the primary self and a secondary self. The secondary self ordinarily is subservient to the primary self, but "in cases like that of Minnie Gallender, it rises to the surface of the consciousness to assert itself and produce the hallucinations."

Leibowitz stressed the testimony of his neurologist in his summation. The District Attorney ridiculed it, emphasizing Minnie's youth, innocence and Cinderella status. The jury deliberated long enough to smoke cigars, and returned with a verdict of guilty. The "Great Gallando" was sentenced to the penitentiary.

Minnie went back to the Protestant Big Sisters and Leibowitz reluctantly wrote his first big case off as a defeat.

"A gentleman to see you," announced the realty steno, poking her head in the door of his office on a Monday morning two weeks later.

"Well, do your stuff," he grinned.

She hesitated a moment and, lowering her voice:

"It's the assistant to the District Attorney."

"Send him right in."

The prosecutor's greeting was a handshake and congratulations.

Minnie Gallender had admitted her story was a hoax. The scars were self-inflicted. She didn't know why she did it. She said she "came to" as if emerging from a trance after her father went to prison. Leibowitz and his neurologist had been vindicated.

"WHY," chided Raffal Mayer, the butcher, "do you wait so late to buy your meat this Saturday?"

"We were all day with friends in Astoria, L. I.," apologized Mrs. Bessie Warnelas, "and I had to undress the baby and put her to bed before I came down."

"It is," explained Mayer, "that I am in a hurry to get to Daniel Kornstein's, the tailor, before he closes. He is pressing my Sunday suit."

"I will have some of your best lamb chops," said Mrs. Warnelas.

"I have no lamb chops, but I have pork chops."

"Let me look at them."

Mayer vanished into the icebox and returned with eight choice loin cuts. He spread a piece of waxed paper on the glass disc of the scales, tossed the cuts thereon, and he and his customer concentrated their attention on the weight pointer. It gyrated half way round the dial, reversed and quivered to a stop at two pounds plus. Mayer paused to let the full significance of the excess impress itself upon Mrs. Warnelas, then:

"To you sixty cents."

"Fifty-five," said Mrs. Warnelas.

"Sixty," he replied firmly.

She counted out a quarter, three dimes and a nickel, received her purchase, bade him goodnight and left.

The shop was on the sidewalk level of a three-story tenement building at 109 Ten Eyck Street in the Williamsburg section of Brooklyn. It was a hot summer night and the neighbors were either congregated on the front steps or sitting by windows and open doorways for a breath of fresh air. A few of them idly watched the butcher hanging up clean paper bags on the racks of hooks in the two front windows, a decorative custom in meat markets over holidays and weekends.

Presently the ceiling light was extinguished and the place was in darkness. Only for a moment, though. A lightning flash of flame illumined the interior. The plate glass panes of the front windows bent outward, crashed to the sidewalk and the neighborhood was rocked by a terrific explosion.

It was 11:59 o'clock when Isaac Ludgate, acting chief of the 35th Battalion, responding to his bedside alarm, leaped into his boots and turnouts to negotiate the mile distance from the fire house to the butcher shop in two and a half minutes. Engine Company No. 216, commanded by Captain William H. Bedell, was already there and stretching hose. Hook and Ladder Company No. 108 and Engine Company No. 213 arrived within thirty seconds.

The fire was confined to the shop and was soon under control. Ludgate groped his way through the smoke to determine the origin. He was accompanied by Bedell. Simultaneously they halted in the rear of the shop, simultaneously they knelt and began sniffing. A suspicious odor had assailed their experienced nostrils.

"Kerosene," surmised Ludgate.

"I'm not sure," mused Bedell, "it may be that or gasoline. It's some kind of volatile oil."

"Must have been a wicked explosion to bust those windows," observed Ludgate.

"It's arson all right," replied Bedell.

The trained beagles of the department, whose specialty was solving incendiary crimes and running down firebugs, were soon on the job. Assistant Fire Marshal William B. Anderson, "Old Sherlock Holmes," as he was called, arrived at 2:30 A.M. He not only detected kerosene but found a butcher's apron and a quantity of rags soaked in oil. He summoned his colleague, Assistant Fire Marshal Jacob Winkler, who contributed the discovery of two broken bottles, apparently kerosene containers.

Sniffing about on hands and knees, Winkler scooped up a handful of sawdust.

"Smell this," he said to Anderson.

"Ha! More oil," affirmed "Old Sherlock."

"I'll take it along for evidence," said Winkler.

The Police Department was represented by Detective Thomas J. Carroll, who had started his investigation thirty minutes after the fire was reported. He first interviewed Harry Samuelson, proprietor of a laundry across the street from the meat market. Samuelson, who turned in the alarm, had seen plenty. He was looking when Mayer hung up the paper bags and turned out the light. He saw the lightning flash of flame, the explosion, and "a man running out the front door in a stooping manner with his straw hat over his face."

Mrs. Agnes Blez, standing by the door of her home at 106 Ten Eyck Street, identified Mayer as the man she, too, saw running. Mrs. Margaret Murillo, sitting by a window of her first floor apartment at 102, heard some one yell, "Get a-hold of him," and also saw Mayer running.

Carroll, after advising with Anderson, went to the butcher's home, stalked into his bedroom and ordered him to "get up and get dressed."

"What's the matter?" asked Mayer.

"You know what's the matter; your place caught fire."

He took him to the Stagg Street police station where

Anderson questioned him. Was his place insured? Yes, for
$1,800. Had he ever had a fire before? No. Did he sell
kerosene? No. Why did he have it around? To clean the
scales. Suddenly Anderson shot at him:

"What did you want to do, get rid of the shop? Burn
it up?"

"No, I didn't want to get rid of it," protested Mayer,
"I am doing a good business."

But he spent the night in custody. The sleepless beagles,
stalking the trail like bloodhounds, located Mike Yukulas,
a former roomer at the butcher's home, who said Mayer
had offered him one hundred dollars to set fire to the shop.
It was the decisive link in the circumstantial chain of evidence. Mayer was arraigned in Magistrate's Court, bound
over to the Grand Jury and indicted for arson in the first
degree. The case was going great guns. "Old Sherlock"
had got his man again.

In the District Attorney's office of Kings County,
Brooklyn, in 1921, a new face appeared—a shrewd-eyed,
pug-nosed, Irish face, crowned with a fighting mop of
white hair—the face of William F. X. Geoghan, an assistant who was to justify the weighty name by his heft
as a prosecutor. The careers of Geoghan and Leibowitz
were to run parallel and in conflict for more than ten years
—the one insatiably ambitious for a record of convictions
to further his progress toward that shining goal of the
political bar—the New York State Supreme bench; the
other equally ambitious for a record of acquittals to establish himself as New York's foremost criminal lawyer.
Both egoists, both unyielding fighters, both inflexibly
tenacious of purpose, they were utterly non-assimilable.
They loved each other like poison.

Leibowitz, in the summer of 1923, when he was retained as Mayer's counsel, had achieved a formidable local reputation. He had appeared in one thousand cases—felonies and misdemeanors—in the Kings County and Brooklyn courts, with a batting average on acquittals of slightly better than .800 per cent. His uncanny success had given rise to a saying, "When Leibowitz steps into a case it's two strikes on the D.A.'s office." It didn't make the young lawyer a bit sore. He admitted he was pretty good.

The battling Irishman and the battling Jew faced each other October 15, 1923, before a jury in County Judge Franklin Taylor's court-room. The mass of evidence assembled by the fire marshal's office was so tremendously conclusive and the defense case relatively so hopeless, that it seemed a waste of the taxpayers' money to try it.

Geoghan opened with Acting Battalion Chief Ludgate on the stand, who testified to the "strong odor of kerosene," and how he searched for an oil tank and couldn't find it. He was followed by Captain Bedell of Engine Company No. 216, whose testimony was similar. Leibowitz was interested in details of their sniffing ability. He prodded them with such questions as:

"Did you smell burning fat?"

"Did you smell burning grease?"

"Did you smell the pulp in the wood?"

"Did you smell burning paper?"

"Did you put your nose on the floor?"

"Did you put your nose to the wood?"

"Was your nose able to tell you where the kerosene came from?"

"Was your nose able to lead you to the spot where it was?"

"Old Sherlock" Anderson reviewed his examination of

Mayer and his investigation of the premises. Leibowitz, after Geoghan had finished with him, wanted to know if he could distinguish "between the odor of gasoline that has been consumed in a fire and the odor of kerosene."

There was a different smell between the two, the marshal believed.

"Can you tell this jury now that you are able to distinguish between the smell of the remains of a fire in which kerosene had been consumed, and the remains of a fire in which gasoline had been consumed?"

"I think so."

"I don't want your thinking."

"I say I think so."

"I don't want your thinking, I want to know whether you say positively that you can distinguish. You can answer that yes or no if you want to."

"I have answered it, I do not think so—I think so."

"Which is it, you do not think so, or you think so?"

"I think so."

"Well, do you know?"

"I cannot swear positively that I can distinguish between the two of them, but I could tell either one of them."

"Will you please describe to the jury the smell of a fire that had contained gasoline?"

"I cannot describe the smell."

"You cannot describe the smell?"

"And you cannot either."

"Can you give us any idea how it smells?"

"I cannot describe a smell."

"Can you give us any idea how a gasoline smell is, can you describe it?"

"I said I cannot describe a smell."

"Can you give the jury an idea what the difference is between the two?"

"No."

To Assistant Fire Marshal Jacob Winkler, Leibowitz put the question:

"In all your experience as a fire marshal, have you ever heard of an incendiary fire in a butcher shop?"

Winkler's answer was, "No."

Leibowitz whacked away thus at all the State's witnesses, attacking their qualifications as experts. With Harry Samuelson, the laundryman, who had seen everything and turned in the alarm, he was mercilessly persistent as to motive. Hadn't Samuelson and Mayer had words because Mayer got tired of supplying him with change? Hadn't Samuelson taunted Mayer with being "a Polack"? The laundryman's answer was "No" to both questions. Leibowitz shifted to the night of the fire:

"You saw policemen there?"

"When the fire engine arrived there were policemen there."

"You stood there and talked for three hours with people?"

"Everybody talks when there is a fire."

"You talked for three hours with people?"

"Yes."

"But you did not mention a single solitary word that night about the fact that a man had run out of the building, and that there was a firebug, did you, as you have told us before?"

"I had nobody to mention."

"You had seen a man run out of the store that was blazing?"

"I saw a man run out of a store that was blazing."

"Very suspicious, wasn't it?"

"It appeared to me."

"It appeared to you that a man had set fire to the store?"

"Yes."

"You knew that when you called the fire department?"

"I knew that it was my duty to ring the alarm."

"You rang the alarm?"

"I rang the alarm when I saw the fire."

It was one of those neighborhood quarrels. Mayer in his halting English told about it during his direct examination by Leibowitz. Samuelson's boy had bounced a rubber ball against his show windows:

"I chase him. The laundryman comes out and says, 'You dirty Polack, you keep your hands off my boy,' and I say, 'You better take your eyeglasses off and come this side of the street and I will show you how I am a dirty Polack.' "

Since which the butcher and the laundryman had not spoken.

As for Mrs. Agnes Blez and Mrs. Margaret Murillo, the other eyewitnesses, they were embattled housewives, according to the defense testimony, and aligned with Samuelson. Why, people even repeated to Mayer Mrs. Blez' remarks:

"She say, 'I don't like to buy meat from him. He is a very strong fellow; he should work in a factory. Why do you go to his shop?' "

Mike Yukulas, the former roomer, who testified Mayer offered him one hundred dollars to start the fire, had tried to make love to Mayer's wife. She had chased him with a broom and he had called her an "outkayer" and a "nagina," meaning a yellow pine tree. Mayer had ordered him from the house and he had threatened, "I am going to fix you."

Yukulas had testified he moved from the Mayer home on June 9. Hearken to Leibowitz:

Q. How do you know it was June 9? A. That time when I left on Saturday I looked at the calendar, and it was the 9th.

Q. You are positive? A. Yes.

Q. What calendar did you look at? A. It was hanging in the room on the wall.

Q. Did you go to the calendar and look at it to make sure it was June? A. It was hanging in my room and I looked at it.

Q. You remember particularly it was June 9th? A. I imagine, but I am not positive it was the 9th.

Q. You told us before you were positive. A. Yes, I did say.

Q. Did you make a mistake before when you said you were positive? A. I am not positive now.

Q. Did you make a mistake before when you said you were positive? A. Then I must have made a mistake.

Q. Was it an English calendar? A. Yes, sir.

Q. Do you read English? A. No, sir.

Q. What does "Sat." in English mean on a calendar? A. I could not tell you.

Q. What does "Fri." in English mean on a calendar? A. I could not read English so I could not tell you.

Leibowitz had trapped him cold. He further impeached his testimony by subpœnaing his employer, Peter Atkochaites, a garment contractor, to whom, Yukulas said, he had confided Mayer's offer to start the fire. Atkochaites denied Yukulas had ever mentioned it.

Geoghan, however, caused Mayer to spend an uncomfortable two hours in cross-examination. After obtaining admissions from him that he was satisfied with his business and intended to remain in it, he produced an advertisement inserted by Mayer in a Lithuanian paper. Translated it read that the shop was "a very good, nice, worked-up place" and could be bought "very cheap." Mayer couldn't account for money he had withdrawn from the bank.

There was a gas stove in a small rear room. His wife had lighted it early Saturday night to "boil some fat." He didn't know whether or not it was still burning when he left. Yes, there was kerosene in the shop. He used it to clean the gold-plated metal of the scales.

Betting favored the prosecution when the case went to the jury. It deliberated ten hours, nine of its members holding out for conviction, two for acquittal, and the twelfth noncommittal. Its foreman reported to Judge Taylor it was hopelessly deadlocked and he dismissed it.

Four months later, in February, 1924, the second trial was begun, County Judge Alonzo G. McLaughlin presiding. The Leibowitz strategy was characterized by two innovations.

(1) The spearhead of the defense was John C. Olsen, a chemist, graduate of Knox College, Illinois, Chicago University, Johns Hopkins, Professor of Analytical Chemistry at the Polytechnic Institute of Brooklyn, and Secretary of the American Institute of Chemical Engineers.

(2) And Raffel Mayer was kept from the witness stand.

The Professor, as he was addressed, finished what Leibowitz had started. He proved the fallibility of the fire department's expert sniffers.

Leibowitz had Professor Olsen prepare some fifteen

small glass vials containing water, kerosene, gasoline, benzol and other volatile oils. Each of these vials had a label bearing a number, and Leibowitz kept a key in his pocket indicating the contents of each. He presented this series of vials to each State witness in turn and asked him to smell and identify the contents for the jury. The result was surprising. One witness swore that the odorless water was gasoline, while another insisted with equal vehemence that it was benzine. To confound the witness even further Leibowitz produced from his pocket another vial, also containing a colorless liquid, but this time the contents were concentrated kerosene. After inhaling the pungent vapors, one of the witnesses now insisted that each of the vials which he had already smelled contained kerosene.

Leibowitz's purpose in all this was not only to demonstrate the fallibility of the sense of smell, but also to try to prove that the odor detected by the firemen and others upon entering the butcher shop was that of creosote which is an odor given off from burning wood which has been saturated with fatty oils, in this case the fatty oils coming from meats.

The jury after a four-day trial voted a not guilty verdict and Geoghan smarted under the sting of another defeat—by Leibowitz.

The young lawyer's notebook after 1922 was devoid of mention of accordion practice. Its pages were devoted to law practice. Leibowitz was on his way.

Since the Monday in June of 1919 when Izzy the Goniff, the "Millionaire Pickpocket," scouting for promising talent, had retained him as counsel, he had been swamped with clients. Many of them, in the vernacular, were punks, but they had the cash in hand. Leibowitz had boosted his retainer fee for felony cases to $5,000. His feats were the talk of the underworld.

Big Business of the Volstead era had not yet discovered him, but it was going to. And he was to be wined and dined by the country's foremost rising Public Enemy for a dizzy exploit.

CHAPTER FIVE

LITTLE RED RIDING HOOD

IT is a tale of Hell's Pavement, which runs down to
the docks where the tall ships lie. It is a tale of
the East River; of the "Rose of the Waterfront," and
of rollicking, landlubber buccaneers who lived and loved
and died with uproarious gusto. . . .

Blue-eyed, flaxen-haired Anna Lonergan remembers the
house in Brooklyn where she was born because it had
a small garden in the rear and she used to play in it.
"You were brought up with the flowers," her mother
said.

She was enrolled in the Sacred Heart Sodality as soon
as she was able to walk, and confirmed, when she was
nine, in the Church of the Assumption. The Sisters of
the parochial school were fond of her and would let
her run errands and accompany them on shopping tours.
Her favorite saint was Theresa of the Little Flower.
Whatever you asked of Theresa—if it was for your good
—she gave you, but you must pray nine successive weeks.
Anna had rheumatism of the heart. She always carried
about with her the medallion picture of Theresa, along
with the gold medal of the Sacred Heart of Jesus, and
her rosary. She hoped to take the veil and be a nun.

95

One morning her mother dressed her in her best bib and tucker. A horse-drawn van came and the household furnishings were stowed into it. The Lonergans were migrating across the River to Manhattan. The new home had no garden. It was a tenement in the parish of St. James Church, 23 Oliver Street. Anna was four years old.

The day she saw her first shooting she was playing on the sidewalk at Roosevelt and Cherry Streets. Men with popping revolvers appeared from everywhere; advancing and deploying, skirmisher fashion; scurrying from tree to tree, seeking cover between houses and in doorways, as they fired and reloaded. People scattered. Anna was left alone, clapping her hands in childish glee at the exciting noises. The belligerents were Monk Eastman and her Uncle Jim and their respective yeomanry.

"Jiggers! The cops!"

The cry caused hostilities to end as abruptly as they had begun. Uncle Jim eased up to his niece, who was wearing a long, red cape with a hood attached. She had pushed the hood back. Uncle Jim dropped something into it and whispered:

"Get going. Take that to your mother."

It was a big revolver and the barrel was smoking hot. The contact with her spine made Anna squirm.

"Keep your hands off it," warned Uncle Jim.

She trotted home and delivered the weapon to her mother. The incident gave Uncle Jim a grand idea. Thereafter Anna was his companion on sundry expeditions involving the possible elimination of bothersome enemies. Nobody could suspect a man of sinister designs who held a baby cuddled in his arms.

They lived close to the Fulton Fish Market, Pier 20,

the East River, where Uncle Jim was employed as a cooper.

The family later, when little Anna was five, moved back to Brooklyn, settling in "Irishtown," in the shadows of the Manhattan and Brooklyn Bridges.

John Lonergan—the doughty "Pinky" of the local prize ring—was Anna's father. He fought bare knuckled and drank his liquor straight. He was one of John L. Sullivan's sparring partners. His intermittent earnings were inadequate to support his rapidly increasing brood—which eventually was to number sixteen—so Anna at fourteen went to work, first in a department store at three dollars a week, then in a shoe store at five dollars a week.

Pinky opened a bicycle and hardware store in Bridge Street, not far from McLaughlin Park and St. James Pro-Cathedral. The gun battles continued. Anna, out for a stroll of a summer's evening, almost ran into one. The firing started as she was nearing the Park. Dusk had fallen and the tiny spurts of flame gleamed like dancing fireflies. It was a thrilling sight.

"Oh, you should have heard those nineteen or twenty guns going," she reminisces.

The Irish and the Italian boys were exchanging pleasantries. The Irish were led by Anna's brother, Richard, who lost a leg under a train, bought an artificial one and was nicknamed Peg Leg. But it was a misnomer. A peg leg, explains Anna, is straight, merely a stump. Richie, as she calls her brother, had a wooden leg or limb. He paid $150 for it and could make its toes wiggle.

Prominent among the Italians were a couple of youngsters known as Frankie Yale and Al Capone; tough, smart, ambitious and fiercely race conscious. They weren't going to let the Wops be pushed around by shantytown Irish.

In a little while the police were swarming through the Park, but it was as silent and deserted as the churchyard across the street. The bluecoats, after putting the usual futile questions to tight-lipped neighbors, climbed into the patrol wagon and left. Richie, in the Lonergan home, told Anna:

"There are some nice guns down there in the cemetery. I'd like to go after them but I don't dare."

Anna volunteered. A picket fence, sharply spiked, surrounded the churchyard. The headstones, thickly clustered, loomed in ghostly outline. Her mother, carrying a market basket, stood outside. They talked in whispers. Methodically Anna began her search and in a few minutes it had yielded three revolvers. She passed them through the pickets.

"That's plenty," said her mother.

"But Richie says there are a lot of them," continuing the quest.

"God, Anna, don't step on the graves."

"They can't feel it, Mom."

She had just handed the ninth gun through the pickets.

"Come on, Anna, the priest is calling for the mass."

"Not till I find them all."

The basket held eleven pieces of artillery when Anna finally shinned the fence again. Five belonged to Richie's boys and six to the Italians. Highly pleased, Richie telephoned their headquarters:

"You fellows lost quite a few biscuits last night. I am returning them tomorrow."

He wrapped each weapon in tissue paper and Anna next day took them to the headquarters—a poolroom

in City Park at St. Edward's Street—and delivered them
to the Italians' leader, Ralph Filsey D'Amato.

In Brooklyn's Irishtown there dwelt a lusty-blooded
youth, son of a dockside watchman at Pier 20. His name
was William Lovett and his parents, devout Catholics,
wished him to prepare for the Franciscan Brotherhood.

Encouraged by his sister, Lillian, whom he idolized,
he dutifully thumbed his textbooks, but study was irk-
some. His animal spirits rebelled. He could endure it
only so long. Then he must loose his pent-up feelings
in some strange wild prank, as when he hurled a brick
at a policeman and got six months in jail to think it over.

America entered the World War April 6, 1917. He
enlisted April 7, and was doughboying it in France six
months later. He was over there two years, winning a
D.S.C. His sister died meanwhile. He came back "Wild
Bill" Lovett.

Dennis (Dinny) Meehan, a two-hundred-pounder, was
boss of the White Hands, supreme in the Red Hook
section from the Brooklyn Bridge to the Gowanus Canal
and beyond; controlling the loading and unloading of
ships, likewise of trucks, and the working time of those
who toiled along the docks. Barge and wharf owners as
well paid tribute.

Wild Bill came back with his tinware and citation,
and mustard gas eating at his lungs. Meehan, arrogant
with power, had expanded into dope, a racket from which
the White Hands had traditionally remained aloof. Meehan was in bed in his flat at 452 Warren Street the evening of February 29, 1920. Three men entered through
the kitchen.

"Don't go in there," said Meehan's four-year-old son, indicating the bedroom, "my papa's asleep."

One of them handed him a nickel, patted him on the head and led him to the door:

"Don't worry, sonny. Run out and buy some candy. Your daddy won't wake up."

The youngster sped downstairs and to the confectionery store on the corner. The three men were gone when he returned and his father was dead with nine dum dum bullets in his brain and heart. Over night the White Hands transferred allegiance to Wild Bill—all, that is, except talkative Bill Quilty. His body was found slumped outside a Red Hook speakeasy.

Chicago gained an unexpected visitor following an argument in an Irishtown restaurant between Wild Bill and an Italian, in which the Lovett Army .45 had the last word. There was a hostile eye witness, which meant heat. Wild Bill decided a change of scene would be beneficial. He boarded a freight train incognito and met up with a world war veteran, Paddy Carroll, who displayed his honorable discharge. It was a fatal error. He died that night in a hobo jungle of an overdose of lead, and his fellow bum became Paddy Carroll for the duration of the Chicago sojourn.

Returning to New York he resumed his identity and responsibilities as chief of the White Hands and boss of the docks. Testing the metal of a new recruit was a hobby with him. He would balance a tin can on the rookie's head and let fly with his .45. He was a dead shot. If the rookie trembled and he missed, he would yell:

"You're yellow. Beat it."

Perhaps because of his reading while studying for the

Franciscan Brotherhood, he had a discriminating ear for English. One of his men invariably pronounced "thirty" as "dirty." It annoyed him. He would sit for an hour at a time teaching him the correct pronunciation. Always, however, the pupil would relapse into "dirty," and Wild Bill would bellow:

"If I didn't know your mother, I'd end you."

As his grunting, sweating crews labored at their tasks he would roar out the songs of the trenches:

The infantry, the infantry, with dirt behind their ears,
They can whip their weight in wildcats and drink their
weight in beers ...

Our grease ball is a dirty, God damn bum,
Our grease ball is a dirty, God damn bum,
Our grease ball is a dirty bum,
He bails out the swill and makes the slum,
Hinky dinky parlez-vous.

and for an encore:

Digging a ditch, you son of a bitch.

Wild Bill was as gargantuan in his drinking as in all else. His normal consumption of liquor was two quarts a day, and his eating in proportion. When he was drunk, therefore, it wasn't maybe. He was that way the night he dropped in for a social call on hot-tempered Eddie Hughes and two other acquaintances. An eight-gallon crock of home brew was standing in a corner. Wild Bill bet he could spit in it. He won the bet with no takers. He yanked off his shoes, tossing them carelessly across the room. One splashed in the beer.

"I'm going to sleep here tonight," he announced, and stretched himself on the bed.

Hughes waited till he was snoring then fired a bullet into his left breast near the heart. It woke Wild Bill up. He leaped from the bed and chased the three men down the stairway to the street, yelling:

"You're yellow. You're three to one and I haven't got a gun. Come back and finish it."

He staggered to the telephone, summoned a taxi and rode to the Cumberland Street Hospital. It happened that Anna Lonergan's mother was a patient there. When Anna came to visit her, she said:

"Bill Lovett is in the ward here, and dying. You should go down and speak to him."

"I don't like him," said Anna. "Who wants to see that gunman?"

Her brother Richie, Wild Bill's good friend, was wounded in the arm a few days later in a speakeasy brawl, and was also brought to the hospital. He, too, asked her to "go down and see Wild Bill; he likes you." But Anna was stubborn. Or was she shy? Her thoughts were temporarily diverted from the hospital. Her mother had gone home and her father, John Lonergan, had been shot to death. Wild Bill, weak as he was, managed to attend the funeral. During the ride to Calvary Cemetery he changed from one carriage to another to elude his enemies who were gunning for him. That was on a Sunday. The next day Frankie Healy, a White Hander, was killed on his way to the docks.

Mrs. Lonergan, meanwhile, had been arrested, charged with her husband's murder. It was then that Anna accepted Wild Bill's attentions and advice.

"Let her stand trial," he said; "if she loses we can try an insanity plea later."

She didn't. She won a speedy acquittal. Pinky Lonergan, who had developed into a wife-beating drunkard, had threatened to kill her. She had fired in self-defense.

A bullet had overtaken Eddie Hughes and the police had seized Wild Bill. He was in the Raymond Street jail with bail set at $10,000. Anna visited him every day and he wrote her a letter every night with a special delivery on Sunday. She could only raise security for bail of $7,500. She was trying to get it reduced to that amount. A month elapsed before she succeeded. The day Wild Bill was freed she was waiting for him. Said he without preliminary:

"We'll go to Manhattan and get married. You're my bodyguard from now on."

They went to City Hall, obtained their license and were married by a deputy clerk. They waited an hour for a taxicab to take them to the Lonergan home in Brooklyn because Wild Bill refused to ride in any but a green one, the occasion being what it was.

The honeymoon was spent in New Jersey and Wild Bill was the life of all the parties. He would improvise ditties about the bride:

"Anna took out her false teeth, hung her ear on the wall, put her cork leg in the corner," etc.

Now that he was married he didn't want to make scenes in public. He had a penchant for shooting out the lights in street cars. He appointed Anna his guntoter. She packed the .45 in her purse. Thinking it over she decided it would be still better if the weapon remained at home, so she bought a monkey wrench and substituted it.

"Got the biscuit?" Wild Bill would ask as they were starting out for an evening's pleasure.

"Yes," Anna would say and he would give the bulge in the purse a satisfied pat.

The subterfuge worked till a bartender refused to serve him with a drink because he was stewed. He demanded the gun. Anna was forced to open the purse.

In the center of Wild Bill's forehead was a circular birthmark which in moments of emotional stress denoted the stages of his rising choler. Normally pinkish, it deepened to dull cherry, then warm rose, brick red and finally lurid crimson—incandescent, a baleful, blazing Cyclopean orb.

Reaching into the purse for the gun and finding a monkey wrench, Wild Bill went mute. The orb was in full splendor when he said to Anna:

"If I wasn't so nuts about you, I'd brain you with it."

She was the only woman he ever loved. He loved her so much, in fact, that when the honeymoon was three weeks under way, he stood her off ten paces, remarked, "I want to see what kind of stuff you're made of," and let go with a bullet. It clipped the big toe of her left foot.

Anna didn't whimper. She could take it. Wild Bill roared his delight. Anna was happy, too. She had found her man. Occasionally, to be sure, he would express sentiments that troubled her, especially when they were alone and discussing the mysterious things of life and death and what makes the wheels go round.

"Anna," he would say, "there ain't no God; there's only electricity."

It seems elementary even to mention that his code proscribed squealing. The proprietor of a saloon at Jay and York Streets, Brooklyn, called the police one evening when he was indulging in hilarious target practice with the lights. They had to club him into submission. In court next morning the magistrate gazed at his battered head and asked:

"What happened to you?"

"Well, Judge," grinned Wild Bill, "I'm going to tell you the truth. I was running for a seat in the patrol wagon and slipped and fell."

So many times had his scalp been broken by police clubs and so many times stitched up, that the suture formed a semicircular ridge around his forehead. He liked to swim, and Anna, when all other means had failed, would convoy him to the beach to sober up after a prolonged spree. On one such occasion he dived into three feet of water, hitting the bottom with such force that the scalp popped open, flapping like the visor of a cap. Anna hurried him to the office of a near-by doctor, who restitched it. After the job was completed Wild Bill examined it critically in a mirror, the birthmark turning crimson. Walking over to the doctor he slapped him down with the remark:

"A hell of a lot you know about stitching."

Another killing had occurred and the police, seeking as always to question Wild Bill, raided a flat where he was visiting. A .25 caliber revolver was found and the coppers accused Bill of its ownership. Contempt was in his voice and bearing as he replied:

"I don't carry cap pistols."

A bunch of his friends were talking of his numerous arrests.

"If the Brooklyn Bridge fell down they'd blame me for it," he said.

He and Anna were still honeymooning in New Jersey —they had been married four months—when he slipped out of the house one afternoon and went to Brooklyn. He telephoned her next morning. It was the first time he had spent the night away from her.

"I'm drunk," he said. "but I love you. I'm all right. I slept with a fireman."

He wanted her to come and get him but her feelings were hurt and she hung up the receiver. Almost immediately she regretted it and boarded a train for Brooklyn. She tramped Hell's Pavement till after midnight, visiting his old haunts. One she overlooked—a combination speakeasy and gang headquarters at 25 Bridge Street. Wild Bill reeled in there, blind, flopped into a chair and went to sleep. Four of the patrons eyed him gloatingly, whispered together and surrounded him. One had an iron bar.

Anna, resuming her search next day, remembered the speakeasy and telephoned its owner.

"He's gone," he told her.

"What time will he be home?" she asked, and the reply came over the wire:

"He won't be home. He's dead."

Anna identified him at the morgue. His head was bashed in—twenty-four fractures. His father wanted him buried in consecrated ground if "I have to carry him in on my back."

"No," said Anna, "he lived an atheist and he died one. I will not have them refuse him a church funeral."

They buried Wild Bill with military honors. They fired a salute and they sounded taps. He sleeps in the National Cemetery, Brooklyn, and—what a laugh he would get—on one side of him lies a detective and on the other a patrolman.

The "Rose of the Waterfront" was to be a widow less than two months. She was to marry upstanding Matty Martin, pal of Wild Bill's—but here the story leaves her and continues with the White Hands and Peg Leg Lonergan, who assumed their chieftainship after Wild Bill's death.

The Italians under Cira Terranova, the artichoke king, controlled the vegetable and market shipments along the East River dockside of Brooklyn. Wild Bill, content with his own racket, had not bothered them.

Peg Leg was more ambitious—and he needed money. Following the father's death the Lonergans had lost the bicycle and hardware store, their only source of income. Peg Leg broadcast that he would invade the Terranova field and the White Handers started muscling in. There were sluggings and stabbings. Peg Leg toured the waterfront, swaggering through its dives, boasting he would "run all the foreigners out."

Volstead, with its crazy sumptuary legislation, had spawned the illicit booze industry. Peg Leg wanted a share of the fabulous profits, and again he defied the Italians, who controlled the traffic along the waterfront. They consulted with Frankie Yale and others. The rash Irishman had issued a challenge that demanded but one kind of answer.

CHAPTER SIX

CAPONE

M IDNIGHT was striking.

"Here's luck; bottoms up," boomed the foghorn voice of Jack (Stickem) Stabile, barkeep, and glasses clinked in the Adonis Social and Athletic Club as elbows were crooked to down the toast. Even the pianist, the fiddler and the drummer gratefully abated their labors to join the wassail, for it was Christmas night of 1925, and the drinks were on the house.

By and large, one might say, joy was unconfined, especially among the female help, including Helen, the singer; May, the waitress; and Olga, the checkroom girl. The party of swarthy gentlemen at table No. 1 had been generous with their purchases and lavish with their tips.

And what mattered if each of their right coat pockets did bulge and sag a trifle?

The place was a speakeasy owned by two Italians, on the first floor of a decrepit two story tenement at 154 20th Street, South Brooklyn, in the Gowanus Bay section. Entrance was through a hallway, where wraps were checked. The café itself consisted of one room, forty by thirty feet; a bar, and a small quadrangular dance floor in a hollow square of tables. Orange colored bulbs in wall fixtures provided the illumination.

Agreeably mellowed by their Yuletide tipple, the musicians sentimentalized with the "Blue Danube" waltz, and presently three of the swarthy gentlemen were dancing with the girl employees to its seductive rhythm. Bartender Stabile went to the basement to tap a fresh keg of beer.

The interruption, timed as it was, had elements of wild west melodrama.

Peg Leg Lonergan had left his home at 9 P.M. to buy lights for the family Christmas tree. Dropping in at a saloon frequented by the White Hands, he encountered five acquaintances—Cornelius (Needles) Ferry, Aaron Harms, James Hart, Joseph Howard and Patrick (Happy) Mahoney. He bought a round of drinks. Each of the others bought a round. The house bought a round. Amply oiled, the six hailed a taxi and toured the neighborhood oases.

Sober, Peg Leg never would have crossed the Fulton Street deadline to set foot in the Adonis Club, hangout of his deadliest enemies. Not that he lacked courage, but that he was circumspect in keeping to his own bailiwick.

Midnight had just struck when he and his companions lurched through the entrance. Table No. 1 flung quick glances at them, then exchanged looks pithy with meaning. Peg Leg leered his contempt. A toothpick protruded from the left corner of his mouth and he constantly worked it about, screwing his lips into preposterous shapes. This business accentuated his insolent attitude.

Ferry, attracted by a pretty girl, went to the bar and struck up a conversation. They were soon having drinks together. He noticed the couples dancing and guffawed,

"Hey, look at the dames dancing with them dirty dagoes."

A beer bottle crashed over his head and he slumped to the floor. Peg Leg who, with the other members of his party, was seated at a near-by table, reached for his gun, but the "dirty dagoes" beat him to the draw. The lights went out. . . .

Patrolman Richard Morano of the Fifth Avenue station, traveling his beat at 3:30 A.M., stumbled over a man's body in front of the club. His flashlamp disclosed a red trail leading to the door, which was locked. He kicked it open. The flashlamp cut a silver cone through the darkness and framed in a circle of light, in a corner by the piano, lay two bodies face up.

One was that of Peg Leg, plugged in the brain and heart, his right hand on the butt of his gun, still in its armpit holster; the toothpick was intact between his graying lips. The other body was that of Harms. The third, on the sidewalk, that of Ferry.

The club interior was eloquent of battle—over-turned tables, shattered window panes, and bullets imbedded in the walls and back bar. The fiddle and the drum had been smashed, and the pianist's stool shot from under him. Scattered about the floor near the White Hands' table were five revolvers, all undischarged.

A couple of hours before Morano made his discovery, Patrolman Thomas McGrath saw a man crawling on hands and knees in Flushing Avenue near Troop Street. He was James Hart, wounded in the right thigh, and he collapsed after relating that he was standing on the corner when shot at by an automobile party of Christmas revelers. McGrath called an ambulance and sent him to the Cumberland Street Hospital. The only members of

the Lonergan gang who had escaped injury were Howard
and Maloney.

Deputy Inspector John J. Sullivan, in charge of Brooklyn detectives, directed the police investigation. He started
in by questioning Hart, Howard and Mahoney, then the
three girl employees and Stabile, the bartender. The killings had occurred the morning of Saturday, December
26. It was midafternoon of that day when Sullivan issued
instructions to bring in Al Capone, and hardly had the
message hit the teletype when Leibowitz received a telephone invitation to attend a dinner the same evening, in
Brooklyn's Williamsburg section.

Supposedly visiting his mother, Capone was really in
hiding here, as was his partner, Johnny Torrio. They were
in the midst of the machine gunning campaign in Chicago
that was to establish Capone as the Volstead Mussolini
of the city's $100,000,000 a year vice, booze and gambling
rackets—also of its politics, likewise a racket. The going
had become too hot for them. Enemy mobsters had blasted
Capone's car into the junk heap, narrowly missing the
Big Shot himself, and, ambushing Torrio as he was
motoring with his wife, had shattered his jaw with a load .
of buckshot.

The Gennas had risen. They were six brothers, born
in Marsala, Sicily, who immigrated to America in 1910
to settle in Chicago. They had with the advent of prohibition developed alky cooking into a $10,000,000 a year
industry, supplying the basic ingredients for the synthetic
bourbon, rye and Scotch whiskies peddled by bootleggers.
They were ambitious to rule the Unione Sicilione, a power-
ful political organization, whose founder and president,
Mike Merlo, had died. He was, by the way, the only one
of its seven presidents from 1924 to 1930 to die a natural

death. The Gennas contrived to seat their toughest brother, Angelo, in Merlo's chair, before Capone suspected what was up. His choice for the presidency was Antonio Lombardo, commission broker and cheese merchant. What happened is best told by the coroner's record for 1925:

> May 26: Killed: Angelo Genna
> June 13: Killed: Michael Genna
> July 8: Killed: Anthony Genna
> Nov. 13: Killed: Samuel Samoots Amatuma

The inquests were annoying and, besides, a forthright mayor, William E. Dever, and an honest chief of police, Morgan A. Collins, were smashing at Capone with ruthless raids on his gambling and vice dens in the notorious 22nd Street district.

Chicago temporarily had become decidedly unhealthful for the rising young No. 1 Public Enemy. So his fadeaway to Brooklyn. He was eventually to return, but without Johnny Torrio. Johnny had had enough. He was going to enjoy permanent sanctuary in the comparatively pious quietude of the purlieus of Long Island.

The lawyer's confessional, like that of the cleric, is sacrosanct. Leibowitz, therefore, while letting us view his client close-up, now, as on a later and more memorable occasion, shows us only the outward man, the impenitent Scarface. We are excluded from the legal shriving. We do not see him, *mea culpa;* we do not hear his cry *"Peccavi."* The inner Capone remains still the baffling enigma, the abysmal riddle of our generation—and perhaps will so remain for generations yet to come as the soul of the errant John Brown of the Noble Experiment goes marching on to meet its maker.

Al was guest of honor at the dinner Leibowitz attended. It was a stag affair with thirty diners seated at a long table, the chef d'œuvre being spaghetti, and at the conclusion of the meal Leibowitz had mapped his strategy.

Picture a tight rope walker trying to do a Blondin with nine men on his back and you visualize the delicate task confronting Leibowitz. Not only had he to defend nine men, but two of them, Joseph Howard and Patrick Mahoney, were members of the deceased Peg Leg's party—strange bedfellows the criminal law makes. The others, all Italians, were, besides Capone: John Stabile and Anthony Desso, bartenders; Sylvester Agoglia, owner of the club; Ralph Filsey d'Amato, George Carrozza and Frank Pizza.

The police were prepared to charge the nine with murder—the usual procedure—and Howard and Mahoney were thrust upon Leibowitz because the Capone partisans felt it was peculiarly incumbent upon them to take care of the surviving White Hands. Our Lawyer Blondin must negotiate his tight rope with his entire load intact, for if but a single passenger tumbled off (into police hands), the whole nine were lost. Leibowitz, that is, had to safeguard against the third degree with its possibility of a confession.

Try as they might the police had been unable to obtain information justifying grand jury action. Despite the number of persons present none would admit having seen the shooting—let alone having participated in it. The only hope of the police was for "a break." Pending that, they wanted above all else to question the key figure, Capone.

Capone wished otherwise. Leibowitz started his game of touch and go with the police by having Capone remain in hiding Saturday night. Then on Sunday morning he and d'Amato met at the Leibowitz home and, after breakfasting, motored to downtown Brooklyn, parking their cars on a side street two blocks from the 16th Street station house. The dragnet had pulled in the others the night before.

Leibowitz strolled over alone to tell Captain John J. Ryan of the detective bureau that, if he would pledge his word, to arraign Capone immediately, Leibowitz would produce him along with d'Amato. Ryan readily agreed and Leibowitz brought in his clients.

His object in surrendering them on a Sunday was to avoid the line-up at headquarters, which is not staged on that day. His purpose in exacting the promise from Ryan for immediate arraignment was to prevent the police from taking the prisoners to the "massaging room" at police headquarters and there subjecting them to the third degree. Leibowitz could say:

"I am handing over these men in good shape. They have been examined by witnesss and there are no marks upon their persons. You don't dare 'massage' them."

Headed by Ryan and Leibowitz the men walked five blocks to the Fifth Avenue court, where they were arraigned before Magistrate Charles Haubert, and held without bail for hearing the following Tuesday morning before Magistrate Francis A. McCloskey in homicide court. They were charged with homicide, and Capone was fingerprinted and locked in a cell at the Raymond Street jail. It is a fact to ponder on that during a brief visit in New York Capone should have been subjected to those processes of the law which he escaped altogether in the ten years of his sanguinary career in Chicago.

Representing the police, Captain Ryan had a shade the

better of Leibowitz in the second round of the touch and go game. Magistrate McCloskey not only refused to admit the nine to bail, although Capone's friends were present with $500,000 for that purpose, but adjourned the hearing another forty-eight hours until Thursday so that Captain Ryan's detectives could continue their investigation. Leibowitz' protests were of no avail.

The third round was a seesaw. Ryan asked for another forty-eight hours' delay—the police had been unable to find witnesses to sign a formal complaint. Leibowitz, pointing out that five days had elapsed since the triple killing with no evidence adduced against his clients, argued for dismissal of the charges, and Magistrate McCloskey acceded, discharging the prisoners. It looked like a victory for Leibowitz, but as the men walked from the courtroom a squad of Ryan's detectives seized them, hustled them into a patrol and started for police headquarters four miles away.

So what? Leibowitz had anticipated the strategy. He drew from an inside pocket a folded document and handed it to a young man at the curb astride a motorcycle with idling engine. The machine was soon speeding in and out of traffic. It made Borough Hall in three minutes flat. The youth dashed up the steps to the chambers of Supreme Court Justice William B. Carswell, who affixed his signature. The motorcyclist's next stop was police headquarters. The patrol hadn't yet arrived.

Ryan planned to circumvent Leibowitz through one of the White Hands' own members, James Hart, who was still in the Cumberland Street Hospital recovering from his wounds. The idea was to book the nine for felonious assault. It was good strategy, for in New York state defendants in such cases may be held until their alleged victim leaves the hospital. Thus the police would have opportunity "to work" on Leibowitz' clients.

The patrol arrived at headquarters. The detectives herded their prisoners inside. Ryan was waiting to book them. Up stepped the motorcyclist and handed him the document. It was a writ of habeas corpus calling for immediate court arraignment. Back to the patrol filed the prisoners, to be haled before Magistrate James J. Golden. Leibowitz was already there. His triumph was short-lived. Golden refused his application for bail, remanded the prisoners to jail and adjourned hearing on the assault charges for forty-eight hours. Said Golden to Leibowitz when he persisted in his demand for bail:

"You're too smart."

"If you want to get personal, I may get personal, too," barked Leibowitz.

"Get that man out of here," ordered Golden.

"Get me the minutes of this hearing," demanded Leibowitz of the court stenographer.

"There won't be any minutes," said Golden, closing the episode.

Round three was the law's by a wide margin.

One of the outstanding Leibowitz traits is doggedness. The reverses suffered at Golden's hands only stimulated his ardor. He visited Hart and obtained from him an affidavit that he had been shot by a stranger as yet unidentified, and that none of Leibowitz' clients was involved. Armed with this paper he appeared on Friday, January 1, before Supreme Court Justice Carswell, with a petition for the release of the prisoners on bail. It was granted and next day the charges were dismissed. Leibowitz had won round four and the decision in the game of touch and go.

Hiring a hall in Fourth Avenue, Brooklyn, the Italians celebrated the feat with a Lucullan repast. Capone, Johnny Torrio and Frankie Yale delivered speeches, and again and again the counsellor was compelled to bow his acknowledgment of cheers and shouts of "Viva Leibowitz." Champagne, gushing inexhaustibly at the diners' elbows, abetted the felicities.

Not present were Joseph Howard and Patrick Mahoney.

LEIBOWITZ in 1925 had moved from the side room cubicle in the realty broker's office to commodious quarters in the Brooklyn Chamber of Commerce Building. These seemed adequate to accommodate his expanding practice for years to come and would have been had Leibowitz remained the ordinarily successful criminal lawyer. By reason of his uncanny record of acquittals he became something more in the eyes of the public—his public. The superstition inherent in the human breast invested him with an aura of invincibility. His name was a magic symbol. He became a cult. It was inevitable, therefore, that he should outgrow Brooklyn. His unique talents demanded the larger stage of Greater New York City.

.

CHAPTER SEVEN

LET FREEDOM RING

JAIL delivery floor is forty-two stories up, at 225 Broadway, lower Manhattan. Double doors open into an anteroom. A young woman receptionist, pleasantly sophisticated, fetchingly tailored, sits behind a railing at a typewriter desk flanked by a telephone switchboard. She is calm of eye, persuasive of manner, and her voice is soothing with an Ethel Barrymore huskiness. She guards the portals of the Leibowitz sanctum. She is a lion tamer.

She divides her time between the typewriter and the switchboard. She lifts the French phone from its bracket and addresses the mouthpiece:

"Mr. Leibowitz's office. Yes, Mr. Blank."

Then the conversational formula varies. It may be any one of:

"Have you an appointment?"

"Mr. Leibowitz will give you fifteen minutes tomorrow morning at 11."

"Mr. Leibowitz is too busy to take the case."

"Mr. Leibowitz is in conference."

"Mr. Leibowitz is in court."

"Mr. Leibowitz is out of the city."

The visitor sees on his right a long bench filled with waiting clients, such a cross section of humanity as one might encounter in a subway train. The faces of both men and women—whether gangster or citizen, gun moll or housewife—have one expression in common—hope.

A Lilliputian catapults out of a side passageway, bounding past the clients' bench, volleying greetings in English and Italian. He has jack-in-the-box springs in his feet. He thrusts a sheaf of papers at the receptionist, turns and bounds back whence he came. He bristles with authority. Diminutive as a bantam gamecock, he has the head and features of a man wise beyond his years. He piques curiosity.

On the visitor's left is a table holding three tomes bound in black leather, bearing on their respective covers the inscriptions in gilt lettering: "Newspaper Reports (of) Famous Cases Tried by Samuel S. Leibowitz"; "Homicide Cases, Samuel S. Leibowitz"; "General Criminal Cases, Samuel S. Leibowitz"; and a duodecimo volume titled "Let Freedom Ring," a profile published by the *New Yorker*.

Head-high around the wall is a macabre frieze—the Pilgrim's Progress of a criminal lawyer, told pictorially. It is a series of framed photographs, action shots by newspaper cameramen, of climacteric moments in Leibowitz cases. The legends are self-explanatory:

"The Gravesend Bay Rowboat Murder Trial; Acquitted December 3, 1927."

"Grandma Angelina Mecili Murder Trial; Oldest Woman Ever Tried in New York; Acquitted June 21, 1928."

"Maurice De Near, Triangle Murder Trial; Saved from the Chair January 22, 1929."

"Daniel Chieppa, Honor Slayer Murder Trial; Acquitted November 21, 1929."

"Max Becker Murder Trial; Becker Hears Jury Say 'Not Guilty,' March 12, 1930."

"Ernest Wente, Dream Slayer Murder Trial; Acquitted December 8, 1930."

"Vivian Gordon Murder Trial, January 30, 1931."

"Four Gun Sweeney Murder Trial; Saved from the Chair March 11, 1931."

"Amy Conlin, Gigolo Murder Trial; Acquitted November 11, 1931."

"Vincent Coll, Baby Killer Trial; Acquitted December 28, 1931."

"Matteo Di Gregorio, Phantom Slayer Murder Trial; Acquitted October 22, 1932."

It might be called the trophy room of the big game verdict hunter. The visitor's scrutiny is interrupted by the receptionist. Mr. Leibowitz will see him. She gestures toward the side passageway. The private office is five steps to the right and a turn to the left—a spacious room done in restful browns, paneled in American walnut, with a fireplace, recessed bookshelves, comfortable chairs, a red leather divan and a massive glass-topped walnut desk.

Leibowitz, plumply undramatic, stands beside it. His thinning hair, prematurely gray, is parted on the left side and combed over. He is bald almost to the crown of his head. His brow is high, broad and sloping. His eyes are amber, his mouth wide and full lipped. His shoulders are square but stooped. His fingers are long and tapering. He wears a double-breasted blue suit with a vertical pin stripe, a soft shirt with collar attached, and a blue polka dot tie.

His greeting is robustiously genial—a hearty hand-shake, a heartier slap on the back:

"Hello; how's the old boy? Let me look at that handsome face. What's on the mind? How're the beer pipes?" He bandies wise-cracks. He is boyishly exuberant. His laugh is infectious. His face, placid in repose, lights with animation. The eyes grow warm and crinkle at the corners. The mobile lips come into play. His voice, a rich baritone, has timbre, power and gamut. He instrumental-izes with it as he does with his accordion.

Leibowitz is theater. He is always in character. His attitudinizing is instinctive rather than conscious. He is geared to the courtroom rôle he has so long enacted. He is the thrall of habit. He is the veteran actor forgetting to doff the sock and buskin. The bailiff's gavel is his callboy, and the twelve men in the jury box his audience. He analyzes the rôle, the versatility required:

"A criminal lawyer has to be a combination of a Belasco, a John Barrymore, an Einstein and an Al Smith. It's auto-intoxication, a species of complete submersion of self in a cause."

He recalls Eugene Brieux's play "Accused," in which counsel for defense in a murder trial, after the jury has brought in a not guilty verdict, explains to his mother why he pleaded for a client whom he knew to be guilty. In an advocate there occurs a kind of mysterious doubling of the personality, a power that becomes independent of him who speaks. Words are stronger than he. They take possession of him, enslave, enrapture, drag him on! One glowing phrase begets another, more vivid still. He wills an acquittal. Nothing shall stand in his way. His only object is to force the jury to see it.

"It's an emotion I've always gone through," says Leibowitz, "an exultation in the knowledge I was making the jury cry, molding it like clay. It's just the technique that thrills you. The criminal lawyer in the courtroom is like a surgeon. A surgeon never worries about the pain he causes the patient. He worries about the technique. If the criminal lawyer's technique is correct, the result must follow inevitably. That is, acquittal."

The horror play "Dracula," with its clutching hand, so stirred his vivid imagination that he looked under the bed the night he saw it. He has never forgotten it. He speaks of its atmosphere and draws a parallel:

"A courtroom is a stage, and atmosphere is everything. Take that Hoffman case. There the science of ballistics was simplified, dramatized, and brought down to the understanding of the men in the street, the jurors."

The technique! That is everything:

"There isn't a question I ask that I don't know what the answer will be, or that I'm not reasonably sure I know. I never ask a witness 'Why?' That is one of the failings of lawyers. They give the witness a chance to lambast them with stuff they don't want in the record. That three-letter interrogative has ruined more criminal and civil cases than any other single question."

He expounds his fundamental theory of "popularizing" the evidence; of "making every abstract or trite thing live":

"I would not ask a witness, 'How long did it take you to get there?' I would put it, 'It didn't take you more than a couple of snaps of the finger (illustrating) to get there, did it?' I have created a word picture. I would not ask, say, 'Did you get there quickly?' I would phrase it, 'You got there in a hop-skip-and-a-jump, eh?'

"Consider credibility. I have frequently shot the question, 'Have you ever told a lie in your life?' Invariably the witness blurts out 'No.' That calls for a laugh, for there isn't a man living who hasn't told a lie. I jab the dagger deeper and twist it around with, 'Are you telling the truth now?' I have destroyed the whole effect of the testimony of a witness who has been on the stand for three or four hours with those two questions."

Leibowitz pushes a button and a deep red glow suffuses the synthetic logs in the fireplace. The visitor is surprised. He thought they were real. Leibowitz chuckles boyishly.

"It's quiet up here," he muses; "you're away from things. I like an office like a home. A man spends half his life in it, you know."

He walks to a south window, commanding a sweeping view of lower Manhattan and the Bay. Dusk has fallen. Gleaming above Bedloe's Island is the torch of Liberty, enlightening the world.

"A great place for a criminal lawyer's office," he half soliloquizes. "God, it's an awful strain, though. I think sometimes I've lived a million lives."

Sight of the Statue has recalled the early days. He talks of the immigrant mother and her boundless pride in the son who was graduated from the great American university. He was delivering his first public address in a small neighborhood auditorium in Brooklyn. His parents were occupying aisle seats down front. He had hardly begun speaking when the mother arose and bustled up on the platform to pluck a raveling from the trousers of his tuxedo.

"Sam, you're late for dinner." It is the voice of the Lilliputian, stern, peremptory, rebuking.

"Yes; what time is it?"

"Seven forty-five; you were to be home at 7:30."

"Did you phone the missus?"

"Yes; you're to be there at 8."

The Lilliputian is John Theodore Capozucca, nicknamed Terry, whilom jockey and flyweight boxer. Leibowitz in the early twenties defended a Tony Muzio, charged with slashing the throat of a Frank Tuorto. Much to the amazement of Tuorto's relatives, among them Capozucca, his cousin, Leibowitz won an acquittal. Curiosity and grudging admiration getting the better of his bitterness, Capozucca visited Leibowitz at his office. He has been with him ever since.

A rare understanding exists between these two. They complement each other. They are inseparable. Terry is Leibowitz's eyes and ears and hands and feet in all matters of professional and personal detail. He thinks for him. He anticipates his every wish. He watchdogs him, bullies him, tyrannizes over him.

Leibowitz one afternoon was deep in a discussion of the Negro question. He had just returned from Decatur, Alabama, where he had served as chief counsel in the famous Scottsboro case. Harlem had staged a tremendous demonstration for him and he had been deluged with invitations to address mass meetings throughout the East. He was leaving that evening by plane to fill a speaking engagement in Washington, D. C.

"It has given me," he was saying, "a vista of 14,000,-000 people of whom the greater proportion are fettered in the chains of bondage. I shall remain active in this case as long as there is a breath of life in me."

"Sam," cut in Terry, "you gotta have a clean shirt."
Leibowitz ignored him:
"It is not the cause of the Negro alone; it is the cause
of my own people. What a glorious opportunity it was to
fall to the lot of a Jew to strike a blow for the emancipa-
tion of the colored race. The Scottsboro case has awakened the Negro masses. Only yesterday the Negro in the
street of Decatur was a cowering, beaten individual.
Today he—"
"Sam, you gotta have a clean shirt."
Leibowitz continued talking. Terry left the room. He
was gone about fifteen minutes, returning with an oblong
parcel. He undid the wrapping, removed the pins from
the shirt and spread it out on the glass-topped walnut
desk.

"Now put it on," he ordered, and Leibowitz obeyed.

Terry is czar of the office. His knowledge of legal
routine is matched only by his efficiency. He has an ency-
clopedic memory for names, dates and incidents of Leibowitz's cases. Like his employer he came up from the city
streets and when alone they talk the patois. With Terry,
then, it is "Sam," but when in public it is "Mr. Leibowitz."

"It took me twelve years to cure him of the ponies,"
says Leibowitz. "When the horses would start running at
the Metropolitan tracks each summer he would be off
like a schoolboy on vacation."

Except for his home and family, Leibowitz lives for
the courtroom. He has no outside interests. He is stolidly
bourgeois, a thoroughly domestic husband and father.

"I'm not colorful like Fallon," he says a trifle impa-
tiently; "I'm prosaic."

He has a singular and refreshing naïveté that expresses

itself unexpectedly. The writer had mentioned Clarence Darrow and compared a certain detail of his technique in the Loeb-Leopold case with that of Leibowitz.

"Oh," he exclaimed, waving his right hand with a gesture of finality, "but Darrow is a great lawyer."

Then with a wry grimace:

"The public's romantic picture of a criminal lawyer is that of a flamboyant, cavalier figure swaggering picaresquely through the city's night life and the Broadway hot spots with a sycophantic retinue of big-time criminals and racketeers. The real picture is the reverse. The successful criminal lawyer is surrounded by a pack of wolves, awaiting the opportunity to leap upon him and destroy him. He must watch his every step.

"Let me explain that there are two kinds of criminal lawyers—the trial lawyer and the fixer lawyer, who wins his case outside the courtroom by conniving with crooked police officers and shady prosecutors. It is the trial lawyer that the district attorney wants to get. Suppose the trial lawyer has lost a first degree murder case and his client has been sentenced to the chair. The district attorney goes to him and puts a combination question-answer like this:

" 'Well, they tried to put it over for you, but it didn't work. Who framed the testimony—Leibowitz?'

"The client wants to save his life. He answers 'Yes.' It's an old game.

"They don't love me in the D. A. offices. They know when I go into a case I'm out to win. I ask no quarter and give none. Perhaps I've put a crimp in a lot of political ambitions around New York. Losing a big case doesn't help a district attorney's career."

He has a hobby. It is collecting. He collects human

faces. He collects them on the street, in the subway, at the theater, the race track, the ball park; in cafés, hotel lobbies, on trains and in airplanes—everywhere.

We were strolling across the teeming esplanade of city hall park during a noon hour. Leibowitz, stalking his prey with the ardor of an entomologist bagging specimens, would halt every so often to gloat over a find.

"See that bird," indicating a thick-set man in his late fifties, with a dimpled chin and firmly compressed lips. "He'd be a washout as a juror. He's a born hanger."

Next a tall, bespectacled man with a long narrow face:

"Couldn't take that fellow; a churchman type, bigoted."

A youngish man, round faced, blue-eyed, passed:

"Ah! there's a natural; sympathetic; he's a let-liver."

He indulges in a dissertation:

"Men who travel much—commercial salesmen, say— make fine jurors. I like them young, too. They're still interested in people and they have a sense of brotherhood because of their fraternity ties. They're not set in their ways. They're tolerant. They're good listeners.

"Frequently judges have tried to hurry me in the selection of my juries, prodding me with the admonition, 'One citizen is as good as another,' and seeking to inhibit me by limiting my range of questioning. I refuse to be admonished or hurried. The jury is the pivotal factor. If my client is to have a fair trial, I must know the kind of men I'm talking to; trying to convince; entrusting with my client's fate. As a youngster I used to try to please the judge by hurrying. I've quit that.

"A criminal lawyer is a failure unless he's a born psychologist. He has to know and to feel human nature. He has to be able to tell from a man's face what's going on in his mind. The human race, so far as jury service is concerned, classifies into two groups—whether young or old, rich or poor—the 'rope pullers' and the 'let-livers.'

"Doubtless it is because of my melting pot background; my association as a boy with almost every nationality and every type of individual; but I've always been profoundly interested in people. I like to look at a man and try to figure out what sort of a fellow he was in his infancy. Was he a cry baby? Or was he smiling and friendly and no worry to his mother? Most cry babies grow up to be reformers. I can spot them a mile away. I want no reformers on my jury.

"Self-made men of the assertive type are to be shunned. Their attitude is always one of contempt for the defendant. They compare their status with his. They have no sympathy for him. He is a victim of his own weakness. The self-made man will send your client to the gallows or the chair without compunction.

"Then there are those men of conscious rectitude; self-righteous and impatient of the peccadilloes to which all of us are prone. They dot their i's and cross their t's in the moral sense. They would cheerfully send culprits to the pillory or the stake if our laws permitted.

"Some big business men make acceptable jurors; some, especially those with close set eyes, tight lips and square jaws, don't. They have a pompous disdain for the underdog. They are your true snobs."

Also included on the Leibowitz blacklist are "sea lawyers" who, he says, deadlock juries; writers, because they invariably construct their own case, based upon dramatic values, and ignore the law and the facts; professors and those who live cloistered lives generally, because they are too easily shocked by the raw facts of life; former policemen and private watchmen, because the chances are at one time or another they have been outwitted by criminals and have an obsession that all persons accused of a crime are guilty.

All the world's a stage peopled with potential talesmen for Showman Leibowitz. Their turn will come some day. They will file into court for his critical appraisal. A hundred, 200, 300, 400, 500 may pass in review, but eventually twelve will remain seated in the jury box, and Leibowitz will have finished casting for another performance of "Not Guilty."

CHAPTER EIGHT

TECHNIQUE

THIS is a fish story.

A jury in Kings County court, Brooklyn, was hearing the case of Vincenzo Santangelo, charged with first degree assault. The complainant was Patrolman Thomas P. Fitzgerald of the Bath Beach station.

Summoned to Santangelo's home by neighbors, who said he was beating his wife and threatening to kill her, Fitzgerald testified he found two women struggling, for possession of a revolver, with Santangelo, who wrested it away from them, jumped behind a curtain and shot Fitzgerald three times, sending him to the hospital for six months. A year elapsed between the shooting and the trial because Santangelo could not be found. The prosecution contended he had gone into hiding.

The defendant, however, denied he had assaulted the patrolman or that he had disappeared. He explained under the kindly ministrations of Leibowitz, his counsel, that he had been working in a Manhattan fish market and living with his employer, Salvatore Santaperio. Assistant District Attorney Barshay, listening cynically to his story, whispered to a court attendant, who left the room and returned with a small covered basket.

"So you were working in a fish market," drawled Barshay, when he started his cross-examination. "Now let's hear you tell this court and jury what you know."

He opened the basket, displaying a dozen different varieties of fish.

"What's this?" and with thumb and forefinger of his left hand he lifted out a halibut by the tail, holding it at arm's length so all might view it.

"A flounder," replied Santangelo unhesitatingly.

"And this?" exhibiting a butter fish.

"A sea bass."

"And this?" holding up a fat perch.

"A mackerel."

"And this?" showing a codfish.

"A porgie."

Santangelo guessed wrong twelve times. The prosecution complacently rested its case and Leibowitz sat back till time for his summation. Then:

"I want you, Mr. Rabinowitz, and you, Mr. Epstein, and you, Mr. Goldfogle, and you, Mr. Ginsberg, to explain to your fellow-jurymen the fraud which has been perpetrated on my client. You see through it; they do not. Was there in all that array of fish a single pike, or pickerel, or whitefish, or any other fish that can be made into 'gefullte fisch'? There was not. My client told you that he worked in a store at 114th Street and Lexington Avenue. The prosecutor knows that is a Jewish neighborhood, and he did not show a single fish that makes 'gefullte fisch.' What a travesty on justice! My client is an Italian who works in a Jewish fish market, and they try him on Christian fish."

The verdict was not guilty. The case presents the versatile Leibowitz technique at its artful best, maneuvering adroitly around the law and the facts to exploit an adventitious circumstance. Often, however, it employs tactics just the opposite, surprising judge and jury with the boldness and frankness of its strategy.

A certain client was what is known as a bad egg; a confirmed criminal. He was charged with murder. Leibowitz put him on the stand and here is the court stenographer's transcript of the Q and A:

Q. What is your occupation? A. A professional pickpocket.

Q. How long have you been thus employed? A. Twenty-four years.

Q. In the event of your acquittal in this case, what will your future occupation be? A. A professional pickpocket.

Leibowitz tells why he did it:

"Before we went into court he asked me what occupation he should give. I told him to tell the truth. He protested he was a pickpocket. Well, I protested, too; but, as I told him, since he was actually innocent of this particular crime he'd better tell the truth no matter how painful.

"He was being tried, not for picking pockets, but for murder. I didn't mind having the jurors know he was a bad one; but I did want them to know he didn't commit this murder. My job wasn't to sanctify him, but to free him.

"He didn't even have an alibi either, and that's a thing a criminal can think up in a twinkling. I refused to let him manufacture one. That man, a known criminal, told nothing but the truth in that courtroom. The jury recognized it, too, and I won an acquittal."

An ordinance passed by the village board of Island Park, Nassau County, L. I., made it a misdemeanor to appear on the beach with the upper part of the body uncovered. Three children—6, 8 and 9 years old—were playing in the sand one afternoon. Their father, in the rôle of nurse, was sitting near them talking with an acquaintance from Manhattan. The two became so interested they forgot about the children. A village policeman hove alongside.

"Which one of you do those kids belong to?" he asked.

"Me," said the father.

"Here's a summons."

The children were scampering about with the tops of their bathing suits down. The father tried to argue but the copper was adamant. The case was set for hearing next day. The Manhattanite knew Leibowitz and prevailed upon him to represent the father. He pleaded him not guilty.

After the officer had told his story before the local magistrate, the village prosecutor called the father, who confirmed him. It seemed as if there wasn't much to do except wait for the court to impose the fine. Leibowitz asked the policeman to take the stand. The Q and A:

Q. You say, officer, that the children were in their trunks; no tops; that's why you gave the summons? A. Yes.

Q. You consider that indecent? A. Yes.

Q. You wouldn't want your wife to see it? A. No.

Q. By the way, do you ever go to the fights here? (Boxing bouts are held weekly at the Island Park stadium and are social events. The whole village turns out for them.) A. Yes.

Q. Take the wife? A. Yes.

Q. You are on duty at these times? A. An officer is always on duty.

Q. And the wife enjoys the fights? A. Yes.

Q. What do the fighters wear? A. Trunks.

Q. The upper parts of their bodies are bare? A. Yes.

Q. Have you ever arrested those men for indecent exposure? A. No.

"Your Honor," said Leibowitz, turning to the magistrate, "that is my case."

The magistrate dismissed the charge and invited Leibowitz up to the house for dinner.

Matteo Di Gregorio, admitted slayer of Bernard Ernest, 19-year-old high school student, was on trial before Judge Richard W. Hawkins in the Suffolk County court, Riverhead, L. I. Ernest, returning from a dance, was killed as he drove past the suburban home of Mrs. Katherine Gray, near East Hampton, L. I., Di Gregorio blasting at him with a double-barreled shotgun.

The newspapers dubbed it "The Phantom Murder Case" because Di Gregorio was in his underwear and looked ghostly in the moonlight.

The testimony disclosed there had been a spirited rivalry for Mrs. Gray's affections between Di Gregorio, a bathing pool proprietor, and Leslie Loomis, an automobile mechanic. The latter, after a long courtship, had been rejected in favor of Di Gregorio, who was calling on Mrs. Gray the night of the murder.

Loomis, however, was a persistent suitor. He, too, called that night—surreptitiously. Mrs. Gray, a comely divorcee, told about it on the witness stand.

Her mother and brother were away and, fearful of prowlers, she asked Di Gregorio to spend the night. He consented. She retired to her bedroom and he to a couch in the parlor. However, before so doing, he draped his trousers over the back of a chair. A neat dresser, he desired to preserve the crease. The chair was adjacent to a window in her bedroom. She was awakened by the beam of a flashlight. A voice she recognized as that of Loomis asked, "Where is he?" A hand was thrust through the window and the trousers disappeared. She aroused Di Gregorio, who immediately made for the chair and demanded:

"Where are my pants?"

They were the only ones he had brought with him! Armed with the shotgun, he dashed out in his bare feet to recover them. He had arrived at the driveway in front of the house when Ernest drove past. Leibowitz' defense was that Di Gregorio tripped and the shotgun was discharged accidentally. In his summation to the jury he contended that a man had a right to use reasonable force in recovering his property. Judge Hawkins and the jury upheld him and the verdict of acquittal was a perfunctory gesture.

It was technique plus keen observation and a break that enabled Leibowitz to score a spectacular coup at the trial of the hoodlum, Vincent Coll, in the famous "Baby Killing Case."

Five children had been wounded, one mortally, when a touring car sped through a Harlem street, raking it with machine gun fire. The crime horrified the city and nation. Rewards totaling $30,000 were posted. Coll and a sidekick, Frank Giordano, were captured in a raid two months later and speedily indicted. They were charged specifically with the murder of five-year-old Michael Vengalli.

For once it seemed Leibowitz had undertaken the impossible. Every element, human and circumstantial, was arrayed against him. General Sessions Judge Joseph E. Corrigan, presiding at the trial, was noted as the "terror of gunmen"; public sentiment, which always reflects itself in the jury box, was clamoring for the death penalty, and the police had found an eyewitness who positively identified Coll and Giordano. Among the state's exhibits was a bullet riddled baby carriage, wheeled into the courtroom the opening day of the trial.

The eyewitness was a mysterious George Brecht, whom the police had zealously guarded for four months, maintaining him at a Manhattan hotel and putting him on the police department payroll. A squad of detectives, assigned to entertain him, had taken him to theaters, night clubs, ball games and prize fights. He was not allowed to meet strangers or speak to any one. Leibowitz didn't even know his name. The day of the shooting, he testified, he was walking in East 107th street, where children were playing on the sidewalk:

"My attention was attracted by a sound like a backfire. I turned and saw an automobile with five men in the middle of the street, and they were shooting. There were two men in the front seat, two in between in small seats like you have in a big car, and one in the left hand side of the car in the rear.

"First I saw the man in the rear was firing a pistol out of the window. The man directly in front of him was shooting with some kind of firearms, going round about."

Asked to explain what he meant, he made motions similar to those of a man pumping cartridges into the breech of a rifle or a shotgun.

"Was the car going slow?" asked James T. Neary, Assistant District Attorney.

"Yes, very slow. When I heard the first shot I saw the

car moving. The man in the rear seat was firing and the man in front of him was firing. There was no other firing from the car. And then the man in the rear seat turned to speak to the man in front of him.

"The man in the rear seat had curly brown hair and a dimple in his chin. He wore a blue suit. The man in front of him had a high forehead and black hair slicked back. The other man with him was a heavy set fellow who looked like he needed a shave every day or two."

"Do you see in court any of the men you saw in the car?" asked Neary.

"Yes, I see two."

He stepped down from the witness stand and standing in front of Coll and Giordano, said:

"These are the men. They were doing the shooting."

Leibowitz' first question on cross-examination was:

"For whom did you last work?"

"I don't care to answer that. I've got a wife and two children I want to protect."

"What was the nature of your employer's business?"

"He was an alderman."

Brecht would not reveal the name of the city in which the alderman lived and when Leibowitz pressed him, Judge Corrigan interrupted sharply:

"You are not going to make him tell where he worked."

"Where were you born?" asked Leibowitz.

"Missouri."

"Is the alderman from Missouri?"

"Maybe."

"When did you quit your last job?"

"In July."

"Who has been supporting you since?"

"The police department."

"You read in the papers that rewards totaling $30,000 were offered for the murderers?"

"No, I only read the funny papers."

"How many windows were in the automobile the gunmen used?"

"I don't count windows."

"The witness should not be so fresh and clever," protested Leibowitz.

"Why not set a good example?" remarked Judge Corrigan.

It was Brecht's crowded hour. The courtroom atmosphere was distinctly anti-Leibowitz. He began hammering away at Brecht's veracity.

"Is there a park in the vicinity of the shooting?"

"I don't look for parks."

"How many floors were there in the building at 2060 First Avenue where you say you sought a job selling belts?"

"I don't count floors."

"Were you moping around East 107th Street, as you said yesterday?"

"No, I was just a man of leisure."

"You know there is no belt factory at 2060 First Avenue?"

"I can't help that."

"You're not positive these are the men; you just think they are, don't you?"

"If I didn't know they were the men I wouldn't be here."

Hour after hour Leibowitz continued the cross-examination, his eyes never leaving Brecht's face. Finally he turned to Johnny Terry and whispered:

"He is an ex-convict. He has been expertly coached;

he speaks clearly and crisply, but every once in a while he forgets and lets a sentence fall out of the corner of his mouth, with his lips tightly closed. He's been in one of those penitentiaries where inmates aren't allowed to talk to one another, and so hold conversations by stealth. He's from outside New York state because the silent system has been abolished in all the prisons here."

It was Terry's cue. He left the courtroom, and the Leibowitz office went into action with an investigation utilizing the grapevine of the underworld which travels far and wide, reaching into the high places of law enforcement and the archives of penal institutions.

Leibowitz himself employed the time playing a cat and mouse game with his recalcitrant witness. Brecht had testified he peddled Eskimo pies. Leibowitz sent out and bought one, then asked Brecht to describe the label on the wrapper. He was unable to do so. Leibowitz offerred the wrapper in evidence, but Assistant District Attorney Neary objected, so he offered the whole pie.

His cross-examination of Brecht was resumed next morning, and spectators and jurors sat up and took notice as he developed his line of questioning.

"I asked you yesterday," he began, "whether you had ever been in court before on the witness stand, and you answered you had not?"

"I did."

"You came from St. Louis?"

"Yes, sir."

"You were a witness in a court trial there, were you not?"

"Yes, sir."

"You testified for the state when two members of the Cuckoo Gang were tried for killing Dr. August H. Sante.

They were acquitted. Did you identify these defendants, too?"

Assistant District Attorney Neary objected, and Judge Corrigan sustained him.

"You were before a judge in the Juvenile Court in St. Louis, charged with stealing diamonds, weren't you?"

"Yes, that was the charge."

"You were convicted and sent away, weren't you?"

"Yes, sir."

"Why did you say you had not been a witness previously when you were asked that question yesterday?"

"I didn't tell because I didn't want any one to know where I came from on account of my wife and children."

Leibowitz, smiling blandly, bowed to court and prosecutor and offered to submit his case to the jury at once without summation, but was overruled. His office had learned of Brecht's past through Joseph Gavin, a probation officer in the Children's Court of Brooklyn, and for seventeen years a probation officer in St. Louis. He told his story in chambers to Judge Corrigan, Police Commissioner Edward P. Mulrooney, and Assistant District Attorney Neary.

The prosecution's sole identifying witness had been unmasked as a perjurer, jailbird and professional "surprise" witness. Judge Corrigan, the "terror of gunmen," had no alternative. He issued an order directing the jury to return a verdict of not guilty. He had just completed this formality when Leibowitz arose and said:

"I move that Brecht be committed for perjury."

"That is a matter for the court to decide," rejoined the judge. "This court will mind its own business and prefers that you mind yours, Mr. Leibowitz."

Was there a conspiracy to swear away the life of the

accused so that public clamor might be placated? Not in the opinion of the presiding judge. He exculpated both the police and the district attorney's office in a statement declaring that "they were honest and fair throughout."

But dumb?

Aside from Coll's vicious record, Leibowitz' greatest handicap in this case was the status of the codefendant, Frank Giordano, a condemned man. Two months previously he had been tried and sentenced to the electric chair for the killing of Joesph Mullen, a beer-runner. He was brought down from the Sing Sing death house, appearing in court each day with six prison guards. Leibowitz did not represent him. His attorney was Edward V. Broderick.

Criminal lawyers prefer separate trials for their clients. Sharing the courtroom spotlight cramps their style and jeopardizes their chances of an acquittal. However, when there is a joint indictment for the same crime, they have to make the best of it. Leibowitz, encumbered with Giordano, was facing no new experience. He had been somewhat similarly handicapped in the celebrated Gravesend Bay Rowboat Murder Case.

It was a life insurance plot, concocted by Joseph Lefkowitz, 42 years old, a gentleman of exemplary personal habits—he never smoked and he never drank, but was a graduate of Elmira Reformatory and had once engineered a fire in a clothing store that had gone inexplicably bankrupt.

His co-conspirator was Benjamin Goldstein, 22, a psychopathic weakling, whom he had insured for $30,000 with the New York Life Insurance Company and for $40,000 with the Metropolitan Life Insurance Company.

He had kept up payments on the policies for four years to allay suspicion.

The idea was for Goldstein to go rowboating, fall overboard and be accidentally drowned. He was to be picked up by a motor boat hired by Lefkowitz and put aboard a ship bound for Honolulu, where he was to remain until Lefkowitz collected the insurance, of which he was to receive half.

So Goldstein believed. The real idea was to have him drown, and for that purpose Lefkowitz had retained the services of Irving Rubinzahl, 18, and Harry Greenberg, 17. Rubinzahl was the assistant master mind. Lefkowitz had paid him twenty-five dollars earnest money, with a promise of $1,000 after Goldstein's demise.

One pleasant summer's morning Rubinzahl, Greenberg and Goldstein motored out to the beach and donned bathing suits. Goldstein carried a traveling bag containing four suits of clothes to wear on the voyage to Honolulu. They seated themselves in a rowboat with Goldstein at the oars. Lefkowitz, who had driven out alone, watched them through binoculars from the dock.

They were a quarter of a mile off shore when Goldstein and Rubinzahl arose to change places. As they passed, Rubinzahl's hands shot out and Goldstein went overboard. Rubinzahl took the oars and rowed away. Goldstein's voice came faintly over the water. "Help, help, help, help." He couldn't swim. Lefkowitz could discern his head bobbing about like an apple. Finally it disappeared. Lefkowitz turned to go.

"Hey," some one shouted at his elbow, "did you see that? A fellow just drowned and the two men in the boat didn't try to help him."

The speaker was Rabbi Moses Pollack, living at No. 11

Bay Terrace, Coney Island, who was taking a stroll on the beach and had seen everything. Lefkowitz hurried past him, climbed into his automobile and drove back to the city. That afternoon he paid Rubinzahl $250 on account and bought Greenberg a $27.50 suit of clothes.

Goldstein's body floated ashore and an investigation was begun, which resulted in the arrest of Rubinzahl and Greenberg. Both confessed, but Greenberg protested he didn't know a murder was intended. Rubinzahl, admitting the plot, turned state's evidence and was allowed to plead guilty to second degree murder. He was sentenced to twenty years in Sing Sing.

Lefkowitz and Greenberg, pleading not guilty to first degree murder, were tried together before Justice Harry E. Lewis in the Supreme Court, Brooklyn. Lefkowitz was represented by Attorney Harry Sacher, and Greenberg by Leibowitz. Star witness Rubinzahl spared neither of his former associates in crime. Lefkowitz was a bloodthirsty Shylock, and as for Greenberg:

"He said to me on the way back to Manhattan after the drowning, 'Huh, I could have saved him a hundred times.' "

Considered for his impression upon the jury, Lefkowitz was no asset for the defense. Softly fat, greasy, with squinting eyes, heavy nose, pendent lips which he licked incessantly, he was a picture of cringing guilt. Frequently, too, even under examination by his own counsel, he would shout his protests at certain questions. The trouble was that Attorney Sacher had no control over his client.

Not so Leibowitz. Young Greenberg, the smart aleck moron of the Ghetto streets, was as docile as a ewe lamb, as modest as a violet by a mossy stone.

"This boy," cried Assistant District Attorney Joseph V. Gallagher, unconsciously tendering Leibowitz a left-handed compliment, "is an actor, and has been acting on the stand."

Greenberg was dressed in character. He wore a threadbare sweater and a pair of nondescript trousers. He answered questions hesitantly and often his counsel had to repeat them.

Both Leibowitz and Sacher had a jolly time lambasting star witness Rubinzahl. He was "a murderer," "a roustabout," "scum of the earth," "a crook," and, testified Greenberg:

"Rubinzahl pushed Goldstein in. I said: 'For God's sake, why did you do that?' He said to me, 'Shut up. If you try to help him, I'll kill you.'"

Lefkowitz on the stand shouldered the blame on the dead youth. Goldstein had devised the scheme; Goldstein had voluntarily made him the beneficiary of the insurance policies. Rubinzahl and Greenberg were blackmailers. Lefkowitz said to Rubinzahl after the drowning, "'Should I give you money for killing my best friend and partner?' and Rubinzahl said, 'Yes, you big bum.'"

Tears streamed from Lefkowitz' eyes and perspiration dropped from his brow.

Sacher in his summation had to admit Lefkowitz' participation in the insurance plot, but he argued that he at no time "sought or planned the death of his friend and partner." Leibowitz, who had contended that his client had been sweated for eighteen hours to force a "confession," referred to Greenberg in his plea to the jury as:

"This little atom of humanity, 17 years old, who never

knew a father—16 years old and still in the Five-A grade at school."

And further along:

"The code of the East Side—the code that every boy on the East Side knows—was brought to bear when Greenberg said this drowning was an accident. The look which Lefkowitz gave this kid in the elevator after their arrest was all that Greenberg needed to frighten him into a lie."

Lefkowitz was sentenced to the electric chair. The little atom of humanity was acquitted, only to be arrested later charged with filching $500 and a diamond ring from a trusting young woman.

PERHAPS a lawyer less sure of himself would have bolstered his defense of Greenberg with an alienist's findings, but Leibowitz has seldom availed himself of that device. Only rarely has he ever used medical science itself. A notable case in which he did was that of the "Dream Slayer" Ernest Wente, 62-year-old German carpenter-gardener of Valley Stream, Nassau County, Long Island.

Oiling up his rusty .38 caliber Smith & Wesson, Wente loaded it to go gunning for his pretty wife, Clara. He found her in a shoe store, walked her to a corner and shot her four times. He put one bullet in her brain, and, as she fell, knelt beside her and sent three more into her body.

"Now," he cried, shaking his fist at her, "you suffer as I did for three years."

To eyewitnesses he said:

"Okay. I killed her. I'm not sorry for it either."

One of the eyewitnesses, Mrs. Catherine Afflen, told

how he had entered the store without a hat, wild-eyed, "like a man out of the woods." He was indicted for murder in the first degree.

Leibowitz' investigation disclosed that Wente had married his wife, fifteen years his junior, after a three weeks' courtship; that she left him soon after to live with a man in Valley Stream; that she made a practice of thumbing her nose at him when she passed him, calling him "You Old Dutchman"; that she taunted him with her amours; that when he importuned her to return to him, she laughed and spoke of "his senility," saying she preferred younger men.

Superimposed upon all this at the trial was the medical testimony that Wente was suffering from arteriosclerosis, and that the resultant constriction of the arteries and veins so impeded and diminished the flow of blood to the brain as to induce in moments of mental stress, a semicomatose condition.

Wente, on the day of the killing, Leibowitz proved beyond a reasonable doubt, was in a dream state, laboring under such "a defect of reason as not to know the nature and quality of the act he was performing or that it was wrong."

Verdict: Not guilty.

As the connoisseur discerns in a landscape painting, certain subtleties of tone coloring and mass balance, and exclaims, "Ah, a Corot!" or observes in the tapering symmetry of a church steeple, a rhythm of line and plumb, and knows it for a Sir Christopher Wren; or sees in a detail of carving, in the splat of a chairback, the hand of a Chippendale, so it was with the discriminating multitude comprising the Leibowitz cult.

Scanning the public prints and the chroniclings of sob

sister and feature writer, it appraised the daily record of crime, hot off the presses—phantom, dream and honor slayings; wife, husband, sweetheart and in-law killings—biangles, triangles and quadrangles—until finally its critical eye encountered that particular case, compact of color, balance and detail; a case in which police and district attorney were invariably and invincibly confident of a conviction.

"Ah," the multitude would exclaim, "that is a Leibowitz!"

CHAPTER NINE

TO THE LADIES

THERE was Grandma Angelina Mecili.

Leibowitz, pausing in the tour of his art gallery, indulged in a sly chuckle as he pointed to her picture. "Oldest woman ever tried for first degree murder in New York State," the legend read.

She looked her sixty-seven years, with her plain, squarish face, seamed and worn; her sunken cheeks; the sagging, cleaving line of her wide tight-lipped mouth, which formed a grim crescent that accentuated the thrust of her heavy chin. Her brooding eyes, deep socketed under a broad high forehead, were poignant with sorrow.

Puffing at his No. 3 pipe, the one with the huge bowl and long curved stem—an infallible index of the detective lawyer mood—Leibowitz propounded:

"She shot her son-in-law, Anthony Colantuono, as he sat at the breakfast table. The autopsy, performed by Assistant Medical Examiner George Ruger, disclosed fragments of cheese he was eating still in the larynx. Death, therefore, had taken him by surprise. Otherwise he would not have been intent on masticating his food. Grandma Mecili, in fact, sneaked up behind him and fired two shots from a .38 caliber revolver squarely between his shoulder blades."

Leibowitz allowed himself a couple of extra puffs to enhance the dramatic value of the next sentence:

"I got an acquittal on a plea of self-defense."

The murder was committed the day after Christmas. Colantuono, a former special policeman, burly, domineering and an inveterate wise cracker, had a pet name for his mother-in-law, which she didn't fancy. He called her "Old Crooked Mouth."

Quarrels, it seemed, were frequent. Grandma Mecili felt she was tolerated only because she owned property that her daughter and son-in-law hoped to inherit at her death. She was worth around $20,000, representing the life-time efforts of herself and her late husband, both of whom were immigrants from Sicily. The world is cluttered with Grandma Mecilis—unwanted women who have outlived their cycles of wife and motherhood—but the world seldom hears of them because they do nothing to break into the newspaper headlines.

The Colantuonos had been married three years and had a seven months' old daughter, Madeline, whom the grandmother idolized. She and the son-in-law agreed to a Christmas truce for the baby's sake. They had a tree and a special dinner and Grandma bought Madeline the biggest doll she could find. The truce lasted until the morning of December 26 when, as Grandma stepped from her bedroom, Colantuono greeted her with the hated:

"Hello, Old Crooked Mouth."

Only Madeline, lying in her crib playing with the new doll, saw Grandma run to the bureau where Colantuono kept his gun. . . .

Leibowitz at the trial didn't dispute the findings of the assistant medical examiner as to the cheese fragments. He couldn't. His defense was that Grandma feared for her life because Colantuono that same morning had marched her into the kitchen, stood her before a leather chair, and, seizing a butcher knife, twice plunged it up to the haft in the upholstered back.

"That's the way," he jeered, "I'm going to kill you—maybe—or maybe I will just shoot you, Old Crooked Mouth." And then he had added, "Go wash your dirty neck."

It was the knife threat that terrorized Grandma. Testifying in her own behalf she said, "It was just like as if he had stabbed me. Everything went black. My head whirled. I don't know what happened. All I remember is the police coming in to arrest me."

Mrs. Rose Colantuono, whose original story had caused her mother's arrest, declared on the witness stand she hadn't seen the shooting. The jury after deliberating two hours returned its verdict of not guilty.

The cameramen surrounded the grinning Leibowitz and his client.

"Smile, Grandma, smile," they urged. "Show them how glad you are that the jury acquitted you."

But Grandma only continued to weep and wring her hands. Under the Sicilian code, members of a family who receive a slayer back into the fold condone the crime, and the blood relatives of Colantuono had vowed to avenge his death. Rose told her mother she didn't dare take her in again. And so Grandma's tears.

"What have I to smile for?" she cried to the cameramen. "I wish, now, they had sent me to the chair. I am free, but nobody wants me, nobody loves me. I am just

an old woman going to enter an old ladies' home. I wish
I was dead."

LEIBOWITZ had passed on to another of his art gallery
exhibits. "Funny," he was saying, "how the newspapers
tag them. They dubbed this 'The Gigolo Murder Case.'
It was a double trial—Mrs. Amy Conlin and her lover,
James De Pew."

De Pew was earnestly defended by two barristers; he
was given thirty years in Sing Sing.

Leibowitz counseled Mrs. Conlin; she was freed.

It seemed she was one of those misunderstood wives
and therefore unhappy with her husband, John T. Conlin,
cabaret owner and bootlegger. She left him and filed suit
for separate maintenance. A month later at a friend's
house she met De Pew, lately released from Eastview
Penitentiary.

Mrs. Conlin, who confessed to 37 years, was lean and
angular, her bony olive skinned face shadowed by an
overwhelming expanse of nose. De Pew was 22, a blond
pretty boy, with easy manners and ingratiating ways. So
began a romance that meandered from rooming house to
rooming house with occasional lapses when Mrs. Conlin
stayed with her sister and De Pew hunted a job. Then
there were letters.

Amy to James:

"I was so sorry I wrote you the way I did but I didn't
mean it only that I was worried about my boy. I also
sent you the ring. It isn't much but I hope you will like
it. . . . I hope to dream of my darling, too."

James to Amy:

"Dearest darling, I sure was happy to get your letter.
. . . I would love to be near you always. I adore you,

mother darling. I would love to have you watch over me all the rest of my life. ... Thanks for the dollar. ... Lovingly yours, Sonny."

Mrs. Conlin went to her home in Astoria, Long Island, for some clothes. Her husband persuaded her to stay and give him another chance. Posing as the forgiving wife she continued to have De Pew as a clandestine lover. They planned a Reno divorce and marriage.

But they must have money. Wherefore on a night in April Conlin was held up in the vestibule of his home. The robber had a gun. The gun went off. Conlin was taken to the hospital and died ten weeks later.

In the meantime De Pew was picked up when Mrs. Conlin sent him a money order for fifty dollars and a message to stick around under cover, till the heat abated. He poured out everything to the police. Mrs. Conlin was arrested and the romance was ended. The erstwhile lovers staged a talking marathon in an effort to shift blame for the killing on each other.

A pre-mortem identification of De Pew as his assailant by Conlin was allowed in evidence when the case came up before Judge Frank Adel in Queens County court, Long Island City. So were statements taken by the police from both defendants.

Leibowitz, however, brought out in cross-examination of Detective John A. Dust, Jr., that De Pew was chained to a steam pipe with the steam on while being questioned and that Mrs. Conlin was held eight hours without food.

And neither statement lived up to its police press agent reports. De Pew admitted that he had held up Conlin; but insisted that the shooting was accidental. Mrs. Conlin knew he was going to hold up her husband but begged him not to. She, in turn, stated that she had known of the robbery plans and that De Pew had not intended to shoot her husband.

Nurses testified to a conversation between De Pew and Conlin in St. John's Hospital in Long Island City before the cabaret owner died.

"Do you know Amy Conlin?" Conlin asked.

"Does it matter?" De Pew side-stepped.

"Did you ever meet Amy at the Inn in Greenwich Village?"

"I'd rather not answer."

"As long as you got my money why did you shoot me?"

"I didn't intend to."

When the state had completed its case Leibowitz moved for a dismissal of the indictment because of lack of evidence connecting Mrs. Conlin with the crime. To his surprise, for he had often made similar motions only to have them fall on deaf ears, Judge Adel concurred; the indictments were quashed and Amy was put back in circulation.

De Pew, then, was allowed to plead guilty to second instead of first degree murder because his prison record showed he was mentally deficient. Judge Adel sentenced him to 30 years in Sing Sing.

"I'm sorry he has to go to prison," Amy said. "I'd be sorry for any one, but I don't love him any more. I don't want romance in my life again—or marriage."

PLUMP, curly headed Bessie Lensky was 32; her rival, Mrs. Mary Behrend, was 48. And between the two Samuel Lensky lay dead, stabbed with a bread knife.

"She killed him," said Mrs. Behrend.

"It was an accident," said Leibowitz.

"Not Guilty," said the jury.

It was a new version of "we both grabbed for the gun." It happened in Brooklyn on the Fourth of July. Mrs. Lensky asked Mrs. Behrend to come to her home for a showdown. She led the "other woman" into the kitchen where her husband was sitting smoking a pipe, resting his elbows on the washtub.

"How many times did you have dealings with this woman?" Bessie wanted to know.

He looked at Mrs. Behrend, then at his wife, then at the floor:

"Twice."

"What do you think of her?" Mrs. Lensky persisted.

"I think she's a rat."

Up to that point prosecution and defense agreed. Mrs. Behrend's version of what happened next was:

"Bessie entered the dining room, opened a drawer and brought out a bread knife. She plunged the knife through his stomach. I ran from the room. She chased me. I yelled one word—murder. She dropped the knife and I fled out of the vestibule."

Leibowitz insisted on the other hand—he didn't put Bessie on the stand—that it was Mrs. Behrend who had the bread knife, that she lunged at Lensky and Bessie tried to save her husband but in the struggle he was killed.

A jury took two hours and twenty-five minutes to acquit her.

It wasn't always via the murder route that women came to Leibowitz for legal aid. Sarah Sachs, for instance, the eighty-seven pound whirlwind—"Two Gun Tillie" as she was headlined—who did nothing more serious than walk into a Coney Island poker game, line up six players, frisk

Policeman Joseph Walsh of seventy dollars cash and a diamond ring, pull off his shield and spit in his face.

"So, you're a cop, eh," she taunted and backed from the room with her two male companions.

"One of them looked like a prize fighter."

That was the only clue the police had. Detectives Anthony Grieco, Thomas Reilly and Thomas Kenny went to work on that. Grieco bought $20 worth of ring fan magazines. A picture of Bobby Green, retired punch drunk featherweight, who had dropped from sight two years before, was identified by the victims of the holdup.

Days and nights spent around training quarters and gymnasiums resulted in another clue. Bobby Green, whose real name was Abraham Sachs, lived at 110 West 73rd Street. He had a wife. They arrested her at the apartment, picked him up when he arrived and the third member of the gang, Herman Rosen, when he came calling.

Voluntary confessions were secured from all three. Sachs, who had a long police record but was clearly a mental case, was sent to Dannemora prison for the criminally insane and Rosen was given a sentence of from seven to fifteen years in Sing Sing.

Leibowitz defended "Two Gun Tillie." Conviction for her in this case on a first degree robbery charge would have meant a life sentence since she had a felony record. Neither the fact of the robbery nor her confession was denied by Leibowitz in his defense. He put her on the stand before Judge George W. Martin in King's county.

"Why did you take part in this robbery, Sarah?" he asked.

"He made me do it, my husband made me do it."

She told the story of her life in the courtroom, a sociological document rather than a sob story.

"I was born October 10, 1907, in New York City in an Eldridge Street tenement. The family consisted of three brothers, mother and father. He worked at anything he could find, usually peddling. I was seven when I went to the first orphan asylum—The Children's Nursery on Bleecker Street. Mother voluntarily put me there.

"She and father had separated in court. They lived together off and on. Father was Roumanian, mother, Russian Pole. I was in the Children's Haven for a few months; then to the Italian Boys' Home. From there to the Brooklyn Orphan Asylum. I went to public schools and took five and a half years to complete the eight year course. I wanted a home and a mother. I never knew mother love.

"I ran away from the asylum when I was thirteen. I went to my mother's home in Bridgeport, Connecticut. I was treated as a servant there. Mother was not glad to see me. She was living under the name of Birkell. A man posing as a boarder was supporting her. Mother said she was sorry I was ever born.

"I refused to live under the name of Birkell. She said to me, 'Either you live under that name or you don't live here.' I took three dollars and went to my father in New York. He put me out boarding. I went to Bushwick High School for a year and a half and then transferred to Girls' High School. Did well in studies. Had boy friends. Ruined when fourteen. Soon I went to live with a man.

"I met him by flirtation. Was all made up. He was about 31 years of age at the time. We went to a movie and he asked me to stay with him that night. I went to his apartment and we made up to live together. He was a gangster. His name was Lou Kramer and he went to prison later.

"I was still going to school. He would meet me after school. I was happy with him. I met the boys. They were all gangsters, members of the Dropper gang. I did not partake in any crimes with him. Crime was never discussed in my presence. We had a layout of opium in the place. I didn't smoke it. All kinds of parties would be taking place. I just drifted along waiting for something to happen. I left him at the time Jack Kaplin was killed. I saw too much gun fighting and I was frightened. I lived with him two years. I was sixteen when I left him.

"While I was living with him I was carrying on with other men without his knowledge. I was afraid of getting in trouble but could not break away from doing wrong. I never knew any one who was good and willing to give me a chance.

"I went back to my mother but she treated me like a servant and wouldn't give me any money. My brothers had me arrested for running away from home and the Judge sent me to a mission at Westhaven. I stayed there one year and ran away again.

"I went to Oswego and worked in a factory; I lived with a family. I met a coast guard and became engaged to him. The wedding was set for May 20 and I was arrested on May 9 for running away from the mission and recommitted. I stayed there a month and ran away again.

"Met a working boy from the east side in New York. Became pregnant. He sold his business and went to Cuba when I told him I'd have him arrested if he didn't give me money for an abortion. The baby was born at the Cumberland Street Hospital. I told my name as Sally Reed. I put the baby out to board at five dollars a week but I didn't pay the board and was arrested. The case was dismissed.

"I met Abe Sachs on 12th Street and Broadway. I was trying to get a cab. One stopped in front of me and Mr. Sachs was in it. He told me to get in and he would take me where I was going. I went out with him every night. I met a girl in jail that I knew and we went to her mother's home in Philadelphia. I tried to steal a coat in a store and was arrested. Got out on bail and came back to New York.

"I was married to Abe Sachs at City Hall, December 20, 1926. He, too, was a drifter. We lived together six months and I left him. He was a man of violent temper. He beat me. I got tired of it.

"I packed my things and took my baby over to my mother. She wouldn't take it. Neither would my mother-in-law. I took it to an orphanage.

"Somehow my husband found me and beat me up so bad I had to go to the Post Graduate Hospital with concussion of the brain. Then I was arrested in New York for skipping bail in Philadelphia and put on probation. My husband came to the jail and said he would help me if I would come back to him. He threatened to blow out my brains if I refused.

"So I went back. But my mother-in-law told me to leave him as he would kill me, she was afraid. I did, but one day I was at my brother-in-law's office and my husband came outside in a car with his gangsters. He came up and asked me to live with him again. I took one look at the car and said yes. He didn't have any money so they planned this robbery. They needed another man but he said to take me instead.

"I refused to go. He said 'You won't? You know when I laid you up in the hospital? This time they'll take you to the morgue.'

"I went."

Judge Martin directed the jury to return a verdict of acquittal on the grounds that insufficient proof had been given to break down her defense that she had taken part in the robbery only under threat and duress.

Sarah went back to the Brooklyn orphanage.

STEEPED in his craft, Leibowitz is sensitive to its backgrounds, settings and atmosphere. During trial of one of his cases he strode into the corridor muttering to himself and scowling blackly.

"What's the matter, Sam?" asked a friend.

"Hell! There's no feeling of murder in that courtroom. In olden times they held murder trials beside the body of the victim, over the gaping wounds. Nowadays you're so far away from the murder you don't know it happened. A murder trial today is simply a problem in mathematics."

Not all of them. One, especially, still thrills the blasé Leibowitz. It was held in the shadow of prison walls with guards and state troopers walking post and the defendant manacled like a wild beast.

"The hardest case I ever had," says the man who has lived a million lives.

CHAPTER TEN

AND LEIBOWITZ FAINTED

SUNK into Leibowitz' memory is the scene in the prison hospital ward—the white metal bed in the corner by the grated window and the tortured wretch sprawled lugubriously like a frog, belly up. His legs were outspread. Steel bracelets with chains attached encircled the ankles. The chains were padlocked to the bedposts. Parallel strips of adhesive tape around his chest secured a bandage on the left side. He had been shot through the lung and he breathed stertorously, wheezing shrilly at times like a penny whistle.

In the bed opposite lay another, similarly manacled, his head swathed in rolls of gauze and resembling that of a mummy, except that there were apertures for eyes, nose and mouth. Part of his face had been shot away. As soon as he recovered, he and two other felons, now in solitary confinement, would be going to Sing Sing to be electrocuted. Maybe the wretch in the white metal bed would go, too. A jury would decide. Guards paced to and fro.

Leibowitz with his genius for dramatization—his instinct for stepping outside himself to hear himself talk and watch himself act—sees in that scene the prologue of the starkest courtroom drama of his career.

Lawyer and client were having their first conference. Max Becker, burglar convict, was gasping out his story of the red Wednesday in December of 1929 when Auburn prison was turned into a shambles, eight inmates dying in a break for freedom after they had killed Principal Keeper George A. Durnford, wounded a half dozen guards and captured Warden Edgar S. Jennings and members of his staff, holding them as hostages.

For six hours the convict mob was in control. It was led by tough Steve Pawlak, lifer, whose 125 pound body bore the bullet scars of three savage battles with policemen. He it was who sent the ultimatum to the then acting governor, Herbert H. Lehman, that Jennings would be executed if the mutineers were not granted safe passage through the lines of state troopers and militiamen. Lehman's reply was an order to storm the prison, and his soldiery went into action with machine guns and tear bombs, quelling the riot. Pawlak, with seven of his desperate crew, died fighting.

Becker was charged with first degree murder in an indictment naming him as Durnford's actual slayer. He had also been identified by Warden Jennings as one of the mob leaders who held him captive.

Leibowitz, listening to his story, asked him pointblank: "Becker, did you shoot Durnford?"

"As God is my judge, Mr. Leibowitz," he said, "I swear I didn't, and if the principal keeper was here today you'd know I'm innocent."

He said it feelingly, but Leibowitz was not surprised. It is a formula answer with those accused of murder, and Leibowitz, going to Auburn in January of 1930, was a veteran of the criminal bar, with a record of seventy-five

acquittals in first degree murder cases, including that of
Harry L. Hoffman.

What impressed him primarily was the wholly different
setting and cast of characters involved in this Becker
case. It appealed to his dramatic instinct. Here was a
crime whose entire action occurred inside prison walls—
a real life epic of the Big House. He was savoring a new
experience.

His professional interest was challenged because the
alleged perpetrators had already been adjudged guilty by
prison officials in star chamber sessions participated in
by the district attorney's office. Leibowitz must take one
of these extra-legally condemned felons into court and
with other felons as his only witnesses convince a jury
of his innocence.

The prosecution, backed by the authority of Governor
Franklin D. Roosevelt, had had in the preparation of its
case the coöperation of every agency—state troopers, police officers and investigators from the Department of
Correction, in addition to prison officials.

Leibowitz, a lone individual, had only a court writ to
permit him to interview whoever might care to volunteer helpful information. He encountered among the
guards a barricade of silence and evasion, and among the
fifteen hundred inmates fear, prejudice and childish
ignorance. Typical of the run of the mill convict attitude
was that of Isadore Weinstein, a burly Russian, doing
fifteen years for a jewelry robbery. Weinstein could have
established an alibi for Becker because he was exercising
with him in the prison yard shortly before the mutiny
started.

"Yes, I could testify for him," he said, "but I don't
dare; I got my bit licked."

"What do you mean?" asked Leibowitz.

"I've done six years; I've only got nine more to go and I don't want to get in bad with the screws."

"But," remonstrated Leibowitz, "a man's life depends upon your testimony."

"Nothin' doin'; I got my bit licked."

Auburn, county seat of Cayuga County, population 36,000, thinks prison, talks prison, lives prison. The grimy ramparts of New York State's oldest penal institution, situated less than three blocks from the little city's main thoroughfare, dominate its skyline as the institution itself dominates its economic and industrial life. Bankers, merchants, manufacturers and farmers are beholden to it. The mayor of Auburn at the time of the Becker trial was Charles Osborne, son of Thomas Mott Osborne, founder of the Mutual Welfare League, most of whose officers were exiled to Dannemora after the mutiny.

Not in fifteen years had a Cayuga County jury acquitted a convict accused of murder in a mutiny. Leibowitz' initial move was to file a motion for a change of venue. It was denied.

The harsh prison atmosphere of the prologue was maintained in the courtroom drama, which opened February 17. State troopers sat on either side of Supreme Court Justice Benjamin B. Cunningham, presiding judge, and stood post at doors, windows and in aisles—forty in all, augmented by fifteen deputy sheriffs.

Becker, a wisp of a man, appeared manacled to two guards, his chains clanking as he shuffled to his chair. He was preceded and followed by state troopers. His prison gray uniform was newly pressed, with the jumper collar turned down at the throat, disclosing a white shirt and a blue cravat. His black hair had been trimmed and slicked back. Leibowitz greeted him, arose and addressed the bench:

"Your Honor, the presence of the defendant, surrounded by guards, with shackles on his wrists, deprives him of that fair and impartial and constitutionally guaranteed trial to which he is entitled. I move that the shackles be removed."

The court: Motion denied.

Leibowitz: Exception.

That bald colloquy, with its staccato note of finality, recurred again and again, running through the trial like a motif, setting a grim tempo in keeping with the atmosphere.

Jury selection occupied seven days, 260 talesmen being examined. Leibowitz wanted men of low dialectic polarity, as it were. The twelve chosen included seven farmers, two truckmen, a carpenter, a mechanic and a florist. All lived outside Auburn except the florist.

Justice Cunningham halted the third day's proceedings long enough to sentence to the electric chair Claude Udwine, William Force and Jesse Thomas, fellow inmates of Becker involved in the mutiny. It was Udwine who lay in the hospital ward with part of his face shot away. The fifth day Leibowitz was summoned home to Brooklyn by the death of his mother, Mrs. Isaac Leibowitz.

Court was recessed for two days.

A MURDER trial is a modified game of chess, refereed by twelve men in a jury box, in which the opposing players—the attorneys—seek to maneuver a key piece—the defendant—into one of two positions—that of guilt or innocence—through the use of human pawns or occupants of the witness chair. Manipulation is by word of mouth, and the game is won by that side with a preponderant strength of testimony.

Comparing sides in the Becker case on this basis, the prosecution is seen to have an overwhelming advantage. Its master pawns, or chief witnesses, were all prison officials; those of the defense all convicts. Juxtaposed, the two sides contrast thus:

PROSECUTION	DEFENSE
Warden Edgar S. Jennings, colonel in World War, brigadier general N. Y. National Guard, identified Becker as armed with a pistol and threatening him.	Abe Stein, serving twenty years for robbery, established alibi for Becker as exercising in prison yard when mutiny started.
Captain Claude Dempsey identified Becker and "saw" his pistol duel with Principal Keeper Durnford; "heard" him threaten warden.	Thomas Riley, manslaughter—ten years; another alibi witness.
Captain Milton J. Ryther identified Becker as armed, and also heard him threaten warden.	James Benson, stick-up, fifteen years; "saw" Ernest Pavesi, a forty year termer killed in mutiny, running toward Durnford with a gun in his hand.
John McTaggart, foreman woodworking department, saw Durnford shot and Becker with a gun.	Bert M. Ainesworth, forgery, five to ten years; "heard" Pavesi say, "I got the P.K."
Captains Timothy J. Donohue and Patrick Goff, who "missed" Becker just before the mutiny started.	Max Becker, thirty years for burglary, who took the stand in his own behalf.

Besides the foregoing the prosecution had witnesses who further involved Becker. Hugh D. Hawthorne, supervising nurse of the prison hospital, who attended Becker, asked him when he was brought in who shot him and Becker said, "The P. K.", but next day when Hawthorne renewed his questioning Becker, apparently with a clearer head, said, "The P. K. didn't shoot me." Captain Harry F. Butts, ballistics expert of the New York City Police Department, identified the bullet extracted from Becker's lung as having been fired from Durnford's gun.

The defense was doubly handicapped in that Becker was charged with attempted escape—in itself a felony—in addition to murder. It gave the prosecution what Leibowitz described as a double-edged sword because the law provides that any one involved in a felony in which a person is murdered is equally guilty with the actual slayer. In other words, the prosecution, if it couldn't prove Becker fired the shot that killed Durnford, could still send him to the chair by proving he was feloniously present when the murder was committed.

Becker's trial opened on a note of triumph for the State. District Attorney James Hosmer the week before had won a conviction against Udwine, Force and Thomas. They had been defended by Auburn lawyers appointed by the court. Facing Leibowitz, Hosmer, newly elected, retained as his associate counsel his predecessor in office, Benn Kenyon, to whom Leibowitz yielded the accolade, "One of the shrewdest district attorneys I have ever seen in a courtroom."

Play started then in this human chess game with the state seeking to move the key piece, Becker, from a cell in the north wing of the prison down to the lower corridor of the administration building, where the action of the mutiny transpired. A time element was involved. The State must have Becker in the corridor by 10:30 if he was to shoot Durnford.

Guard Captain Donohue was in charge of Becker's company. Guard Captain Goff had orders "to keep an eye on him." Both testified that Becker with thirty-three other convicts was marched across the prison yard to the shower baths in the south wing at 9:45. Goff noticed he was carrying an extra bundle under the pit of his arm. The implication was that it was a gun. Neither could find him after the company returned from the baths at 10. He wasn't seen again so far as the state's testimony was concerned until around 10:30 when—

Warden Jennings, touring the prison, had reached the lower corridor of the administration building. He was seized by three convicts—one armed with a revolver, one with a knife and one with a razor. They hustled him into the near-by kitchen of the Mutual Welfare League and there, flourishing a pistol, was Max Becker.

"We're in this to go through with it, Warden," he said. "We've got plenty of ammunition."

Jennings' hands were tied behind him. The kitchen door opened and Captains Dempsey and Ryther and Shop Foreman McTaggart were herded in. They with Jennings were lined up against the wall. Convicts were milling around and discussing their plans to use the officers as shields in their break for freedom. Jennings was marched out of the kitchen to the south wing to be held a prisoner in the punishment gallery. He heard shots but saw nothing.

Dempsey followed him on the witness stand. He had seen and heard much more—Becker, for instance, saying:

"Come on, Warden, no stalling on your part. If you

do, or if you do anything to prevent this escape, I'll kill you."

And when Dempsey was led out of the kitchen into the corridor for the march to the punishment gallery, he saw Principal Keeper Durnford step out of an enclosed stairway, step quickly back and shut the door. He heard some one shout, "Come here," and:

"Max Becker rushed by me and over to the door with a gun in his right hand and pulled the door open and the firing started immediately into the stairway. Durnford returned the fire and it is possible that five or six shots were fired from Becker's gun and possibly two or three from Durnford's. . . . As I got just west of the stairway I looked to my left and saw Becker in a half sitting position, hanging onto the door knob with his left hand." He was wounded in the left lung.

McTaggart heard two shots in the corridor and saw Durnford fall. Becker had a gun but McTaggart didn't see him use it. Ryther was a better witness. He saw Becker in the kitchen and heard him boast, "We have plenty of ammunition and mean business." His account of what happened in the corridor differed from that of Dempsey:

"Durnford pushes the door open, and he puts up his gun and he shoots and the fellow right side of me shoots. Durnford closes the door and the fellow runs forward, pulls it open and then there is two shots."

Did Ryther know the "fellow's" name? Sure—Max Becker.

THUS the state's case as revealed by the six chief witnesses under District Attorney Hosmer's direct examination. Becker was as good as strapped in the electric chair.

The betting odds were one hundred to one against him with no takers.

Leibowitz began whittling down the case in his cross-examination of Donohue, the first witness. There were two hundred men exercising in the prison yard when Donohue was looking for Becker:

Q. You didn't peer into each man's face, did you? A. No.

Q. Of course not. So you can't say, as a matter of fact, that Becker wasn't in the yard, can you? A. No.

Goff was a hostile witness who insisted upon prefixing a Mister to each convict's name. He had a stock answer, "I had an order to look for Mr. Becker," which he used again and again. Leibowitz let him perform for an hour. Suddenly:

Q. You don't like a convict very much, do you? A. What's that?

Q. You don't care much for a convict, do you? A. I haven't got any dislike for a convict.

Q. Did you ever use an ammonia gun? A. Yes, sir.

Q. May I ask you if you have ever used an ammonia gun through a barred door with a convict inside his cell? A. Yes, sir.

JURISTS have pronounced Leibowitz's cross-examination of Warden Jennings a masterly example of defense technique in a murder case. The warden, a man of unimpeachable character and distinguished presence, had made a profound impression upon the jury. His testimony as it stood at the conclusion of direct examination seemed unassailable. Even without Dempsey's eyewitness account of Durnford's killing, it would have been sufficient to send Becker to the chair. Leibowitz cross-examined him for two days. The warden went on the stand a witness for the state and left it a witness for the defense.

It was, in the beginning, as if Leibowitz were his guest on a stroll about the prison grounds: a nice, friendly, chatty stroll. He was deferential, understanding, sympathetic, tactful. He had forgotten his client. He was interested only in the tour of inspection:

Q. And you started out through the prison? A. Yes.

Q. You went through the guardroom? A. Yes.

Q. Somebody let you into the chapel hall? A. Yes.

Q. Then you went downstairs? A. Yes.

Q. Then you went into the kitchen? A. Yes.

Q. And then do I understand you worked your way through the kitchen out into the yard again? A. Yes, sir.

Q. Then you got to the shops, did some work down there, made some inspection, and you started on your way back? A. Yes, sir.

Q. You were wearing glasses? A. Yes.

Q. It was bitter cold outside, wasn't it? A. Very.

Q. And then you started to come back, didn't you? A. Yes.

Q. You finally got back to the kitchen? A. Yes.

Q. Very hot in the kitchen, wasn't it? A. Yes.

Q. Extremely so, Warden? A. Steamy, yes.

Q. Your glasses were cold? A. Yes.

Q. And this steamy atmosphere that you came into clouded your glasses with moisture? A. Yes.

Q. So that you couldn't see clearly through the glasses? A. Yes.

Q. Now, with the lenses of your glasses steamed and watery you proceeded from the mess hall into the lower hall; that's true, isn't it? A. Yes.

Q. How? A. I carried my glasses in the mess hall.

Q. Then you put them on again? A. Put them on just before, like that (indicating), just as I came down the hallway.

Q. And they were still—? A. Still steamed.

Q. Still steamed. So that before you got into this hallway you put your glasses on again? A. Yes.

Q. You had taken your glasses off for the purpose of being able to see clearly in the mess hall? A. Yes.

Q. Now you say three men held you up; one man approached you holding a piece of paper in his hand? A. Yes.

Q. That was Ernest Pavesi was it not? A. That was my thought. I am not positive.

Q. You have identified Pavesi's picture here, haven't you. A. Yes.

Q. Are you uncertain as to whether it was Pavesi because of the moisture on the glasses? You couldn't get a good look at him, you couldn't see his face clearly? A. The man that approached me, I didn't see his face clearly.

Q. Was that because of the condition of your glasses? A. Yes.

Leibowitz conducted him into the Welfare League kitchen, where he testified under direct examination he had first encountered Becker:

Q. There isn't much ventilation there? A. No.

Q. There is a steam boiler in there? A. Yes.

Q. Pretty hot in there, isn't it? A. Quite.

Q. You still wore your glasses in the little cubicle there, the kitchen? A. Yes.

Q. Of course when these thugs stuck you up they didn't give you an opportunity to take your glasses off, did they? A. No, I think not.

Leibowitz, satisfied he had convinced the jury that the Warden's vision was temporarily blurred, shifted his attack.

Q. You don't know whether, from your talks with people or from any other outside ·consideration, your mind has been refreshed as to the details of what occurred there the day of the riot? A. Oh, yes, it has been refreshed; many things I knew nothing about have been brought to my attention.

Q. Have you suffered any nervous trouble since the riot? A. Yes.

Q. And has that somewhat affected your recollection by reason of the ordeal you went through that day? A. I don't know.

Q. You don't know. In other words, you don't know how much it has affected it? A. No.

Q. How many inmates were in Auburn prison on December 11th, 1929, or approximately? A. Over fifteen hundred.

Q. I dare say, Warden Jennings, that you wouldn't know these fifteen hundred inmates, every one of them, would you? A. No.

Q. Did you know Max Becker personally before December 11th, 1929? A. I have no recollection of having met him.

Q. May I ask, Warden Jennings, if you have a good memory of faces? A. Fair.

Q. Who was the man that put the gun up to you? A. I didn't make a positive identification.

Q. Who was the man that had the knife that you spoke of? A. Pavesi had the knife.

Q. Who was the third man, that had the razor? A. I didn't identify him; in fact, I didn't see his face.

Q. Warden, the uniforms these men wear in prison have a tendency, as far as your own personal experience is concerned, to make it difficult to form a clear picture of a man's face unless you pay particular attention to his face, or unless you know him personally for some time, that's so, isn't it? A. Any uniform has that effect.

Q. Well, explain what you mean by "that effect" so the gentlemen of the jury will understand. A. Why, uniformed groups of men, the same clothing, the same type of hats, and all that, it is harder to identify the individual.

Leibowitz' technique with Jennings was superbly demonstrated in his approach to the central, ugly fact of Becker's participation in the mutiny. He marshaled in the foreground every circumstance and detail favorable to his cause, secluding in the background those inimical. He deftly evaded the fact itself. He came up to it and he fulminated and blustered at it, but avoided contacting its incriminating essence. He maneuvered around it with a smoke screen of questions that effectually concealed his artistry from the yokelry in the jury box:

Q. There was quite some confusion in that kitchen, was there not? A. Yes, it was crowded full.

Q. How many convicts in that kitchen would you say you are able to identify outside of Becker? A. Pavesi and Sullivan.

And why didn't the warden, pressed Leibowitz, immediately go to the prison ward for a look at Becker instead of waiting three weeks to identify him? The warden explained that eventually he and the guards did go to the hospital and sat behind an improvised screen as the inmates were brought in one by one, ostensibly to be interviewed regarding their personal records. There was no line-up.

Yes, he was told Becker was to be among them. Yes, there were discussions behind the curtain and these were conducted by representatives of the district attorney's office. No, the inmates didn't suspect what was up. By the time Leibowitz had finished with this phase of his cross-examination the jury, if it were so inclined, could feel that the warden's identification of Becker was influenced decidedly by the comments of his behind-the-curtain confrères.

Later, in re-direct examination, the warden told District Attorney Hosmer that he had seen Becker frequently during October and November, thus repudiating his admission to Leibowitz that he hadn't known him before December 11, the day of the mutiny.

"How do you reconcile your contradictory testimony?" asked Leibowitz with acid bitterness.

The warden was silent.

"Do you know the nature and quality of an oath?"

Again silence.

THE state had built its case around Jennings and Dempsey. They were its star witnesses—Jennings to the felony, or Becker's participation in the attempted break; and Dempsey to the revolver duel and Durnford's murder.

Leibowitz with Jennings had performed a psychological operation. He had dissected his mind and let the jury see the wheels go round. He couldn't do that with Dempsey, the lanky, up-state country man who drove a milk wagon before becoming a prison guard. Dempsey had no wheels. His was a simple, belt and pulley mind—grooved and rimmed. So all Leibowitz could do was to flay him alive—which he did, and hung up the skin before the jury.

Q. Was Mr. Durnford a friend of yours? A. A friend of mine?

Q. Yes. Please answer yes or no if you can. A. I never asked him.

Q. Was he a friend of yours? A. He always appeared to be very friendly.

Q. He was your boss, wasn't he? A. Yes, sir.

Q. How many times have you gone over the story that you have just told this afternoon? A. I haven't gone over the story.

Q. How many times have you told it? A. I told it to the Grand Jury.

Q. How many other times? A. That is all.

Q. Is that the first time you told it? A. Yes, sir.

Q. Are you sure? A. Yes, sir—no, I told it in the hospital.

Q. How many other times? A. That is all.

Q. Did you tell it to the district attorney? A. Yes, sir.

Q. Did you tell it to some of the guards? A. No, sir.

Q. What? A. No.

Q. Didn't even tell your fellow guards what you had seen, that you were an eyewitness of the murder of Durnford? A. I told them I was an eyewitness but I didn't go on and relate the whole story.

Q. Did they ask you how it happened? A. Yes.

Q. Did you refuse to tell them how it happened? A. No, sir, not entirely.

Q. Did you keep back from your fellow guards any of the facts that you knew? A. Yes.

Q. Did you know Ernest Pavesi? A. Yes.

Q. Did you see Pavesi in the lower corridor before you went upstairs to the hospital? A. I didn't take particular notice of him, no.

Q. Did you see Tucholka? A. No, sir.

Q. Did you see Sporney? A. No, sir.

Q. Did you see Stefanek? A. No, sir.

(Note: these were among the ringleaders of the mutiny.)

Q. Did you see any of the men who later were killed, in the lower corridor before you went upstairs?˙ A. No, sir.

Q. But you did remember seeing Becker? A. Yes.

Q. You single Becker out of this whole list of names, as having seen him? A. I remember Becker having stepped out of the league room and going back in again.

Q. Then you went upstairs into the hospital? A. Yes, sir.

Q. What for? A. I went up there to get medicine for a cold I had.

Q. Cold in the head, was it? A. Yes, sir.

Q. You weren't feeling so well that morning, were you? A. Well, I had a cold in my head; I wasn't feeling very good, no.

Q. Then you came down the stairs? A. Yes, sir.

Q. You were seized by two men from the rear? A. Yes, sir.

Q. You saw the warden? A. Yes, sir.

Q. Becker was right near the warden with a gun in his hand? A. Yes, sir.

Q. How many men were near the warden? A. One.

Q. Do you remember me being at the prison on a Sunday with Mr. Capozucca over there? A. Yes.

Q. Do you remember the new principal keeper, Mr. Beckwith, being in the hall? A. Yes, sir.

Q. Do you remember my asking you, "Dempsey, just what do you know about this case?" A. Yes, sir.

Q. Mr. Capozucca was present at the time when I asked you that question? A. Yes, sir.

Q. Do you remember saying to both of us, "I am under orders by the district attorney not to talk"? A. No, sir.

Q. Do you remember saying to me, "You needn't worry; I have nothing against Becker, I am not bringing Becker into this"? A. No, I didn't say that.

Q. In the presence of Mr. Capozucca are you sure about that? A. Yes, sir, I am sure about it.

Q. You didn't want to tell me what you knew about the case, did you? A. No, sir, not after I refused to tell you.

Q. Where was Pavesi when you got out of the kitchen? A. I don't know.

Q. Where was Tucholka? A. I don't know.

Q. Where was Sporney? A. I don't know.

Q. Where was Stefanek? A. I don't know.

Q. Can you name one man outside of Becker—

HOSMER: I ask Counsel not to point his finger and shake it at the witness.

THE COURT: Yes, Counsel will make no demonstration.

Q. Can you name one man outside of Becker who was down in that lower hall when you got out of the league kitchen? Yes or no. A. None other than the man who was with me.

Q. Do you remember the color of Becker's shirt that day? A. No, sir.

Q. Do you remember whether or not he had a cap on? A. Yes, he did.

Q. Again starting at the time when you got out into the hall, just repeat again if you please what you told the district attorney on your direct examination in answer to this question, "Now, will you continue and tell what you saw?" You started off, "Mr. Durnford apparently saw—Mr. Durnford stepped out of the doorway." Go ahead from that point and repeat the events again. A. Mr. Durnford stepped out of the doorway, and immediately stepped back in and pulled the door behind him.

Q. Yes, go ahead. A. At the time that he stepped back in somebody from the rear shouted, "Come here." About the same time Max Becker rushed by me over to the doorway.

Q. Yes. A. Pulling the door open. The firing started immediately, and Mr. Durnford returned the fire.

Q. Yes, go ahead. A. There were four or five or six shots.

Q. Yes. A. From Becker's gun.

Q. Yes. A. Two or three from Durnford's.

Q. Continue. A. I then passed on towards the south wing.

Q. Yes. A. As I got about west of the bottom of the stairway or the door where Mr. Durnford stepped out of I looked to my left. I saw Becker in a half sitting position, grasping the door with his left hand.

Q. Yes. A. I then passed on into the south hall.

Q. Did you study this speech at any time for the purpose of testifying? A. No.

Q. Of all the men going in and out of the league kitchen that morning you can't name one man except

Becker. That's true, isn't it? A. That's the only one that I remember.

Q. Well, now when you were in the league kitchen you were in a position to see Becker holding the gun, weren't you? A. Yes, sir.

Q. You were in a position to see Becker have the clips? A. Yes, sir.

Q. When you got out you were in a position to see Durnford step out of the hall? A. Yes, sir.

Q. You were in a position to see Becker pull the door open? A. Yes, sir.

Q. You were in a position to see Becker fire the shots? A. Yes, sir.

Q. And you were in a position to see Durnford return the fire? A. Yes, sir.

Q. That's right. Then you marched along toward the south hall; that's right? A. Yes, sir.

Q. And then you turned your head to the left, in this fashion (indicating) and you were also in a position to see Becker grab the door knob and sink down? A. Yes, sir.

Q. So that you were in a position at every stage of the proceedings to be "Johnny-on-the-spot"—to see everything that occurred?

HOSMER: Now, I object to any such question as that as highly improper.

THE COURT: Objection sustained.

LEIBOWITZ: All right. By the way, Mr. Dempsey, have you ever told a lie in your life?

HOSMER: Objected to.

THE COURT: Objection sustained.

LEIBOWITZ: That's all.

Leibowitz had completed his flaying, but he had one

finishing touch to put on the skin. He did it while the
district attorney had Dempsey on the stand on re-direct
examination. The lanky witness was slouched in the chair
on his shoulder blades, with his long legs crossed and
resting on the rail in front of him. Hosmer was trying
to mitigate the effect of the merciless cross-examination.
He was in the midst of his questioning when Leibowitz
roared:

"Now one minute, Your Honor. May I, out of respect
to this Court, have this witness take his feet off the rail
there—sitting there as if he were in a barroom or a
barber shop."

Dempsey was so embarrassed he forgot his testimony,
and the court stenographer had to prompt him.

"THE People rest."

A liturgic solemnity invests the phrase. It marks a high
moment in the age-old ceremonial of a murder trial. It
has something of the fateful connotation of the question:

"Gentlemen of the jury, have you reached a verdict?"

Hosmer uttered it and sat down. Leibowitz arose. Black
robed judge, guards, troopers, manacled prisoner at the
bar and spectators focused their gaze upon him.

"Rabbi Benjamin Freidman," called the court clerk.

Leibowitz, opening his case, was making a move calcu-
lated solely for its effect upon the jury. He was using
the scholarly, bespectacled rabbi for a first impression.
His testimony, per se, was immaterial, but his value as a
factor in lending a semblance of respectability to the
defense cause was inestimable.

His rôle in the Leibowitz set-up was akin to that of
Mrs. Fanny Becker, the mother, who, heavily veiled and

dressed in black, was escorted into the courtroom each day by her son, Samuel, and her brother, Abe Beloff, to occupy a front row seat separated from her son only by a railing.

It was of course an altogether different Becker that Leibowitz presented for the jury's consideration. At the very moment the prosecution declared him to be participating in the mutiny he was engaged in the benevolent enterprise of buttonholing votes among his Jewish fellows for a committee to collect funds for the Passover celebration. The rabbi, in fact, testified that he was to have supervised the election the morning of the mutiny, but remained at his home in Syracuse that day because of an indisposition.

Abe Stein, twenty years for robbery, followed the rabbi on the stand as the first alibi witness. He had met Becker in the prison yard, "between 10 and 11 o'clock" and they had discussed the celebration.

Thomas Riley, ten years for manslaughter, confirmed his testimony. He was walking with Becker when they encountered Stein. They continued their walk and Riley decided he would go to the Welfare League kitchen for a cup of coffee. Becker accompanied him. They had just stepped inside the lower corridor when Ernest Pavesi, with a gun in his hand, ran past them toward the enclosed stairway. Riley looked around and saw Principal Keeper Durnford, also armed. The shooting started and Riley fled, shouting, "Come on, Max," but he didn't see Max again that day.

James Benson, fifteen years for a stick-up, also saw Pavesi with the gun and running toward Durnford. He heard shots. He had seen Durnford standing at the foot of the enclosed stairway a moment before and had heard him say to Charles Stefanek, a convict killed in the mutiny, "You come here." Stefanek, refusing, had countered with, "I won't, you come here," and Durnford had sent Captain John F. Foster for "the guns." The surprise element of Benson's testimony was that Stefanek was standing by the door of the kitchen, and not Becker as the state contended.

Bert M. Ainesworth, five to ten years for forgery, told of a conversation with Pavesi. He had asked him, "Ernest, do you think you will make it?" Before he could answer, Alex Tucholka, another mutineer, had interrupted with, "We'll either eat Christmas dinner outside, or the Warden won't eat Christmas dinner at all." Pavesi had then said, "I've already got the P. K."

Leibowitz had set the stage for his feature act. With a guard on either side of him, the 26-year-old convict stepped to the witness chair, a dapper figure despite his prison gray uniform. His attorney began the examination with punctilious formality:

"Mr. Becker, you are the defendant on trial here for your life, are you not?"

Yes, Mr. Becker was. Had he gone through public school? Yes, and then he had taken a six months' business college course.

Q. Now while you were 16 or 17 years old were you in the Court of Special Sessions? A. I was.

Q. For what? A. I had a little blackjack, a little club in my pocket.

Q. Now shortly thereafter, while you were still a young boy, did you go to Elmira reformatory? A. I did.

Q. What was that about? A. Stole a bicycle.

Q. Now on this last conviction you got thirty years, did you not? A. Yes, sir.

Q. Was that for stealing some jewelry? A. Imitation jewelry.

Q. From where? A. From a house.

Q. You were sent to Sing Sing, were you not? A. Yes, sir.

Q. And from Sing Sing to Clinton? A. Yes, sir.

Q. And from Clinton to Auburn? A. Yes.

So much for the Becker *Who's Who*.

He hadn't disappeared the morning of the mutiny as Guard Captains Donohue and Goff had testified. He had gone back to his cell to deposit his soiled linen on the bed, and the "suspicious" bundle he carried under his armpit wasn't a gun, as was intimated. It was a cake of soap. He verified his alibi witnesses Stein and Riley. Then Leibowitz continued:

Q. Tell the jury what you saw in the lower corridor, what happened there? A. As I got to this point a mental picture came to my mind—it is a picture that I will remember for the rest of my life.

Q. All right. A. I saw a man rush by.

Q. Did you see anything in his hand? A. A gun.

Q. What happened? A. He rushed toward the north, towards the stairway that leads upstairs to the chapel hall, and at the foot of the stairs Principal Keeper was standing.

Q. Then what? A. As he rushed toward the stairs he stopped a few feet from the stairs and the shots were fired and I felt something slap me in the chest, a sort of wind, hitting a pane of glass, and everything before my eyes started getting black, and I could hear Tom Riley's voice, "Run, Max, run," and I tried to turn around and I must have fainted.

Q. Do you remember anything at all that happened to

you from that moment until you were in the hospital?
A. No, sir.

Q. Have you a faint idea of what happened to you?
A. Very, very faint.

Q. What do you recall of your condition, what was being done with you, and what happened to you? A. Just that I was being carted around, and carted around, that is all I can remember.

Leibowitz was watching the clock; timing his act; waiting for 12:30. He wanted the jury to ponder a certain answer during the noonday recess. He shot the climacteric question just before the bailiff let the gavel fall:

Q. Becker, did you shoot Principal Keeper Durnford?
A. As God is my judge, I swear that I did not and if the Principal Keeper were here in the courtroom today my innocence would be established plain and clear.

.   .   .   .

"The defense rests."

LEIBOWITZ is a great criminal lawyer because of (1) his knowledge of human nature; (2) his prowess as a cross-examiner; (3) his ability as a jury pleader, and (4) his consummate art in analyzing, defining and humanizing a subject. He reasons solidly, for, with, and from the law, and he puts his thoughts into plain, strong words with no rhetorical flourishes or classical allusions. He talks the language of the average man. His naturalness is such that it is as if he were holding a personal conversation with each juror. So, his summation in the trial of Becker:

"May it please the court, the district attorney and

gentlemen of the jury: This is the final moment, gentlemen, the final moment when I have got to make a plea for a man's life. It's a great undertaking. I wish I had the power to invoke the Supreme Father to give me the ability to convince your minds and to touch your consciences.

"I wonder whether any defendant, not Max Becker, any defendant in a criminal case, when he sits in the defendant's dock, with an officer of the law at each side of him, ready to shoot him down if he should seek to go through the door—I wonder if he doesn't start with a burden and a handicap.

"It took seven days—some 260 talesmen sat in that witness chair—before we could obtain twelve men who could honestly and fairly raise their hands to the Almighty God and swear they were not prejudiced by those riots, that they were not prejudiced against this defendant, nor against convict testimony.

"Please remember the cross-examination of the convict Abe Stein. What did the district attorney ask him? 'What is your record, what are you convicted of?' He didn't attempt in the slightest to break down his story. He simply questioned as to his record, what he was convicted of. I knew what the district attorney had in mind by that. He felt secure that because the man was a convict the jury would disregard his testimony.

"Well, what did they offer against Stein to counteract his testimony? Three guards, Donohue, Goff and Hickey. Did they prove that Becker wasn't in the yard? Donohue says he didn't lock Becker in the cell. We don't dispute that. He didn't lock Becker in the cell.

"Goff is called. You remember Goff, a gray-haired fellow, a big, tall fellow with a tough looking face—remember him?—the fellow who squirts ammonia guns in cells—what does he say?

"He says he saw Becker coming in with two bundles. That was peculiar. You remember? Peculiar. Suspicious that a man should come in with two bundles. What does he mean? He means to insinuate Becker had a gun in one bundle. Well, if that was so, what would the normal human being have done? Wouldn't he have gone over to him and said, 'Here, Johnny, what have you got in there? Let's look at this bundle.'

"Gentlemen, am I talking commonsense to you or am I giving you oratory? Am I appealing to your reason, to your intelligence, or am I trying to hoodwink you? If it was suspicious, why did he let Becker pass and go into the bathroom with two bundles? Why didn't he stop him then and there, or apprise his keeper of the fact that Becker had two bundles and there might be something in there that was suspicious?

"I have my faults. There are things that I did in this case, little things here and there, that upon sober reflection I would not do again, but we can't help those things in the heat of battle, in the battle to save a man's life.

"Haven't I, at least, raised a reasonable doubt? That is the question. Haven't I raised a reasonable doubt with Stein's testimony, with the Rabbi's testimony, with Benson's testimony and with Riley's testimony? If there is a reasonable doubt raised—only a reasonable doubt and not proof that they are telling the truth; only a reasonable doubt about it—that Becker didn't steal out into the yard or anywhere else; that Becker was talking to Stein in the yard; that he went into the lower hall legitimately; that he had no part in the holdup of the warden or the guards; that Becker fired no shots; and that Becker must have been wounded in this cross fire between Principal Keeper Durnford and Pavesi. ...

"Well, they brought in the star witness for the state— Dempsey. He is the Babe Ruth, he bats in fourth position, he's the clean-up man; he wields the heavy stick that drives in the home run and they save him for fourth. They put him in the fourth hole as they say in baseball —a player who can bang out a home run and land the bacon.

"He was Johnny-on-the-spot in the cook room, was Johnny-on-the-spot when Becker had the clips, Johnny-on-the-spot when Becker had the gun, Johnny-on-the-spot when Becker said, 'We have got the ammunition and we are going to go through with this,' Johnny-on-the-spot when they came out, Johnny-on-the-spot when the door was opened, and he was Johnny-on-the-spot when Becker did the shooting, and even when Dempsey was being marched with guns stuck into his back he was Johnny-on-the-spot enough to look back to see that Becker was sinking by the stair and got hold of that knob. That was a little too perfect for you sensible men, a little too good to be true, just a little too good. It was meant for a homer over the fence, but it was a foul—that is the trouble with it. ...

"The way this identification was made; wasn't that a shame? Three or four weeks after the riot this scene in the visiting room, these men hidden behind the curtain. Why did they have to hide behind the curtain? Peering over a slit in the curtain like so many people looking into a side show or under a tent in a circus, and then they bring in one of the men and they all come out and the district attorney is there and they make their statements.

"No heart bleeds more than mine for that poor soul that was cut down in the flower of his manhood, Principal Keeper Durnford. He was a brave man and he died with his boots on. I am sorry for his poor family, but what poor consolation to them to take for his death an innocent human being and burn him in the electric chair. . . ."

District Attorney Hosmer's summation centered upon the credibility of the convict witnesses. He said there could be no compromise and reiterated again and again that the jury, if it accepted the defense case, branded Jennings, Dempsey, McTaggart and Ryther as liars and perjurers.

THE jury retired at 1:55 and Becker was allowed a brief reunion with his mother who, Leibowitz had said in his summation, "read her boy's innocence in his eyes." The old clock on the wall above the judge's bench ticked off twenty-three sleepless hours for Leibowitz. He snatched catnaps on the courtroom benches, but mostly he paced up and down. Once in the early dawn Foreman J. W. Houghton emerged to request a reading of Leibowitz' cross-examination of Jennings, Dempsey, Ryther and McTaggart, and Leibowitz remarked wearily to District Attorney Hosmer:

"I guess it's murder first degree, Jim."

It was 12:55 when the jury filed in and Justice Cunningham put the question:

"Gentlemen, have you reached a verdict?"

"We have," was the answer.

"What is that verdict?"

"Your Honor, counsel and defendant," announced Foreman Houghton, "we find Max Becker not guilty."

Up popped the little burglar-convict, raising high his manacled hands.

"The only words I can find in my heart are to thank you for this life you have given me," he quavered. "I hope some day to make it a real life."

Then, turning to the judge:

"And I want to thank His Honor, I want to thank him for the fair and square manner in which he has treated me."

Reporters and camermen stampeded into the railed arena in search of gladiator Leibowitz, seeking the usual interviews, the lawyer-client pictures—the famous victory pose, right arm around the acquitted's shoulder, and the famous victory smile. He seemed literally to have dropped from sight in the pushing, jostling throng. For a full two minutes the search continued. Then a court stenographer discovered a crumpled, inert form on the floor beside his table.

Leibowitz had fainted.

CHAPTER ELEVEN

THE LAST MILE

IT is a comfortable chair, roomy, with broad arms, ample seat and softly cushioned headrest sheathed in rubber. It is fashioned of quartered oak and has the massive solidity of its Seventeenth Century English ancestor, archetypal pattern for all American armchairs. It stands directly under a skylight and its four sturdy legs are bolted to the concrete floor.

Skilled hands tuck the occupant into its snug embrace, adjusting the leather harness and steel appendages, shaped like shepherd's crooks, to bind his legs, arms, waist, chest and neck. Then the two electrodes, one clamped to the tonsured head, one to the calf of the leg. A delicate business this, for it is through the electrodes that the lethal current enters the body. The contact must be perfect. The electrodes are made of flexible wire screen lined with sponges. They are dipped in salt water, an unfailing conductor, and the sponges retain the moisture.

Tall, gaunt, sad-eyed Robert Elliott, the executioner, who gets $150 a job, is stationed in a small alcove at the right and slightly behind the chair. The occupant cannot see him but Elliott has a full view of the mechanical apparatus. A nod or a dropped handkerchief is the signal for him to close the switch.

Leibowitz in eighty-six first degree murder trials has cheated the chair eighty-five times. His eighty-sixth case was that of Francis Howard Reddy, 23-year-old lather, found guilty of slaying a patron in the hold-up of a Manhattan cider stube. One, Joseph Baumann, already sentenced to die for the crime, had won a commutation to life imprisonment by testifying Reddy was his accomplice. The owner of the stube and three customers failed to identify Reddy, but the jury took Baumann's word for it. Leibowitz appealed the conviction on the grounds that Baumann had perjured himself, and obtained a reversal. Reddy, as this is written, is in the Tombs, awaiting his second trial.

Like Clarence Darrow, who has never lost a client to the gallows or the chair, Leibowitz has never seen an execution. He never will. He has an antipathy to it that is almost pathological. Although death by electrocution is perhaps the most merciful form of capital punishment, it smacks of torture to him, and that is unendurable. His attitude is probably racial, a heritage of the long centuries of persecution suffered by his forebears.

The Sing Sing death house itself was for years a sort of chamber of horrors to him. The chances are he never would have set foot in it had not professional exigencies required his presence there. The direct cause was Peter Sardini, "the only man," says Leibowitz, "I ever saw just before he burned."

Sardini and Pietro Matera had been sentenced to die for a double killing committed during the hold-up of a Brooklyn waterfront speakeasy. They were awaiting execution when Sardini absolved Matera in a statement declaring him to be a victim of mistaken identity. Sardini said his real accomplice was a Francesco Locasio, who had fled to Sicily. He added that he had knowledge of a half dozen murders which he would reveal if his sentence were commuted to life imprisonment. Leibowitz had not represented Sardini and Matera at their trial. He was called into the case after they had been put in the death house. He succeeded in having Matera's sentence commuted to life imprisonment, but was unable to do anything for Sardini because investigation disclosed his purported knowledge of unsolved crimes had no basis in fact. He was merely trying to talk himself out of the chair. Even so, Governor Franklin D. Roosevelt granted him three reprieves.

The day the third one was to expire, with Sardini doomed to walk the last mile—at 11 o'clock that night—Mrs. Sardini came to Leibowitz' office and implored him to go with her to Sing Sing. She was accompanied by her five-year-old daughter, Rosy, and she carried in her arms a two-year-old son named for the father. Leibowitz couldn't find it in his heart to refuse. He felt, too, that it was his duty. They took a cab from his office to Grand Central Station to board a 3:06 train for Ossining.

This death house visit, this first and only experience with a man about to burn, stirred a welter of emotions in Leibowitz' fecund mind. He was like one in a trance. He was seized with an uncontrollable impulse to set his reactions down on paper. He is not given to writing. He had neither pad nor notebook, but he had bought a magazine and on a back page, around a cigarette ad, he penciled his thoughts. Quoting:

"Walked around Grand Central watching passengers

leaving on the 20th Century for Chicago ... happy folks
... swells ... movie stars, friends and flowers ... June
Collyer and Stu Erwin ...

"An appropriate day, bleak and drizzling ... we sit in
the smoker ... it is only half filled ... Mrs. Sardini, an
Italian woman with an oval madonna face ... eyes glazed
... unseeing ... mind apart from body ... next to me a
man who appears to be Robert Elliott, the executioner
... he has the black bag in which he carries the precious
electrodes ...

"Only affable person is the chubby conductor ... he is
chewing gum ... his train has carried many men to Sing
Sing ... he wears a shamrock in his coat lapel ...

"The pelting rain beats a dirge on the train windows
... the tenements are dripping ... even the railroad tracks
seem deserted ... no laborers ... we pass a junk yard
filled with iron scraps ... I am going to another junk
house filled with human scraps ...

"A deserted shipyard on our left ... a deserted house-
boat ... mist over the river ... not even a gull aloft ...
station platforms empty ... all the world seems to be in
mourning ...

"We arrive at Ossining ... squeaky cab ... two minute drive to Sing Sing ... we get in Black Maria for ride
to death house ...

"In the visitors' cage Mrs. Sardini meets a cousin,
Tony, who has two youngsters with him ... Mrs. Sardini's
baby is nursing its milk bottle ...

"Sardini is in the prisoners' coop facing them through
the steel meshing ... he is short, wiry, rosy complexioned,
with big brown eyes ... his hair is close cropped ... he
presses his lips to the meshing and kisses empty space
... he means the kisses for the baby ... he says to Rosy,

'Poppa'll be home tomorrow'... Rosy pays no attention
... she and the other children are playing leap frog...
Mrs. Sardini, holding the baby, sits mute and motionless
like a frozen image...

"I give him a cheerful 'hello' and tell him I have just
telephoned the governor at Albany... 'Don't worry,' I
assure him, 'I expect word of another reprieve any moment now'... I am lying... I know he is doomed... he
is drinking coffee... the turnkey whispers to me that he
hasn't eaten for three days...

"Would I like to speak to Sardini alone, the turnkey
whispers. I say 'yes,' and he conducts us up to the second
floor to counsel's room... it's almost bare, with only a
desk and a hat tree and two or three chairs... I sit behind the desk... Sardini is in front of me... the turnkey sits in a corner looking through a barred window at
the rain...

"Sardini's hair stands up like brush bristles; he strokes
the tonsored spot... he wears a faded blue shirt, torn at
the elbow; brown trousers, felt slippers... he is a changed
man from the father who threw kisses at his baby... he
is a cornered rat... he complains of the breaks the other
fellows get... he raves hysterically... 'What'll my boy
do? How'll he be able to look any one in the face? They'll
point at him and say, "His dad died in the chair"'... he
turns to the turnkey and asks, 'I got four more hours,
ain't I?' The turnkey doesn't answer... he only stares
out the window at the driving rain...

"A crazed look comes into Sardini's big, brown eyes
... his fingers twitch... he finally blurts, 'I'm going to
squeal; I've sent for the D. A.; to hell with everybody;
I'm going to squeal!'...

" 'Do what you want about squealing,' I tell him. 'Personally I despise squealers' ... I add, 'Don't give up the ship; keep up your courage; we'll hear from Albany' ... he smiles weakly and mutters, 'I got courage' ... I didn't say good-by to him; I didn't have the nerve ... just left him with 'I'll see you later' ...

"He walked the last mile that night—not the swaggering bully and killer his gang had known, but a pitiful weakling, kissing the crucifix at every step..."

SARDINI'S case recalled to Leibowitz another in which blind fate and circumstance played stellar rôles in a near drama of the death house.

"Let me," he said, "tell you the story of Adam Lemansky, known to the police as Adam the Polack.

"I have been asked countless times why in all conscience I could defend thugs and alleged murderers, men I believed to be guilty. He is my answer.

"Lemansky was only twenty-five years old, but his record included five convictions, with one term at Elmira Reformatory, and another at Sing Sing.

"Born in the slums of the Williamsburg waterfront section of Brooklyn, he was a truant from school at 10, a petty thief at 11, and a purse snatcher at 12. His victims were women shoppers in department stores. He had a wiry body, nimble legs and could squirm through crowds like a slippery eel.

"He learned successfully to pick pockets, to burglarize stores and dwellings and finally arrived at man's estate in the underworld as a safecracker and stick-up.

"Adam the Polack was notorious as a copper hater. So dangerous was he considered that the police had orders to use the utmost caution in handling him. He had slashed many a uniform and bashed many a head.

"Now on a February night when a heavy snowfall had piled the drifts high on the city streets, two clerks in an Atlantic and Pacific Tea Store in Lee Avenue, Williamsburg, were counting the day's receipts preparatory to closing. Three men entered. Looking up from their account books, expecting to see belated customers, the clerks stared into the muzzles of three revolvers.

" 'Hi'st 'em,' said the leader of the trio.

"One clerk obeyed. The other whipped out a gun and opened fire. The robbers returned it, making for the door. Their way was blocked by Mrs. Mary Betsch, a housewife, hurrying to make a last-minute purchase. The leader turned his gun on her and she fell, fatally wounded. The three men ran across the street to their car, but it was stuck fast in a snowdrift.

"A taxicab driven by Samuel Kitzman with a woman passenger approached. They leaped on the running board, telling him to 'Drive like hell.' He refused and the leader shot him dead. A truck driven by Joseph Monich happened along. They commandeered it, had Monich drive them across the Williamsburg bridge to the lower east side of Manhattan, where they boarded a subway train, forcing Monich to accompany them.

"They rode in a brightly lighted car filled with passengers to the Van Cortlandt park station. They took Monich into the park, beat him over the head with the butts of their guns and left him for dead in the bushes.

"Long before Monich had finished his subway ride the police were busy—and looking for Adam the Polack. It was the type of stick-up in which Lemansky and his gang specialized, and had occurred in his home neighborhood.

"Peculiarly enough that very night he had disappeared

from his usual haunts, the poolrooms and cheap dance halls. But the police had a hot trail. They caught him at Philadelphia, preparing to board a train for the south.

"They carted him back to Brooklyn and in the detectives' room of the precinct station house he was identified as the trigger man in each killing by the two clerks in the A. & P. store and the woman passenger in Kitzman's taxi. Monich, the truck driver, likewise identified him as one of the three that had taken him for the subway ride.

"Detectives also found a cigarette butt in the tea store with finger prints which they said corresponded with Lemansky's prints on file in the Rogues' Gallery at police headquarters.

"A grand jury quickly started Lemansky on the first leg of his journey to the electric chair. He was indicted for two murders, holdup and robbery, kidnaping and possession of firearms. Pending trial he was lodged in the Raymond Street jail in Brooklyn.

"I was summoned to the jail, soon after the indictment, to confer with him. He protested his innocence. He wanted to retain me as his counsel. He asked me what I thought of his chances.

" 'Whether you're innocent or guilty,' I said, 'you have as much chance as a snowball in hell of beating the hot seat.'

" 'But I'm innocent,' he repeated.

"To myself I thought, 'That's what they all say.'

"Alleged crook and jailbird though he was, however, there was a certain something about the way he looked at me, about his whole demeanor, that caused me to pause, despite the fact that here was a man identified by four persons independently; a man with a terrible criminal record, who was 'on the lam,' before the bodies were cold.

"Not guilty? It seemed impossible.

"The machinery of justice moves slowly. A month elapsed and the trial was not quite a week away, when on a balmy Sunday afternoon, a highway policeman was directing traffic on the Boston Post Road, fifty miles from Brooklyn, at Darien, Connecticut. A touring car with three men failed to stop on the red light. The policeman blew his whistle, hopped on his motorcycle and the car halted. He was set to give the driver the usual bawling out when he caught sight of three revolvers on the floor in the tonneau.

"Forgetting about the traffic violation, he drew his gun, and, standing on the running board took the car to the station. There, after an hour's questioning, the three rather boastfully confessed to a series of robberies, among them the A. & P. store holdup in Williamsburg. They were returned to Brooklyn that night and not only supplemented their confession with details of the double killing but reënacted the crime.

"Again the witnesses were called in and this time they were voluble in their identification.

"The following day the district attorney appeared before the trial judge with a motion to quash the indictments against Adam Lemansky because:

" 'He's an innocent man.'

"What if the red light at Darien had been green instead of red? Or what if the highway policeman had lacked a vigilant eye?

"The four reputable witnesses would have taken the stand. The district attorney would have done his stuff. The judge would have gone through the motions of a charge to the jury. The twelve good men and true would have retired to the jury room, smoked their cigars, and returned with a verdict of guilty.

"Then on a Thursday night around 11 o'clock when all was hushed inside the grim gray walls of Sing Sing, the prison warden would have led a party of citizens along the gravel path to a square, boxlike room whose walls are bare save for one-word placards, 'Silence.'

"The guests would have been motioned to seats in three church pews to listen to the ticking of a clock and the beating of their hearts. Before them on a rubber mat the machine of straps, wire coils and shackles—the hot seat; the instrument the state uses to snuff out the life of one found guilty.

"Presently a tap on the little green door. Flanked by burly guards, Adam the Polack, once chubby, now a shrunken figure in felt slippers, trousers slit to the knees, hair close cropped. One, two, three, four steps. He is in front of the chair. A voice intones:

" 'Lord have mercy on his soul.... Father, forgive them, they know not what they do....'

"Then, perhaps, Adam the Polack asking:

" 'May I say something?'

"And, at an affirmative nod from the warden:

" 'You're killing an innocent man.'

"A hard smirk from the guards. A hard smirk from the reporters.

"They thrust him into the chair. The man the state employs as executioner adjusts the helmet on the head, the mask over the eyes and flits back to his alcove.

"A click. The switch is thrown. A moaning whir as 2,000 volts shoot through the body of a man who a moment ago was pulsating with life, and now is furiously straining at the straps, hands twitching, saliva dripping from his lips.

"A thin wisp of smoke from the helmet, nauseating the people in the pews. A signal from the prison doctor. The current is cut off. Business of stethoscope and—another voice:

" 'I pronounce this man dead.'

"They loosen the straps and shackles. They wheel the body to the medical room. Doctors in black aprons slit it to remove the heart, saw the skull to remove the brain. They sew him up, put him in a pine box, paste a label on it, and the burned and charred hulk for which the state has no more use goes back to the mother as her own, to do with as she sees fit.

"Next morning John J. Citizen, sitting at breakfast with his newspaper propped against the salt shaker, reading details of the execution of Adam Lemansky, would have encountered the line 'You're killing an innocent man,' and he, too, would have said:

" 'That's what they all say!'

"It would have happened just that way except for a red stop and an observant highway policeman at Darien. Who can tell how many Adam Lemanskys have gone through the little green door?"

CHAPTER TWELVE

"A BLOT ON EVERY SHIELD"

E MMANUEL KAMMA, an armorer of the 27th Division Headquarters, New York National Guard, was walking east through Van Cortlandt Park in Mosholu Avenue, the Bronx, at 7 o'clock the morning of Thursday, February 26, 1931.

A white kid glove fluttering from a bush at the edge of an embankment caught his attention. He stepped over to examine it and saw, fifty feet down in a gully, the body of a woman. He hailed a passing gasoline truck driver, Harry Francis. They did not stop to investigate, but immediately telephoned police headquarters.

Patrolman Daniel J. Sullivan and Detective Alfred Sweeney were on the scene at 7:20, the first officers to arrive. They were followed by Dr. Ralph Drews of the Fordham Hospital ambulance service. The woman had been strangled to death with a six-foot length of window sash cord. She was about 40 years old; height five feet four inches; weight 130 pounds; gray eyes, bobbed auburn hair, fair complexion and full face. She was wearing a black velvet dress, trimmed at the collar and cuffs with cream-colored lace; black, pliable, close-fitting straw

hat; gunmetal silk stockings and one black suède pump.
The other was missing.

The vast police machinery of New York City moved
swiftly and efficiently. Within two hours after the finding
of the body fingerprints had been taken and their classifi-
cation telegraphed to the Bureau of Identification at headquarters. The woman was Benita Franklin Bischoff, better
known as Vivian Gordon, notorious procuress and black-
mailer, whose name had been linked with underworld
activities since the days of Arnold Rothstein.

She lived at No. 156 East 37th Street, Manhattan, in
a three-room apartment. She was last seen alive, so far
as the police could learn, by William Wheaton, elevator
operator of the building, who said she had gone out at
11:30 o'clock the night preceding the murder and had not
returned.

He volunteered a bit of significant information. Vivian
was wearing a $2,000 full-length mink coat. Like the
purse and the suède pump, it was missing when the body
was found, as were also, the police soon learned, a platinum ring set with eighteen diamonds, valued at $2,000,
and a diamond wrist watch, valued at $750.

Search of the apartment revealed seven leather-bound
diaries with sizzling entries concerning the woman's varied
and peculiar enterprises, along with the names of three
hundred wealthy "gentlemen friends." Among these were
the late Henry McDonald Joralemon, sportsman and phi-
lanthropist, who had given her $30,000 during the year
preceding her death; John A. Hoagland, baking powder
magnate, and Jefferson Livingston, the catsup king.

Her life, as pieced together by the police, had the raw
material for a Eugene O'Neill play or a Thomas Hardy
novel. It was that of a girl of unusual beauty, born of

good parentage; reared in the quiet environment of a
small town—Michigan City, Ind.; educated in a convent;
growing up to become a respectable married woman, the
wife of one John Bischoff, who came of a fine southern
family. For some reason known only to herself she
abandoned everything to become, first, a street walker
in New York City; then a trafficker in prostitution and a
consort of gangsters and criminals. She ended with a rope
around her neck—and over in a Jersey town her sixteen-
year-old daughter, Benita, who had lived in ignorance of
her mother's calling, committed suicide because she could
no longer face the world for shame.

It was a letter found in the apartment that sent Police
Commissioner Edward P. Mulrooney, himself, into action,
and enlisted the attention of Mayor James J. Walker. It
was signed by Irving Ben Cooper and read:

"My dear Miss Gordon: Your letter addressed to Mr.
Kresel under date of February 7 has been turned over
to me for attention. I should be glad to see you at the
above address on Friday, February 20, 1931, between the
hours of 10 A.M. and 5 P.M."

New York City's police department was under fire in
an investigation of magistrates'' courts and general vice
conditions directed by Samuel Seabury. His chief counsel
was Isadore J. Kresel, and Cooper was Kresel's assistant.

Vivian in her letter to Kresel had stated she had "some
information in connection with a frame-up by a police
officer and others which I believe will be of great aid to
your committee in its work. I would appreciate an interview at your earliest convenience."

Her information, given to Cooper in the subsequent
interview, was that in 1923 she had been committed to

Bedford Reformatory on fictitious charges preferred by
Patrolman Andrew J. McLaughlin of the Vice Squad.
Cooper had told her to bring in proof of this and her
other allegations. She had left promising to do so, and two
weeks later was murdered.

McLaughlin was sought for questioning. He was vaca-
tioning in Bermuda. He had left the city a week before
the murder. Investigation absolved him of any connection
with it.

But the challenge to Mulrooney still remained. The implication was that the police had eliminated Vivian because she knew too much. Press and pulpit thundered de-
nunciations. Said Mulrooney:

"Until the murderer or murderers of Vivian Gordon are
convicted, there will be a blot on the shield of every
member of the police department."

The Patrolman's Benevolent Association, reflecting his
attitude, promptly appropriated a $15,000 reward for "in-
formation leading to the arrest and conviction of the
slayers."

Mulrooney assigned sixty of his best headquarters detectives to the case, in addition to six hundred precinct
men. They were ordered to report daily progress to him
personally. An entry in one of the diaries had interested
him. It was dated July 10, 1929. It read:

"Charles Reuben . . . loan of $1,500 . . . Oslo."

Mulrooney chewed it over in his mind. Mightn't Oslo
mean the city in Norway, and mightn't the money have
been advanced for a trans-Atlantic trip? He put his men
to searching passenger lists of steamships that had sailed
for Norway about the time of the diary entry.

So far not a single clue had been uncovered. Mulrooney
was getting restive. So was Mayor Walker. The men

searched for days. It was March 10 when Mulrooney's private telephone jingled and he picked up the receiver to learn that a Charles Reuben had been a passenger on the *S.S. Bergenfjord,* sailing from New York to Norway July 20 of 1929.

Here at least was something definite to work on. The U. S. passport records were examined and the police obtained a sample of Reuben's handwriting through his signature; also the information that he had declared the voyage was for "pleasure."

The signature was compared with the handwriting of criminals on file at headquarters. It exactly resembled that of Harry Stein, a rascal with a long record and a reputation as a strangler. He had deserted from the United States Army in 1916 and had served terms in Elmira Reformatory and Sing Sing for grand larceny and robbery. He had long since returned from Norway and in 1931 was living at 1312 Park Avenue. Mulrooney assigned a detail to shadow him.

They reported that his favorite rendezvous was a restaurant at 1030 Sixth Avenue where the patrons played cards for sandwiches and drinks. Stein frequently was in conversation with Samuel Greenberg, another fellow with a record. Greenberg was shadowed. Detectives eavesdropping in an adjoining telephone booth one day overheard him call a number and ask for "Harry." Apparently Harry wasn't home for Greenberg instantly hung up. The detectives traced the telephone to an apartment at 300 West 49th Street. The tenant was listed as Harry Harvey, a name new to the police. The telephone was taped, and the listening ears of the department gleaned information that caused Mulrooney to beam with joy. The trail was getting warm.

DAVE BUTTERMAN, oldtime fence and drug peddler, and his wife Anna, were roused from their slumbers early the morning of April 5, more than five weeks after Vivian Gordon's murder. Six detectives questioned them in their apartment at 639 West 173rd Street. Hadn't Harry Stein telephoned them between 2:00 and 2:30 A.M. February 26? Yes, he had. Mrs. Butterman had talked to him. He had made an appointment to meet her husband the next morning at Broadway and 96th Street.

"We ate breakfast," said Butterman taking up the narrative, "and then went to a house at 294 Riverside Drive. The landlady, Mrs. Madeline Tully, let us in and we went to the kitchen. Stein showed me a lady's diamond wrist watch. I asked him how much he wanted for it and he said, 'The boys are asking $100.' I told him it was worth only $50 to me. He would let me know, he said. He showed me a full-length mink coat and when I asked his price he said, 'The boys would like $400 for it.' I cut out the lining, spread the coat on a couch, and tried to obliterate some factory marks by rubbing ink on them. I splashed some of the ink on the couch cover."

Butterman took the coat to Max Mishkin, a dressmaker, at 2228 Broadway, for appraisal; and the wrist watch to William Rosenfeld, Butterman's brother-in-law, a dealer in diamonds, living at the Edison Hotel, in midtown Manhattan. Rosenfeld didn't want the watch, Butterman reported to Stein. Well, then, how about a platinum ring set with eighteen diamonds, for which Stein was asking $1,000? Rosenfeld didn't want· that either. Butterman had decided he couldn't use the mink coat— it was too hot—and the deal was off.

The case was going great guns. The police had established that Stein the day after the murder was hawking Vivian Gordon's personal belongings.

Still they hadn't linked him with the crime itself. Again the tapped telephone rendered yeoman service. It revealed that the mysterious Harvey was Harry Schlitten, a taxi driver, who at 8 o'clock the night preceding the murder had rented a seven-passenger Cadillac sedan from an auto agency at 123 Suffolk Street. He had returned it at 1 o'clock the next morning.

Schlitten, taken into custody and confronted with this fact, broke down and confessed. Stein had offered him $1,000 to act as chauffeur for himself, Greenberg and Vivian. Schlitten had been eyewitness to everything.

Stein brought Vivian to the sedan in a taxi and introduced her to Greenberg, who was posing as "a sucker with $250,000 worth of diamonds." She got into the car, seated herself between the two men and immediately concentrated on the "sucker" with the remark, "Where have you been all my life?"

They started for Van Cortlandt Park, sharing drinks from a bottle of Bourbon. Soon Schlitten heard scuffling. He looked around and saw Stein and Greenberg tightening the rope around Vivian's neck.

"She's finished now," he quoted Stein as saying to Greenberg.

The car continued on to the spot in Van Cortlandt Park where they dumped the body into a thicket. The night Schlitten told his story, the police arrested Stein and Greenberg, and within the week they were indicted for first degree murder. Schlitten received immunity as the state's witness.

So the mystery was solved. None was more pleased than

Mulrooney. With Mayor Walker sitting by, smiling approval, the good, gray commissioner said:

"The detective work reflects the highest credit on the department. It is one of the most intelligent, persistent efforts that has been carried out by detectives in many, many years."

THE trial was held in Bronx County before Supreme Court Justice Albert Cohn. Greenberg was represented by three attorneys—John D. Sullivan, Abraham Berman, and John F. Reidy; Stein by one—Leibowitz. District Attorney Charles B. McLaughlin designated an assistant, I. J. P. Adlerman, to direct the prosecution. The state had forty witnesses; Greenberg, four; Stein, two.

Schlitten on the witness stand, facing Leibowitz June 18, 1931, represented the supreme effort of the New York City police department in "its biggest case in years," to quote Mulrooney. He was much more than a star witness; he was the state's whole case. The remaining thirty-nine witnesses were incidental, their testimony either supplementing or corroborating sequential details.

In the direct examination conducted by District Attorney Adlerman, Schlitten recited the story that seemingly damned the defendants to the electric chair. Stein had approached him in the restaurant in Sixth Avenue two days before the murder. He wanted a car because, "If I don't get a certain party out of the way, a friend of mine is going to wind up going to jail." Schlitten spoke to Izzy English who rented one from Hymie Siegel, owner of the agency at 123 Suffolk Street.

Schlitten, posing as chauffeur, with Greenberg as the
· sucker, waited in the car in front of a house at 1631 Grand Avenue, the Bronx, the night of the murder. Stein

and Vivian Gordon arrived a few minutes before midnight.

"Drive to Max's, please," said Greenberg. It was a code phrase and meant that Schlitten should start cruising over a prearranged route. He hadn't driven far when:

"I heard this awful gasping sound for breath, like a screech, a cackle. I proceeded a little further, and heard Stein say, 'She's finished now.' I turned my head and there were Stein and Greenberg down on their knees with Stein pulling the rope around her neck.

"Stein told me to stop. He got out and grabbed her by the feet; Greenberg picked her up by the arms. They carried her out and dropped her in a ditch. Stein came back then with the mink coat. They got into the car. I started. A little further on Stein picked a slipper of hers off the floor and threw it out the window. (The missing pump.)

"Next he went through her purse. I heard him say to Greenberg, 'There is $2.16 in it.' They gave that to me for a tip. Stein wanted to go back to her apartment to get her diaries, but Greenberg said, 'You're nerts,' and so they didn't go."

Stein met Schlitten four days after the murder and informed him, "We only got $50 for that $750 wrist watch." Three weeks passed and, testified Schlitten, "Stein came to the restaurant all a-flutter."

"All a-what?" asked District Attorney Adlerman.

"All a-flutter, excited." Schlitten went on to explain that Vivian's $2,000 mink coat had been left at the Times Square check room and that Stein, fearful of the police, wanted him to get it out. He refused. Madeline Tully, Stein's landlady, who ran the rooming house at 294 Riverside Drive, finally disposed of the coat.

"Stein told me," Schlitten testified, "what a smart woman this woman was that ran this house. He took the coat up there and she burned it down in the incinerator, and she had some company sitting up in one of the rooms there, and this company smelled this awful stink, and he told me that she told them that the garbage man was downstairs; what a smart woman she was."

These were the essential points of Schlitten's testimony as the state's star witness. Leibowitz's opening question indicated the line of his cross-examination:

"Schlitten, I want to know if you would be willing to tell a lie under oath?"

An objection by Assistant District Attorney Adlerman, sustained by Justice Cohn, saved Schlitten from answering, but Leibowitz had only begun. Schlitten had testified he had never been convicted of a crime. Leibowitz forced the admission he had once gone to Boston to rob an armored car. Then with the lightning shift in questioning he uses when seeking to discredit a witness, he asked:

"Do you know a Chinaman living in Berkeley, California, by the name of Mike Won or Mike Woo?"

Schlitten didn't know a Won or a Woo. Finally, though:

"I know a lot of Chinamen; I did business with a lot of Chinamen."

Leibowitz led him through a labyrinth of Q and A until:

"By the way, you've been engaged, haven't you, in extorting money from Chinamen who were smuggled into this country?"

No, he hadn't. Well, hadn't he been involved in the opium traffic? No, sir.

But Leibowitz was satisfied. He was getting in brush

strokes on a picture for the jury—a shading here, a highlight there. Slowly it assumed outline, form and character:

Schlitten was a guerrilla who sold strong arm protection to millinery shops at fifty dollars a month.

Schlitten had run a poolroom that was a rendezvous for criminals.

Schlitten couldn't remember when or where he was married or by whom. His wife had divorced him. He hadn't supported their three-year-old child.

Schlitten had hidden out for two weeks under an assumed name in a Newark, New Jersey, hotel when word seeped through the underworld that the police were on his trail.

Trying to evade a question that would have compelled an incriminating answer, Schlitten said he hadn't read the newspapers.

"Why?" asked Leibowitz.

"Because my conscience bothered me."

It was a fatal slip.

"So your conscience bothered you?" gloated Leibowitz.

"That's right."

"Was it your conscience that made you confess after the police caught you?"

"That's right."

"Or was it the hope of saving your neck?"

"It was my conscience."

"Did your conscience bother you when you heard the woman's dying gasp?"

"I had company and forgot it."

"Let's see. You testified they offered you $1,000 to drive the murder car?"

"Yes."

"And you accepted?"

"Yes."

"Did your conscience bother you then?"

The answer to that one, of course, was no. Leibowitz had him cornered. The picture was about complete. Schlitten was a much smarter witness than George Brecht in the Vincent Coll case, but whereas Brecht was suave and personable, Schlitten with his barrel torso, hulking shoulders, thick neck, undershot jaw, button nose, shaggy eyebrows and low receding forehead was a carbon copy of Louis Wolheim's "Hairy Ape." He talked gutturally out of the side of his mouth in the argot of the underworld. Wherefore, so feminine a word as "a-flutter" fell ludicrously from his lips.

Leibowitz had him repeat the story of Vivian's last ride. It was identical with that he had told under direct examination. Had he memorized it? Had some one written it for him? Had some one coached him? The answers were "no" as Leibowitz well knew they would be—and cared not. He was getting in more brush strokes.

Schlitten fitted perfectly into a caste worthy of a "Beggar's Opera"—thieves, crooks, jailbirds and cutthroats—Izzy English and David Butterman, principal corroborative witnesses, ex-convicts; Hymie Siegel, from whom the murder car was rented, another Sing Sing graduate; the defendants with their long records, and the victim herself, as infamous a bawd as ever trod the city's streets.

Neither Stein nor Greenberg was put on the witness stand. Both produced alibis. Stein's sister, Miss Marguerite Norris, testified that on the night of the murder Stein had accompanied her to a motion picture theater, later to a Chinese restaurant for chop suey. Four relatives deposed that Greenberg was "sitting shiva" for his mother at the home of Mrs. Sophie Wallenstein. She had died a few days before the murder.

Leibowitz in his summation dwelt almost entirely upon Schlitten's lapses from the underworld argot into such elegancies of parlor diction as "a-flutter," "cackle," "screech," "dumfounded," etc. He attacked Schlitten's motive in testifying for the state. It wasn't because of his conscience. It was because the police had threatened him with the chair. He was a squealer, a rat.

Izzy English, Schlitten's lobbygow, a thug who did his bidding in the strong arm protection racket, was a burglar, vagrant and smoke peddler. As for Butterman, who "dumped the case in Mulrooney's lap," he was a drug trafficker and a fence. Would the jury believe men of that ilk?

Thus the roll call by Leibowitz of the state's spearhead witnesses, interpolated with that shibboleth of the criminal lawyer, "reasonable doubt." Hadn't he established that to the jury's satisfaction?

"The defendants," he concluded, "are presumed by law to be innocent; they don't have to prove anything; they don't have to take the stand. There is no confession here, although Stein and Greenberg were grilled for hours. The burden is on the District Attorney to prove his case."

And the jury voted not guilty.

District Attorney Charles B. McLaughlin, who had sidestepped this "biggest case in years" by designating an assistant to handle it, characterized the verdict:

"The rankest miscarriage of justice I have ever known. Verdicts like that are responsible for gang conditions in America today. Killers are turned loose—scot free—even with the strongest evidence against them. Something will have to be done about it."

The Bronx County grand jury in a presentment to Justice Cohn stated:

"The acquittal of Stein and Greenberg is a great shock to the community."

Mulrooney said nothing for publication, but his action was eloquent. He divided the $15,000 reward among the detectives who had developed the evidence.

Newspaper cameramen got some swell pictures of victorious lawyer and client.

The counsellors Sullivan, Berman, and Reidy, with Samuel Greenberg, also posed.

Leibowitz again had stepped pretty hard on the toes of the police—likewise on those of the district attorney of the Bronx. McLaughlin could sympathize with William F. X. Geoghan, district attorney of Kings county, over in Leibowitz's home bailiwick in Brooklyn. McLaughlin could try to forget it; it didn't happen to him in every case; Leibowitz wasn't his headache. He was Geoghan's. It had been happening to Geoghan for more than ten years, in every case Leibowitz had undertaken.

The fighting Irishman could neither forget nor forgive. He was biding his time to rid himself of the headache. He was a believer in the old saw that all things come to him who waits.

They were to come with a bang for Leibowitz.

.

CHAPTER THIRTEEN

LOCAL BOY MAKES GOOD

ONLY faintly, like the brave music of a distant drum, does the renown of the No. 1 Criminal Lawyer penetrate the secluded tranquillity of the home in Avenue M, suburban Flatbush, Brooklyn. Leibowitz crosses its threshold to become the typical burgher, fond of his slippered ease and armchair solace; a family man of settled habits, who goes to bed on the hour and snores comfortably in his sleep.

He is "Lee" to his wife, Belle, a woman of sparkling charm and rare understanding, devoted to the upbringing of their three children. He has a passion for grand opera—particularly the arias and solos—and also for the homely classics such as "Sweet Rosie O'Grady, "Sidewalks of New York," and "Little Annie Rooney." He croons them to the accompaniment of his accordion after a hard day in court. He likes to improvise on the piano, too.

Now the Leibowitz children—Robert and Lawrence, the twins, and sister Marjorie—have a game they play of evenings. It is to watch for their father's coming, the first one to sight him being the winner.

They watched in vain for him September 29 of 1931, and went to sleep without getting their usual goodnights. It was nearly morning before he came home. He drove into the garage, stepped from the car and switched on the ceiling light. His eyes were bloodshot, his hair disheveled and his face drawn and ashen. He fumbled with a handkerchief wrapped about his right hand, and tied at the wrist, finally loosening the knot with his teeth. He strode over to the side of the garage, raised the hand to the level of his head, fingers outspread fanwise, and plunged it against the white kalsomined wall, holding it there for a moment. When he withdrew it, five black smudges remained. He clenched his fist and shook it at them.

"I'll get you—and you—and you," he shouted, giving to each smudge a name. "I'll get you; I'll get you all, God damn you."

It was melodrama, but it was also a man in anguish of mind and spirit; Leibowitz in his supreme hour of travail; smacked down in midcareer by the grace of Geoghan and the word of a harlot, a pander and a stool pigeon.

A pair of detectives he had known for years—Martin Cannon and Harry Eggolt—had walked in on him that afternoon at his office. Cannon acted as spokesman.

"Sam," he apologized, "we've got a warrant for you."

Leibowitz had been tipped off by telephone.

"Yes, Marty," evenly, "let's see it."

It charged conspiracy to obstruct justice and subornation of perjury. It was based on indictments voted by a Kings County grand jury and it bore the signature of the party of the first part of the eleven-year-old

Agamemnon-Achilles courtroom feud—William F. X. Geoghan.

"I'm ready, boys," said Leibowitz, putting on his hat.

They took him to the Poplar Street police station and gave him the works—booked him, Bertilloned him and fingerprinted him. . . . Right thumb first, on the ink-smeared glass; then over with it to the filing card for the permanent impression . . . gently now, Mr. Leibowitz, so the loops and whorls will be recorded just so . . . right forefinger, next; right middle finger . . . steady, Mr. Leibowitz; don't waggle it or the impression may be blurred . . . right ring finger; right little finger . . . a firmer pressure with that one, Mr. Leibowitz . . . the left hand now.

Detective Eggolt, after it was finished, handed him a can of benzine.

"To remove the ink," he explained. Leibowitz shook his head:

"Thanks, Harry, I'm leaving it on. I'm putting five of these fingerprints tonight in a place where they'll keep; one for each of the rats that framed me. I want them for future reference."

The second stop was the Brooklyn police headquarters, Bergen Street at Sixth Avenue.

"What's the idea?" asked Leibowitz.

"Orders to mug you for the Rogues' Gallery, Sam," said Cannon.

"But the law is that such pictures shall be made only when it is necessary to broadcast the description of a criminal suspect."

"I know; but what can I do, Sam? It's orders."

"It's Geoghan," muttered Leibowitz.

They planted him in the chair so many of his clients had occupied; adjusted the rigid neckpiece and head clamp; trundled the Big Bertha camera around in front of him; trained its glass eye in his face; and the official photographer, a plate holder in his left hand and the shutter bulb in his right, unctuously exhorted him:

"Just look natural, Mr. Leibowitz."

Four times the police artist mugged him—two front and two side views. Leibowitz rose from the chair mopping perspiration from his brow. He was seeing red.

The third stop was the county court building for the arraignment. A delay occurred. The fingerprints had been sent to general headquarters in Manhattan for comparison at the bureau of identification, as was the routine procedure, the purpose being to determine whether a suspect had a record. Leibowitz' prints hadn't been returned, and the regulations stipulated they should be before the arraignment could be held.

"Can't we pass the prints up?" he asked an assistant district attorney.

"I think so; I'll phone the D.A."

In less than a minute he was back with the answer:

"My office says the fingerprints will have to be in court."

One, two, three hours passed....

Word of the arrest had been flashed by ticker, phone and telegraph into the city rooms of the metropolitan press, and reporters and cameramen had taken the trail of the juicy tidbit. Leibowitz had gone when they reached his office; they were too late to catch him at the Poplar Street station, and just missed him at Brooklyn police headquarters.

The pack was in full cry when finally it cornered its quarry—sitting between two detectives—waiting for his fingerprints in the courtroom where he had tried at least a thousand cases and scored some of his greatest triumphs over Geoghan's office. ... These same lousy reporters now firing questions at him had covered them; these same swarming cameramen now pulling their damned flashes had snapped the famous victory smile and the famous lawyer-client victory pose. He leaped snarling to his feet, teeth unfleshed; eyes blazing; his back to the wall; his head half lowered as if to lunge at the pack and trample it down. He was a wild bull of Bashan at bay.

"Congratulations," he bellowed. "Congratulations. Print it! Print it! Let the world know that the character of an honest man can be blasted by a pander, a prostitute, and a sneakthief. They can't hurt me any more now. They've done their worst. But by God I'll hurt them."

The fingerprints had arrived. The court clerk read the indictment:

"How does the defendant plead?"

"Not guilty," said Leibowitz.

1931 was marching into criminal bar history as a lustrous year for the Leibowitz renown. He had successfully defended five police officers in the vice squad trials; obtained an acquittal for Harry Stein in the Vivian Gordon murder case, and in midsummer Capone had asked him to come to Chicago.

Local attorneys had been unable to extricate the No. 1 Public Enemy from his income tax dilemma. A secret agreement with the district attorney's office to plead guilty and receive a two years' sentence had been knocked galley west when an enterprising newspaper sprang the story a few days before the date set for the hearing. The beat cost Capone nine extra years in prison, for the district attorney's office repudiated the agreement and he had to stand trial on a not guilty plea.

The truth was that Capone had become a political scapegoat. Hoover, playing for the dry vote in the forthcoming presidential election, had personally issued the order to make an example of the Peck's Bad Boy of prohibition. It complicated matters.

Capone's S.O.S. for Leibowitz was sent immediately after publication of the newspaper story. He left on the Twentieth Century, arriving in Chicago on a Monday morning, and going direct to the Capone headquarters in the Lexington Hotel, Michigan Avenue and Twenty-second Street. His former client had put on fifty pounds since last he saw him.

They spent the day discussing strategy and conferring with his advisory board. Leibowitz' first suggestion was that they go into court with an affidavit setting forth hitherto suppressed details of the secret agreement but the Chicagoans refused to consider it.

"It's our hometown," as a Capone lieutenant put it. "We have to live here. If we show up that deal we might as well quit."

Leibowitz' alternative suggestion was to carry the fight to "the front step of the White House"; uncovering the trail of corruption that led "right into the Treasury Department." He would begin with a rumor campaign that Capone was going to talk, "spill everything." Of course Capone would deny it but then members of the Capone syndicate would start talking—here, there and everywhere —turning in grafting dry agents; testifying in open court regardless of the consequences to themselves. And the rumor would continue that Capone was getting ready to contribute his share of the revelations. Leibowitz was convinced that such tactics would so terrify Congressmen and influential politicians that they would be quick to put the pressure on Hoover.

Capone couldn't see it that way. He clung to the idea that everything could still be ironed out in some way. Leibowitz refused to consider this. The discussion ended on that note, Leibowitz having to return to New York City to attend to his law practice. He had tentatively agreed to represent Capone, his fee to be $100,000.

The plans of mice and men often go astray. A young man named Chile Mapocha Acuna was the cause of Leibowitz' sacrificing this fat fee. The two had met when Leibowitz was defending the five officers in the vice squad trials. The investigation of magistrates' courts directed by Samuel Seabury had disclosed a graft ring of policemen, bondsmen, lawyers and assistant prosecutors, preying upon prostitutes and innocent women as well.

Acuna, pander and former stool pigeon, had given testimony before Seabury involving some fifty members of the police department, including Lieutenant Peter J. Pfeiffer and four of his subordinates. These retained Leibowitz as their counsel in the departmental trials ordered by Police Commissioner Edward P. Mulrooney and held at headquarters with Deputy Commissioner Nelson Ruttenberg sitting as trial judge.

Taking the stand against each of the five, Acuna glibly recited tales reeking of bribery, extortion, entrapment and exploitation of women. He was shameless in telling how he had connived with Pfeiffer and his men to mulct them of their money. It was pretty slimy but it was life as lived in the Acuna stratum of society and, averred Acuna, "I was always an honest stool pigeon." Leibowitz wolfed at the imperturbable little Chilean, branded him a "pimp, procurer, proprietor of houses of ill-fame," but couldn't feaze him as a witness and it looked bad for the Leibowitz clients until—

Eva Esperanza Mackay stepped unannounced to the stand one day as witness for the defense and utterly destroyed Acuna's credibility by avowing that he had inducted her into prostitution and received a dollar commission for each male customer sent to her apartment; that they had quarreled when she refused to enter a call flat establishment operated by Acuna. With her testimony Acuna was rendered null and void and the case against the five defendants collapsed. The time was January of 1931.

It was the repercussion of this case that caused Leibowitz to be so late getting home the fateful day of September 29. The Mackay girl had mysteriously appeared before the Kings County grand jury in Brooklyn and had not only repudiated her testimony at the police trials but had sworn she committed perjury at Leibowitz' behest; that he coached her as a witness and that she received money from his clients for discrediting Acuna. Specifically she charged:

"Leibowitz wrote out all the questions he wanted me to answer as a witness against Acuna, and I studied them in his office. He wouldn't let me take them away with me."

Leibowitz answered:

"This entire story, coming from a five times convicted prostitute, is an outrageous lie and a foul conspiracy. At the proper time, under the proper circumstances, the absolute falsity of the statement will be demonstrated. Those behind this despicable plot will suffer the full consequences."

Signing a waiver of immunity, he voluntarily went before the grand jury and told his side of the story. Despite that, however, the indictments for conspiracy and subornation of perjury were voted. His professional life was at stake. Conviction on the subornation charge, a felony, would automatically have disbarred him.

The machinery of justice moves slowly. It was not until January of 1932 that the indictments reached the court hopper to be received by County Judge George W. Martin. His action was a vindication for Leibowitz. He threw them out and denounced the witnesses produced before the grand jury by District Attorney Geoghan.

"It is a serious matter to indict any citizen and particularly a member of the bar and an officer of this court," he wrote in his opinion. "To charge any person with a crime, whether the charge be false or true, is a grave matter.

"The type and character of the witnesses produced to sustain these indictments, and their admitted associations and experiences, do not entitle them to very much credence."

Geoghan declined to accept the ruling. He sought to reinstate the indictments by appealing to the appellate division of the State Supreme Court. And while it was pending Leibowitz made a dramatic reference to it. He was defending Hugh T. Cuff, a Staten Island labor leader on trial for manslaughter. He was questioning a prospective juror when he suddenly turned to the whole group of assembled talesmen and asked:

"What effect would it have if you found that some rogues went to the extent of framing a case against a lawyer for personal vengeance in order to destroy him?"

The appellate division in July sustained Judge Martin on the dismissal of the conspiracy indictment but reinstated the one charging subornation of perjury. Meanwhile Leibowitz had rubbed out one of the fingerprint smudges on his garage wall. Acuna had gone to meet his Maker. The cause of his death was tumor of the brain. In August, County Judge Algernon I. Nova upheld Judge Martin and dissented from the appellate division by dismissing the subornation of perjury indictment. Geoghan and Leibowitz faced each other in court. The district attorney had suffered a change of attitude. Said he to Judge Nova:

"One of the witnesses on whom the grand jury relied in returning this indictment was Chile Mapocha Acuna. He died June 22 last. With his death it is impossible for the District Attorney to make out even a prima facie case."

But:

"I don't want to be understood as saying that even if Acuna were alive to testify that his testimony would be accepted by a jury. The jury might not believe a word he said. I move that this indictment charging subornation of perjury be dismissed."

Said Judge Nova:

"Your statement that even if Acuna were alive you don't know whether the jury would believe him appeals to me. This case is of unusual importance because the defendant happens to be Leibowitz, a well advertised and well known criminal lawyer. Character is so easily destroyed that we should be quite jealous to see that the quality of testimony produced against a lawyer is the type and kind that will be believed.

"Lawyers who for years and years built up a good reputation will never be safe if it is our law that an unscrupulous client can walk in and say: 'The lawyer told me to say that.' To ruin and stain a lawyer's reputation, ruin his family life, take away his right to practice upon the word alone, so to speak, of an admitted disreputable prostitute, is carrying it a bit too far.

"I have not always agreed with Mr. Leibowitz in the trial of a case, yet I personally have never known him to do a thing that was not honorable and decent as a lawyer. But it is because of my reading of the testimony before the grand jury that I know I could never personally justify the finding of the indictment.

"I am happy in the opportunity that comes to me in granting the motion of the district attorney to dismiss the indictment and I so do direct that the indictments be dismissed."

Finis had been officially written to a major phase of the classic Agamemnon-Achilles feud. Leibowitz' mobile lips twisted into a sardonic grin as he eyed his veteran adversary.

"Almost," he muttered, "thou persuadest me to be a Christian."

.

CHAPTER FOURTEEN

NIGGER

THE noonday sun burned down on the long line of freight cars as they rattled on their way from Chattanooga to Huntsville. It was spring in the foothills of the Cumberland Mountains, spring in northeast Alabama along the Tennessee River valley.

Round-faced, wide-eyed Ruby Bates and her girl friend, the bored and blasé Victoria Price, were going back home to Huntsville with Lester Carter, ex-chain gang convict and his new-found pal, Orville Gilley, after an overnight jaunt across the state line to Chattanooga.

They'd had a swell time in Chattanooga—Ruby thought so, at least—much more fun than the long night hours they were wont to put in at the frame mill. Clad in overalls the girls and Carter had hopped a freight train out of Huntsville the afternoon before, arriving in the Tennessee town at 8:30 in the evening. Orville made it a cozy foursome when he stopped to borrow a light and stayed to spend the night.

The boys built a roaring fire in one corner of the hobo jungle they had chosen for their night's lodging and hustled out to get some food. They lingered around the

fire, talking and laughing. Orville admitted he was a big
railroad man. Had a railroad nickname, even—Carolina
Slim. His stories entertained the group until they decided
it was time to rest. They were going back to Huntsville
in the morning. Victoria wanted to see her regular boy
friend again, Jack Tiller, whose wife and children made
it too dangerous a risk for him to accompany her across
the state line. They stretched out in the shelter of the fire.
Orville and Victoria slept side by side; Ruby and Lester
found a comfortable nook close to them.

Next day they boarded the half-mile long freight train
that was carrying them back. The train rolled to a stop
in Stevenson and they all got off in search of an unlocked
box car. Finding none they climbed into an open top
gondola car filled with fine gravel or chert.

Six white boys in the gondola next to them asked Gilley
and Carter if they'd stand by and help fight a gang of
colored boys also on the train. They agreed.

The negroes outnumbered their white opponents. One
of them had a pistol, evidently not loaded, and all were
in belligerent mood. Clear from Chattanooga to Stevenson
the white boys had been pelting them with rocks, stepping
on their hands as they walked from car to car, daring
them to fight.

"Unload, you white sons-of-bitches," the colored lads
yelled as they came hurtling into the gondola, accepting
the dare.

Lester Carter climbed into the car where the fight was
raging. A negro let go a punch at him and he quickly
changed his mind and swung to the ground. One by one
the white boys jumped or were tossed off the train. Orville
Gilley was left hanging on the side as the train put on
speed. One of his colored opponents, Haywood Patterson,

rescued him by giving him a hand and pulling him back
into the car.

An hour or so later the train arrived at Paint Rock. It
was met by a sheriff's posse. Men with guns lined the
right of way on either side. The colored boys jumped off
and ran down the tracks but were surrounded. Ruby and
Victoria started to run, too, but were stopped.

"Did the niggers bother you any?" asked W. H. Hill,
Paint Rock station agent, after the girls had been taken
into custody. When they calmly stated that each had been
raped by six negroes the wheels were set in motion for
the world famous Scottsboro Case.

Ruby and Victoria along with Gilley were put in a
limousine; nine negroes, all that were found on the train,
were tied with ropes, put on a truck, and taken to the
Jackson County jail in Scottsboro, where the six white
hoboes who had been bested in the fight were also being
held.

The news spread quickly in the little hill town of
Scottsboro. News that nine niggers were accused of raping
two white girls. Men with guns had met the train at Paint
Rock. Men with guns were hustled to Scottsboro. Men
with guns were to follow the colored boys wherever they
went.

Feeling was so high that the prisoners were rushed
under armed guard to Gadsden, farther from the scene
of the alleged crime, a big town with a strong jail, proof
against mob attacks.

Justice is sometimes speedy in Alabama. The negroes
were arrested on March 25, 1931, and indicted March 31.
Only six days elapsed between the indictment and the
start of the trials on April 6. A special session of Circuit
Court had been convened.

Scottsboro's 1,400 population swelled to 10,000. The whole countryside turned out to see the show and be on hand should justice falter. Armed guards escorted the boys from Gadsden to Scottsboro, from jail to courthouse, from courthouse to jail. Tear gas bombs were added to the already heavy supply of ammunition. Machine guns commanded the entrance to the courthouse. Five companies of national guardsmen patrolled the streets.

Ragged and dirty, wearing the same overalls they had worn on the train ride, the nine colored boys faced Judge A. J. Hawkins.

One was crippled.

One was blind.

One had a peculiar facial twist that contorted his features into a permanent grin.

One was 14 years old.

One was 15 years old.

One had never gone to school.

All were undereducated, strangers in a strange town, friendless, penniless. None was even a resident of the state. Their average age was seventeen.

And they were black boys accused of rape by white girls.

THEY gave their names: Roy Wright, 14 years old; Andy Wright, his brother, 17; Haywood Patterson, 17; Eugene Williams, 15; and Clarence Norris, 19; all of Chattanooga; Olin Montgomery, 17, of Monroe, Georgia; Willie Robertson, 17, of Columbus, Georgia; Ozie Powell, 16, of Atlanta; and Charles Weems, 21, of Atlanta.

When court opened they had no counsel so Judge Hawkins assigned the entire local bar to defend them. It consisted of seven attorneys. One of the seven, however, was appointed special state's attorney to conduct the trial. He named two of his colleagues assistant prosecutors. Of the four remaining three begged to be excused. That left only the elderly Milo Moody as defense attorney with no time to prepare a case.

Steve Roddy, Chattanooga lawyer, appeared on the scene as an interested visitor in behalf of the local boys, but refused to take the case officially as he, too, had no time for preparation.

Justice went into high gear in hillbilly Scottsboro. It required just three days to try the boys, find them guilty and sentence them to the electric chair. They were tried in batches. One of the nine escaped. A mistrial was declared for fourteen-year-old Roy Wright when one juryman held out against the electric chair.

No witnesses were called for the defense. Only the boys themselves testified. Ruby and Victoria were the star witnesses for the state. They painted a picture to the jury and the crowded courtroom audiences that sent the temperature up to the boiling point. It mattered not that the medical testimony, even as brought forward by the state, was scarcely indicative of rape. It mattered not that the white boys were not called to the stand. Two white girls were accusing nine negroes.

Each death sentence for each individual of each batch was separately announced and greeted by the crowds inside and outside the courtroom with lusty hallelujahs, praise-Gods, amens and cheers. This, although members of the jury for the next batch were in easy hearing.

News of the convictions brought a letter signed by Theodore Dreiser as chairman of the National Committee for Political Prisoners, Lincoln J. Steffens, Floyd Dell,

John Dos Passos and a score of others protesting the actions—"No son of a white family would be subjected to that kind of justice."

The International Labor Defense and the National Association for the Advancement of Colored People went into action, the former retaining George W. Chamlee of Chattanooga to aid their chief counsel, Joseph Brodsky, and the latter Roderick Beddow of Birmingham.

Rallies were held in Harlem and in the Bronx.

Negroes organized in the South to protest.

On June 22 after Judge Hawkins had denied all motions for new trials, notice of appeal to the Alabama Supreme Court was filed, automatically staying execution of the sentences originally set for July 10.

Five thousand negroes and whites paraded through the streets of Harlem. Albert E. Einstein added his name to the long roster of those who had issued personal appeals demanding the release of the prisoners. A negro share cropper was killed and five others wounded in a riot following a protest meeting at Camp Hill, Alabama.

Clarence Darrow was asked to handle the case by the National Association for the Advancement of Colored People, but dropped out after accepting because he was not given a free rein in handling it.

The Association and the International Labor Defense couldn't find a basis for agreement. Attorneys for each refused to coöperate with the other. After accusing the I.L.D. of using the case merely for communist propaganda, the Association finally washed its hands of the whole affair. Chamlee then presented affidavits to the Alabama Supreme Court signed by the negroes and their relatives that he and four others had been retained as defense counsel.

Attorney General Thomas E. Knight, Jr., argued the case for the state before a Supreme Court that included in its roster his own father, Justice Thomas E. Knight. Chief Justice John J. Anderson, who presided over the hearing which began in January, 1932, in Birmingham, announcing receipt of thousands of letters and threats, said, "Efforts to bulldoze and browbeat the court will have no influence on the court's action."

Mob spirit attendant on the trial; a lack of negro representation on the grand jury which indicted the nine negroes and the juries which tried eight of them; the hectic speed of the trial; inconsistencies in the testimony of the two girl accusers: these were the grounds argued before the state supreme court.

On March 24, with Chief Justice Anderson alone dissenting, the Supreme Court affirmed the verdict of the lower court on seven of the cases. The verdict in the case of Eugene Williams, who the defense claimed was a juvenile, was reversed and remanded for a new trial.

Justice Knight read the opinion upholding his son's side of the case.

"If there were more speed," he stated, "and less delay in the administration of the criminal laws of the land, life and property would be infinitely safer and greater respect would the criminally inclined have for the law."

Out of Alabama prejudice and bigotry came the one voice yet uplifted in behalf of the Scottsboro boys. Chief Justice Anderson in his dissenting opinion concluded they did not get "a fair and impartial trial as required and contemplated by our Constitution."

Executions were set again—for May 13; then postponed to June when time to prepare an appeal to the

United States Supreme Court was asked. A stay until Fall was granted when the highest court of the country agreed to review the decision of the lower court.

Communists in Berlin, Germany, hurled rocks through the windows of the American consulate. Protest meetings were held in Dresden and Cologne. Ada Wright, mother of Roy and Andrew, toured Europe under the sponsorship of the I.L.D.

Elaborate preparations were made against demonstrations at the National Capitol when the Supreme Court began its review in October. Tear gas and clubs were used to rout one hundred white and colored paraders the day the decision was expected.

When it came it was as a surprise and a blow to Alabama and Attorney General Knight, who had said he "had no apologies to make for the severity of the jury's verdicts."

Upholding the defense argument put forward by Walter H. Pollak, that denial of time for securing counsel constituted an infringement of the due process clause of the Fourteenth Amendment, the Supreme Court went even farther.

"The casual fashion" in which the appointment of counsel was handled by the Scottsboro court was scored in the majority opinion. Stressing the fact that the boys were "ignorant and illiterate," the court pointed out that they were residents of other states and far away from their families and friends. It read:

"However guilty the defendants upon due inquiry might prove to have been, they were, until convicted, presumed to be innocent. It was the duty of the court having their case in charge to see that they were denied no necessary incident of a fair trial."

The judgments were reversed and the cases remanded for new trials.

A year and a half had passed since the long line of freight cars rolled to a stop in Paint Rock. Victoria and Ruby and the white boys had gone their ways, but nine "niggers" still languished in the death house of Alabama's Kilby Prison.

CHAPTER FIFTEEN

THE THIRTEENTH JUROR

I T was spring again in Alabama and Haywood Patterson was on trial for his life for the second time. There was a new backdrop; Decatur scenery, instead of Scottsboro; a new chorus, the good citizens of Morgan County instead of Jackson County. But the atmosphere was the same. No one could say that Morgan County was not as quick to rise to the tempo of the plot as Jackson County had been.

There were, however, essential differences in the leading characters. Victoria Price, as ever, was the accusing angel. But her comrade, Ruby Bates, missing entirely in the first act, was to pop up in a new rôle before the final curtain.

On the judge's bench sat the Honorable James E. Horton, cast in the part formerly played by Judge Hawkins. If he was not billed as star, his fine, steady performance at least brought him press notices away and above those of any of the other characters.

Many new rôles had been created since the last showing. Some parts had been cut and others augmented. There was now some little doubt, even in conservative circles, outside of Alabama, as to the propriety of casting the nine negroes as heavies. But it was the change in the casting for the rôle of attorney for the defense, transforming it into the star part, that created most comment.

Three months before the trial opened Leibowitz had agreed conditionally to conduct the defense.

His introduction to the case was accidental. He had dropped in for a social call on his old friend, Harry Wolkoff, chief clerk of the second district municipal court in Brooklyn and leader of a Tolerance society. Leonard George, a negro lawyer, was discussing the Scottsboro case with Wolkoff when Leibowitz entered.

"There's the fellow that should have tried the case," they chorused.

George next day put the proposition up to William L. Patterson, National Secretary of the International Labor Defense, and Patterson called on Leibowitz.

"Will you take it?" he asked.

"Yes—if . . ."

That "if" meant that Patterson must secure for him the official court records of the first trials and appeals and whatever affidavits he had. Leibowitz wouldn't take the case unless he was certain of the boys' innocence.

Patterson also must call off his communists and give Leibowitz free rein—unhampered and unfettered—to try the case in his own way, and refrain from propagandizing the situation in the courtroom.

Leibowitz would accept no fee; he would pay his own expenses and underwrite his own stenographic and investigation costs.

For two weeks he conned the records of the case. Patterson called again, bringing Brodsky, the I.L.D. counsel.

"I'll take it," Leibowitz told them, "and I'll get a

not guilty verdict. The first trial was a mockery, a trial in name only, as the United States Supreme Court indicated. A terrible injustice was done those negroes.

"Discarding the claims of the defendants as well as the assertions of the prosecution witnesses and using Dr. Bridges' testimony alone as a basis, it is self-evident that there couldn't have been any such assault by the six negroes as was testified by the prosecution witnesses. Now if I can popularize the medical angle, use it as a keystone for the defense, present it in graphic, convincing form so that the layman can understand it, acquittal will be inevitable."

"Not in Alabama," said Brodsky. "You haven't had any experience with these Southern juries."

"Gentlemen," replied Leibowitz in a manner reminiscent of the courtroom, "no matter what the prejudice may be, there is a basic rock of decency in every individual which a little scratching of the veneer will bring out. We cannot lose this Scottsboro case. Take the case of Becker in the Auburn prison riots. The set-up for prejudice was worse there and the case against him was overwhelmingly more convincing of guilt than this flimsy testimony of a woman of no reputation, scientifically rebutted by the State's own witness in the person of Dr. Bridges.

"A Chinaman or a Zulu lawyer, barely able to speak English, must get an acquittal if the evidence we have available is presented to twelve of even the most bigoted, prejudiced creatures that can be corralled into a jury box."

"You'll be a sadder but wiser man, Leibowitz," said Patterson, "when you've finished. We've been down there and know what we're talking about."

"I will buy both you men the finest hats Stetson makes if I don't bring these defendants back with me and dump them in your lap," retorted Leibowitz.

LEIBOWITZ had lost much of his faith and assurance in the inevitability of an acquittal before the trial got under way. A motor trip through the South, the first in his life, gave him a new insight into the difficulties confronting him. Driving through Tennessee and northern Alabama, he angled for local sentiment with shrewdly casual questions. The invariable answer was, in substance:

"It don't make any difference whether they're innocent or guilty. We've got to keep the niggers in their place."

He began to think that Brodsky and Patterson might be right. He began to think that his friends might have been wise when they said:

"Don't go down there. You haven't a chance in the world and you may come back a head shorter."

Maybe Mrs. Leibowitz was right, too, when she said it was a hopeless case. He still had an abiding faith in what the jury must do when it viewed the evidence, but decided an avenue must be left for appeal in case he should be wrong.

His first move was to ask for a change of venue through his assistants. He wanted to try the case in Mobile, which had a Jewish mayor and where he believed he might obtain an unprejudiced jury. But the court decided to move it to Decatur, in Morgan County, a town similar in character and environment to Scottsboro.

WHEN court opened in Decatur's yellow brick courthouse, national guardsmen patrolled the streets of the town, guarding in particular the old jail structure, fifty feet from the courthouse. It had been condemned as unsanitary and insecure and was only used for negro prisoners.

Laying a basis for appeal on the ground of systematic exclusion of negroes from jury service, Leibowitz moved that the indictments returned by the Jackson County grand jury be quashed. Twenty colored residents of the county and six whites were subpœnaed. It was the first time proof had been offered instead of affidavits and contentions.

The Alabama code defining the qualifications of jurors reads:

"The Jury Commission shall place on the jury roll and in the jury box the names of all male citizens of the county who are generally reputed to be honest and intelligent men and are esteemed in the community for their integrity, good character and sound judgment, but no person must be selected who is under 21 or over 65 years of age, who is an habitual drunkard, or who, being afflicted with a permanent disease or physical weakness, is unfit to discharge the duties of a juror, or who cannot read English, or who has ever been convicted on any offense involving moral turpitude.

"If a person cannot read English and has all the other qualifications described herein and is a freeholder or householder, his name may be placed on the jury roll and in the jury box."

A fifty-year-old colored plasterer, John Sanford, was one of the first witnesses called. He said he was a citizen, had never been convicted, could read and understand what he read and had never been examined on his qualifications to serve as a juror.

Attorney-General Knight took the witness. Shaking his long bony finger at him, he started off— "Now, John . . ."

"Will you please move over," cut in Leibowitz, "take your finger out of his eye and call him MISTER Sanford."

"I am not accustomed to that," retorted Knight, as negroes in the courtroom sat up straighter in their chairs and the white section of the audience glared at the upstart attorney from the north.

J. S. Benson, editor of *The Progressive Age* at Scottsboro, called to the stand, said he had been in attendance at the Scottsboro court the greater part of the thirty years he had lived there and had "never heard of a negro being called upon to serve as juror."

"It would be hardly possible to convince me," he continued, "that any but a white man has the sound judgment and training in law and justice which I regard as essential for a fair and impartial verdict.

"I know some good negroes as far as negroes go. But I think that 'sound judgment' part of the statute—I think they can't get around that."

Jury commissioners were called and none could give the name of any negro who had ever served on a jury in Scottsboro or had ever been on the jury rolls. All insisted, on cross-examination, that it was a question of selection rather than exclusion.

Judge Horton announced that the court had decided to hear no further testimony on the question and overruled the motion to quash the indictments. Leibowitz, undaunted, took an exception. Basis for appeal had been laid.

But the question of jury exclusion was not yet finished. The case of Haywood Patterson was called. At the request of the state a severance of the indictment had been granted and he was to be tried separately.

Leibowitz entered a not guilty plea for his client and followed with a motion to quash the venire on the contention that "the rolls from which the jury box was filled, unjustifiably and in violation of the Fourteenth Amendment, excluded negroes solely because of their race."

Morgan County was to receive as searching and thorough an investigation of its jury system as had Jackson County.

Three physicians, a dentist, a motion picture exhibitor, two preachers, an undertaker and a billiard ball proprietor, most of them college educated, were among the colored witnesses called by Leibowitz. In addition to testifying that they themselves were qualified except for their black blood, they read into the record the names of close to two hundred colored acquaintances who were likewise qualified.

Knight sought to discredit their qualifications.

"Haven't you had trouble with your wife?" he asked one.

"If every one who had trouble with his wife in any community was barred from jury duty," roared Leibowitz, "there wouldn't be any juries."

The defense was prepared to bring every colored man on the list to court but Judge Horton agreed to put the names into the record, allowing that further testimony of this sort would be only cumulative.

Then Arthur J. Tidwell, county jury commissioner, stepped to the stand, and the big red book in which the secret list of prospective jurors was kept was brought into court and, over the protests of Knight, offered in evidence for the first time in the history of the state.

"Can you point to the name of any colored citizen on that page?" Leibowitz asked, indicating the first page of the book.

"I don't know whether they are white, black or yellow," answered Tidwell.

Leibowitz asked Knight to stipulate for the record that no names of colored citizens were contained in the book. Knight refused, asserting that the whole line of inquiry was immaterial anyway.

"If you are going to put me to proof, all right," Leibowitz whipped back. "I'll do it if it takes till doomsday."

Names of negroes were checked against those in the big red book—of which there were more than two thousand—and none found. Judge Horton announced that the defense had established a *prima facie* case and it was up to the state to disprove it.

That apparently was accomplished by recalling Commissioner Tidwell to the stand. He stated that "all qualified citizens were on the Morgan county rolls" and, if negroes were excluded that must be because they couldn't qualify. Leibowitz renewed his motion to quash the venire, but Judge Horton denied it.

The next struggle was over selection of the jury.

Out of a venire of 84 farmers, artisans and tradesmen, 25 were excused for having fixed opinions, four for holding scruples against capital punishment and five for prejudice against circumstantial evidence.

All but twelve of the remaining fifty were disposed of in peremptory challenges, two to the defense for each one made by the state under Alabama law. Overalled farmers from rural communities where prejudice was felt to be strong were scratched by the defense while the state used up most of its challenges against young men residing in more urban centers and suspected of favoring liberal ideas.

Three farmers, a draftsman, a hosiery mill worker, a barber, a merchant, two bookkeepers, an automobile salesman, a bank cashier and one unemployed citizen made up the final twelve.

If Decatur had been calm at the beginning of the sessions, it was calm no longer. Sure that the trial would be decided in the one and only way it could be decided to their way of thinking, there had been little outward fuss or feeling at the beginning.

But the challenge to the Alabama jury system, the feeling that negroes were being treated with entirely too much social equality, and the fear that somehow this smart Jew from New York was going to put it over for the boys, quickened their easily roused prejudices.

Leibowitz was a storm center.

It was revealed in the protests of Fred Morgan, postmaster of a nearby town, over Leibowitz' manner of questioning prospective jurors:

"Us jurors in Morgan county are not accustomed to taking charge from the defendant's attorney and we don't like it."

It was revealed in Judge Horton's solemn warning to the venire:

"So far as the law is concerned, it knows neither native nor alien, Jew or Gentile, black or white. . . . It would be a blot on the other men and women of this county, a blot on all of you, if you were to let any act of yours mar the course of justice in this or any other case. . . . I expect

from you a proper restraint and a fair decision, according
to the law and the evidence."

It was revealed in the armed guard of five that Captain
Joseph Burleson of the Alabama state militia posted
around Leibowitz' quarters at a local hotel.

It was revealed in the courtroom whispers.

"It'll be a wonder if he ever gets out of here alive."

"I'll be surprised if they ever let him finish this trial."

And in the whispers along the street as Leibowitz, un-
attended at his own request, each day walked the eight
blocks to the courthouse.

"There goes the Jew son-of-a-bitch."

"That's the goddamned nigger lover."

MORGAN county's yellow brick courtroom seats 425 persons. Jim Crow laws are in effect and the colored spectators are seated in a separate section. There are few
white women in the audience on this opening day of the
trial. Negroes have waited in line since five o'clock to
assure themselves seats. Outside, groups of them loll on
the grass, near the worn and weathered statue of Justice,
or gather round the soldiers' monument, waiting for news
of the trial, for some one to leave the courthouse and
give one of their number a chance to get his chair.

Poorly lighted by five windows high up in the room,
and poorly ventilated because the windows are closed,
the courtroom is smelly and smoky before the day has
well started.

Contrary to northern practice, the jurors sit facing the
judge and the witness chair instead of to one side. They
sprawl in their chairs, feet up on the foot rail and smoke
or chew and spit during adjournments. The spectators

are arranged behind them. Brass spittoons are provided but there are not enough.

The defense table is at the left, Leibowitz flanking the defendant Patterson on one side, Chamlee on the other. Brodsky, chief counsel for the I.L.D., sits beyond Chamlee. Attorney General Knight is at a table on the right with his assistants—County Solicitors Wade Wright and H. G. Bailey and Assistant Attorney General Thomas Lawson. Behind them is the press table, reserved only for regular working reporters. Magazine writers and special writers find their own seats in the audience. Two negro correspondents for negro papers sit near the defense.

Four national guardsmen under the command of Captain Burleson are stationed around the courtroom. Two more stand at the door with rifles and fixed bayonets.

High on the bench sits Judge James E. Horton, tall and spare, with deepset eyes and high, prominent cheekbones, a large strong nose and sensitive, rather thin lips. He has been likened to Lincoln and the resemblance is impressive to many in the audience.

Spread out on a specially built platform close to the witness stand, is a miniature train, complete in every detail with box cars, gondolas, oil tanks, scaled to size, brought into court by Leibowitz. The whole trial centers around it.

There is a hush in the courtroom:

"Let Victoria Price come up and take her seat."

Sullen and moody, Victoria, twice married, and mother of a child, takes the stand. In contrast to her hobo clothes of two years before, she now wears a black satin dress with a white lace fichu, a small blue hat with a red feather in it, and a string of glass beads around her neck. Large and showy rings adorn three fingers of her hand.

A few short questions, a few answers hardly more expansive, and the whole of the state's case is before the jury:

Q. After the boys were put off the train, the white boys, all except Gilley, then what if anything did this defendant do? A. He helped take my clothes off.

Q. What clothes did you have on? A. Overalls, shirt, three dresses, pair of step-ins, girl's coat and girl's hat.

Q. What clothes did they remove from your body? A. Pulled off my overalls and tore my step-ins undone— tore my step-ins apart.

Q. What happened then, Miss Price? A. Well, one of them held my legs and one held a knife at my throat while one of them raped me.

Q. Did Haywood Patterson on that occasion, while one of those boys had a knife at your throat and the other one held you by the legs, did he have sexual intercourse with you? A. Yes, sir, he was the third one or the fourth one. I won't be positive.

There was more to Victoria's testimony than that. There were other witnesses for the state. But that accusation of hers was the basis of the case. It was all the jury needed. It was all Scottsboro had needed.

Before the crowded courtroom she went into greater detail, repeating her accusations against the rest of the colored boys, repeating without flickering an eyelash the raw and rough language she claimed the boys used.

Solicitor Bailey conducting the examination offered her torn pink step-ins in evidence. Leibowitz jumped from his chair to object.

"This is the first time in two years any such step-ins have ever been shown in any court of justice. They were not produced at the first trial or second trial or any of the four trials at Scottsboro. This is the first time in two years any step-ins have been produced in any court."

"They are here now," Attorney-General Knight remarked, picking them up and throwing them in the general direction of the jury. They hit Juror No. 2 in the face and the courtroom hubbub caused Judge Horton to stop proceedings and announce that the court would permit no disorder:

"If you cannot restrain your feelings in this courtroom, the proper place for you is outside."

Leibowitz withdrew his objection.

This was not the last of the step-ins, however.

LEIBOWITZ was leaving no loophole in his carefully planned defense. He was seeking to prove main contentions. They were:

(1) Victoria Price, the prosecutrix and main witness for the state, was not to be believed. This was to be proven by showing her testimony false in several material points. By the denial by Ruby Bates of the whole of it. By patent improbabilities in the whole of it.

(2) The clothes of the girls would not have been cleaned and washed if they had supported the testimony. Further, no one who examined the colored boys found any "mute and telling evidence of rape" as would surely have been found.

(3) The testimony of the physician who examined the girls, a state witness, proved on his own statements nothing more than that they had had intercourse recently. Leibowitz would show where, when and with whom.

(4) Several of the accused boys could not possibly have taken part either in the fight or the rape.

(5) The state kept the white boys, Orville Gilley in particular, from testifying. Why?

VICTORIA was a belligerently stubborn witness for Leibowitz on cross-examination. Many of his questions had to be rephrased because she couldn't understand. Many had to be repeated because she *wouldn't* understand them. When in doubt she answered "no" or varied with "I won't say."

This was her answer when he asked if his freight train replica was like that she had ridden from Chattanooga to Paint Rock.

LEIBOWITZ: That is a fairly good representation of the box car you were in?

VICTORIA: I won't go by that box car.

LEIBOWITZ: How does it differ?

VICTORIA: I won't go by that.

LEIBOWITZ: I asked you if this was a good sample of this big box car.

VICTORIA: Well, it is kinda a little bit built up like one. I won't swear to that box car but I will swear the one the negroes come over was a box car, and then into the gondola.

Victoria was anticipating the defense contention that the fight occurred in a string of gondolas with the girls in a central car away from the box cars. She was also using her favorite ruse when caught in a corner.

Later on when Leibowitz asked her if she ever showed the clothes she was wearing that day to any one and pointed out that on them was the proof of the crime, she again sought refuge in accusation:

"I don't remember whether I did or not but I do know

one thing, that negro sitting over there raped me—Haywood Patterson."

Courtroom photographers snapped her with a long, obdurate forefinger pointed at the defendant.

Leibowitz got so he could tell when she was going to stage her act:

"This part I have forgot," she insisted once, "it has been two years ago, but one thing I do know and will never forget—"

"I don't want any speech," he interrupted.

"Is that that one," she bore on stubbornly, "that one setting over there, raped me."

"You came here," he suggested, "prepared to say he raped you?"

Knight objected and the court sustained the objection but the point was evident.

It was more than evident when after a similar contretemps Leibowitz asked:

"You're a pretty good actress, aren't you?"

"You're a pretty good actor yourself," she retorted.

Again Leibowitz asked her if she was healthy on the 25th of March, 1931, and she answered:

"I was healthy until those negroes raped me."

He was building up to the lack of evidence of a struggle, to the discrepancies in the stories told by the state's witnesses:

"You were not scared when these negroes came into the gondola?"

"Not so very much."

"Did you scream out?"

"Yes, sir, I hollered until they stopped me; some of them smacked me in the head and knocked me down in the gondola."

Q. One of them smacked you on the head? A. With a gun, yes, sir.

Q. Then it started to bleed? A. Well, a little bit.

Leibowitz led her on to talk about the wound. He was to impeach her testimony on that score, refute it entirely by the testimony of another state witness, Dr. R. R. Bridges. He drew her out on where she was supposed to have stayed the night before the all-important train ride. When she said she stayed at the boarding house of Mrs. Callie Brochie in Chattanooga, he had another basis for impeachment. She refused to admit she knew anybody by the name of Lester Carter, or that Lester had accompanied her and Ruby to Chattanooga. She denied staying in the hobo jungle.

He questioned her ruthlessly about the struggle with the negroes, drawing out unwilling answers that tended to show the improbability of the whole story and the character of the girl:

Q. You kept struggling all the time? A. Yes, sir.

Q. You were fighting, were you not, to protect your virtue and to protect your body? A. Yes, sir.

Q. Did you scratch a single one of them? A. I don't know. I won't say.

Q. Did you bite a single one of them? A. No, sir.

Q. Did you kick a single one of them? A. I fought them is all I can tell you.

Q. Did you kick them? A. I couldn't kick them.

Q. Your muscles are quite strong, aren't they? A. Yes, but they finally gave out after awhile.

Then:

Q. Some of these negroes were pretty heavy, were they not, when they were lying on top of you? A. Yes, sir.

Q. With your back on this rock? A. Yes, sir.

Q. They didn't spare you in any way, didn't try to make it comfortable for you in any way? A. No, sir.

Q. Just like brutes? A. Yes, sir.

Q. Was your back bleeding when you got to the doctor? A. I couldn't say.

Q. When you got to the jail did you find any blood on your back? A. A little bit.

Q. You were torn inside? A. I don't know whether I was or not. I felt like I was.

Q. Were you bleeding there? A. A little bit.

Q. Did that blood come out on your clothes? A. Yes, sir.

Q. Did the doctor see that, did you show it to the doctor? A. I reckon I did.

This was denied in the examining physician's testimony.

INTERSPERSED with furious objections by Attorney Knight, Leibowitz drew Victoria on and on, making an obvious basis for impeachment of her evidence:

Q. Of course when Dr. Bridges and Dr. Lynch examined you they saw your coat at the time and it was all spattered over with semen? A. Yes, sir.

Q. Have you got the coat? A. Yes, sir, I have got the coat—they had it cleaned up for me.

Q. You didn't think it was important to preserve it as evidence? A. No, sir.

Q. Did your dresses also have semen on them? A. Yes, sir.

Q. Did you wash them before the trials? A. Yes, sir.

Q. Your story is this, is it not, that six negroes raped you on this train? A. Yes, sir, six raped me.

Q. And six raped the other girl?

"We object," put in Attorney General Knight. Judge

Horton thought the question proper. Attorney Knight still objected.

"But he is putting the words in her mouth," he insisted.

"When I *can* put words in the mouth of this young lady," was the Leibowitz retort courteous.

Again later when Knight objected to a defense line of questioning:

"I am testing her credibility," argued Leibowitz.

"You know that is no proposition of law," answered Knight.

LEIBOWITZ: Address your remarks to the court.

KNIGHT: You make it necessary to address them to you.

LEIBOWITZ: I have been a gentleman, but I can be otherwise, too.

"Wait a minute, gentlemen," broke in Judge Horton. "Don't either of you say anything. Gentlemen, I am not going to have another word between you. Ask the question and the court will pass on it."

Leibowitz took another tack and questioned Victoria about her relations with men before the famous ride.

"That's some of Ruby's dope," she shrilled angrily.

"Ruby who?"

"Ruby Bates," yelled Knight. "And where is she?"

After that Victoria interrupted the cross-examination many times with "That's some of Ruby's dope."

Twice Knight had to warn her to be calm.

Once she protested she could not understand the words Leibowitz used:

"Any word I use, Miss Price, you don't understand—"

"You speak them too fast—"

"I will be only too glad to reframe the question in the simplest possible way I can."

"That is why I said, 'What was it you said?' I don't answer anything I don't know what you are talking about."

Vainly the defense tried to have a conviction of adultery against Victoria read into the record. Judge Horton held that under Alabama law only a state conviction could be introduced.

"We don't care," objected Attorney-General Knight, "whether the woman has been convicted of forty offenses —the charge is rape. She has never been convicted for living in adultery with a negro."

"I will prove that she did consort with negroes time and time again," replied Leibowitz, "and I will prove it beyond a doubt."

The basis for his proof was shown when Leibowitz introduced photographs of the girls taken with negroes and asked Victoria:

"Isn't it a fact that you knew a colored man named Lewis and that you went to his cabin on the outskirts of hobo town jungle and asked for food?"

"I don't know any negroes," she shouted hysterically. "I only associate with white persons. I never was in a negro's home in my life."

Lewis was put on the stand later and identified her as a girl to whom he had given food and talked to several times in the Chattanooga jungles.

When Victoria persisted in saying she had stayed overnight at the home of the mythical Mrs. Callie Brochie, Leibowitz amused the press table by a new line of inquiry:

Q. Did you meet a man by the name of Florian Slappey? A. No, sir.

Q. Do you know a lawyer by the name of Evans Chew? A. No, sir.

Q. Do you know a man by the name of Epic Peters?
A. No, sir.

"I don't think that is relevant cross-examination," objected Attorney-General Knight.

"Is there anything further you want to ask in regard to these parties?" questioned Judge Horton mildly.

"Nothing further," said Mr. Leibowitz, after suggesting that the boarding house lady's name, Callie, came from Octavus Roy Cohen's stories in the *Saturday Evening Post*.

Sufficient motive for false accusation was indicated to the jury in a question put by Leibowitz before Victoria left the stand:

"Isn't this the reason you are making these charges: you were found hoboing on a freight train, you saw the negroes had been captured by the people at Paint Rock and you feared you would be arrested for vagrancy, for being a hobo on a train with negroes; and to save yourself you determined to say they raped you?"

Victoria was not allowed to answer.

As a witness for the state, they called Dr. R. R. Bridges, Scottsboro physician, and he was. But a witness that did far more to support the defense contentions. Even under direct examination by Solicitor Bailey his testimony was damaging. Asked to describe the condition of Victoria Price when he examined her less than two hours after the rape was supposed to have occurred, he said:

"Well, we found some scratches on the back part of the wrist, small scratches, and she had some blue places in the small of the back, low down in the soft part, three or four bruises that ranged, oh, about like a joint of your thumb, small as a pecan, and then on the shoulders between the shoulders another place about the same size, a blue place. We put her on the table and an examination there showed no lacerations."

"No lacerations?" interrupted Leibowitz.

"No, sir," answered Dr. Bridges, "no lacerations. The vaginal examination showed the male element microscopically and we saw the fluid with the eye, that is the fluid that the spermatozoa is carried in."

"From your examination," asked Bailey, "of the genital organs of the woman Victoria Price made on that occasion would you say she had recently had sexual intercourse?"

The answer was yes.

But it was yes again when Leibowitz took the witness and asked:

"The best you can say about this case is that both women showed they had had intercourse?"

Leibowitz also brought out in cross-examination the fact that pulse and respiration were perfectly normal in both girls; that they showed no hysteria; no tears; no evidence of excitement. Dr. Bridges had seen no head wound though he examined the girls with the utmost thoroughness. Neither had he found any fresh scratches, on their backs or any place else. No blood was found on them or their garments. No semen was discovered on their clothes.

And, in addition, Dr. Bridges stated that the spermatozoa he had extracted were found to be non-motile or dead, on examination.

Dr. E. E. Reisman, Chattanooga gynecologist, was called by Leibowitz to add weight to the defense contentions.

"To my mind," he said, "it would be inconceivable that

six men would have intercourse with one woman and not leave telltale traces of their presence in considerable quantities of semen in the vagina."

He added that spermatozoa would live in the female vagina at least twelve hours, several more than had elapsed between the time of the alleged rape and the physician's examination.

In rebuttal the state brought in Dr. J. H. Hamil, who stated that it was entirely possible for a rape to have occurred even though the girls showed no signs of hysteria—"sometimes it is delayed; different people react differently."

Leibowitz saw his chance and took it.

"I will ask you this question: Suppose a woman said she saw blood coming from her vagina. Would you expect a doctor to find that?"

"We object," interposed Knight. "Don't you know that's a question for the jury?"

"Suppose," continued Leibowitz, "she said she was bleeding on her back. Would you expect a medical man to find evidence of that?"

"I'm not going to object," said Knight resignedly to Judge Horton, "I'm leaving it to you."

"It's just too bad, Mr. Knight," commiserated Leibowitz, "when it hurts you squirm around so in your chair."

"No, I don't squirm," was Knight's pettish reply. "I am leaving it to your Honor."

His Honor upheld the objection but a moment later asked the witness a question as damaging as any posed by the defense:

"If there had been semen on the clothing, you could, an hour and a half after that, tell whether there was semen?"

"Yes, sir," said Dr. Hamil, "you could."

PATTERSON was brought to the stand. He denied having seen the girls on the train but admitted taking part in the fight. His story of the fight and that of the five other accused colored boys put on the stand differed materially from Victoria's.

"You were tried at Scottsboro, weren't you?" asked Attorney General Knight in cross-examination.

"No, sir," drawled the boy, "I was framed at Scottsboro."

One by one the colored boys were questioned. Willie Robertson said he had syphilis and gonorrhea so bad he couldn't walk without a cane; he denied that he had anything to do with any white girls or could have raped them had he had the opportunity. He insisted that he had ridden all the way from Chattanooga in a box car.

Olin Montgomery was shown to be completely blind in one eye and almost blind in the other. He had ridden on an oil tank car, he said, and had never left it. He had seen no fighting and no girls.

Ozie Powell said he saw the fight but no girls, and had nothing to do with either. He had never gone to school and had great difficulty in understanding the questions posed by Attorney-General Knight who submitted him to a cruel and searching cross-examination.

Leibowitz protested several times—finally asked Knight:

"Would you mind stepping away from the witness and obstructing the jury's view, Attorney-General Knight?"

"Gentlemen," apologized Knight, "I am sorry if I have obstructed your view. I want the witness to hear."

LEIBOWITZ: He can hear from where you are standing.

KNIGHT: That is all right, I will stand where I want to.

LEIBOWITZ: You are at liberty to climb up in his lap if you want to.

Andy Wright, the boy with the permanent smile twisted on his face, and brother of 14-year-old Roy, testified that he was in the fight but had nothing to do with any girls. He said he saw Haywood Patterson rescue Orville Gilley when the white boy was hanging over the edge of the car.

Their stories all tallied with that told by Lester Carter, a surprise defense witness, called to the stand near the close of the trial. He told of the hobo trip to Chattanooga with Ruby and Victoria, the meeting with Gilley, the night spent in the hobo jungle there preceding the return trip which ended in the Scottsboro jail. He told how the girls and the two white boys climbed onto a gondola, fourth or fifth in a line of eight or more, and how he was thrown off the train when the fight started.

And he detailed episodes of an all-night boxcar idyll, in which he was paired with Ruby and Jack Tiller with Victoria.

The primary object of the defense with Carter was not so much to discredit Victoria as to explain her physical condition at the time of the medical examination.

Neither Tiller nor Gilley, by the way, was called by the state to refute Carter's testimony.

WITH infinite patience Leibowitz had questioned Victoria, forcing her into specific answers, drawing complete details of her version of the Chattanooga jaunt. Point by point and detail by detail her evidence was refuted, in

some cases by witnesses whose general credibility was
not exceptionally high but at other points by persons of
unimpeachable integrity.

Several witnesses, including Assistant Counsel Chamlee,
a resident of Chattanooga, were put on the stand to prove
that there was no Mrs. Callie Brochie, and no such boarding house as the one described by Victoria. In addition,
there were many, Lester Carter among them, to show that
she stayed in the hobo jungle.

Trainmen were called to describe the make-up of the
train and to show that the colored boys were taken off
the train from several different cars and not from the car
in which Victoria and Ruby were riding.

State witnesses who attempted to confirm Victoria's testimony were handled in short order by Leibowitz. Orey
Dobbins, an illiterate farmer, who lived along the tracks
out of Stevenson, fared worst. He had testified at the
first trial, and discrepancies in his testimony were duly
noted. He saw a negro throw Victoria Price back into a
chert car, he said. It was a gondola between two box
cars, he insisted, just as Victoria had, although the official make-up of the train showed that the gondolas were
all together in a string.

"Had you an automobile, and was there a telephone
nearby?" asked Leibowitz.

"Yes."

"You saw a white woman being attacked by a colored
man on a slow freight train and you say you didn't get
to the nearest phone and notify authorities?"

"No."

When Leibowitz asked him how he knew it was a
woman from the distance his answer was:

"She had on women's clothes."

"She had on women's clothes?" echoed Judge Horton in amazement.

"What kind of clothes—overalls?" pressed Leibowitz.

"No, sir, a dress."

Leibowitz smiled benignly. Victoria by her own testimony was wearing overalls.

DECATUR had never been happy about the duty and privilege of retrying the Scottsboro case. It was an expensive proposition and there was some question as to whether the county schools could stay open. It grew less and less happy about it. The fires of race prejudice, which burned with a low comfortable warmth as a matter of habit, were flaming high and wide now. Negro prejudice, Jew prejudice, northern prejudice, city prejudice, New York prejudice—all were just fuel. Lynch talk grew, and the feeling that talk was not enough grew. High spirited townspeople met and decided that they would meet again —for action. But they never did.

Judge Horton was neither deaf, dumb nor blind. When court was called the day after the Decatur lynch meeting he excluded the jury from the room and, rising to his full height, addressed solemn and impressive words to his fellow citizens:

"No unbiased man who has listened to this evidence can say it is not a question for the careful consideration of the jury. If these defendants are guilty of the crime charged, of course the law should be vindicated and they should be punished. If they are not guilty they should be acquitted.

"Now, gentlemen, I want it to be known that these prisoners are under the protection of this court. The court will protect them just as it will any one else engaged in this trial. Any man or men that attempt to take charge outside the law are not only disobedient to the law, but are citizens unworthy of the protection of the state of Alabama.

"You have the authority of this court that the man who attempts the life of these prisoners may expect that his own life be forfeited. If I am in command, and I will be there if I know it, I will not hesitate to give the order to protect with their lives against any such attempt. I absolutely have no patience with mob spirit and that spirit that would charge the guilt or innocence of any being without knowledge of that guilt or innocence. I will say this much: if there is any meeting in this town where such matters are discussed, the men that attend such meetings should be ashamed of themselves. They are unworthy citizens of your town, and the good people of this town look down upon them."

The fire department was ordered to be in readiness to give the cold water treatment in case of mob violence. Guards were redoubled around the jail and a new detachment of militia sent to Leibowitz quarters.

Tear gas, bayonets and guns were in readiness. "Shoot to kill" orders were relayed to the guards.

Leibowitz wasn't worrying, although he knew his final witness would be another for the lynch list. Ruby Bates, long sought by the state to affirm Victoria's testimony, turned up—as a defense witness.

"I call Ruby Bates," he announced in a voice that carried into the corridors of the courthouse. Knight, visibly unnerved, protested, and Ruby in a pathetically cheap but obviously new gray coat and hat walked up to the stand. Her story at Paint Rock, her later story at the four Scottsboro trials, were all false, she said. She corroborated Carter's testimony about the trip to Chattanooga, the stay in the hobo jungles, and all. He was her sweetheart, she admitted. Jack Tiller was Victoria's.

Hatred brooded in the eyes of Victoria Price when she was brought in to be identified.

"Keep your temper," Attorney General Knight cautioned her softly.

"That's the Victoria Price I mean," said Ruby.

"Were you a good girl before you met her?" Leibowitz asked.

"Yes," said Ruby.

She had lied because Victoria told her to, she said.

"Victoria told me I had better tell the story she was telling or we might get long terms in jail."

Knight bit into her testimony viciously on cross-examination. Knight knew his thirteenth juror:

Q. Where did you get that coat? A. Well, I bought it.

Q. Where did you get that hat? A. I bought it.

Q. Where did you get the money to buy it? A. Dr. Fosdick of New York.

Q. He gave you that? A. Yes, sir.

Q. He gave you the money to buy the coat and hat? A. He certainly did.

Q. What about the shoes? A. I've had the shoes a long time.

Q. How long have you had that pocketbook? A. Over a year.

Ruby had gone to see Dr. Harry Emerson Fosdick, distinguished pastor of the fashionable Riverside Memorial church, because her mind was troubled about her testimony at the former trial. He told her to go and tell the truth, whatever it was.

THE courtroom contrast between the defense and the state was etched more clearly as the closing arguments occupied the last two days of the trial:

Leibowitz, direct but suave, urbane, sophisticated, building up his case with mathematical precision.

Knight, thin and nervous, with fluttering hands and wispy hair, quick to take offense—a Kringelein in a courtroom.

Chamlee, mild in manner and speech, a Southerner himself, ready to pour oil for the defense should the waters get too troubled.

Wade Wright, violent, prejudiced, uncensorable; stentor of bigotry, spokesman for the Thirteenth Juror, who on Sunday led the psalm chanters of the All Day Singers, a Bible Belt religious sect.

Brodsky, silent, observing all that went on but saying little, even when he was a point of attack by the state.

H. G. Bailey, a small time man in a big time job, doing the routine work for the state, while Knight did the objecting.

Flare-ups between opposing counsel were inevitable with such a set-up. Outside the courtroom, counsel might be, and were, friendly and courteous, but once the bailiff gaveled the court to order they were the deadliest of opponents—quarter asked but no quarter given.

The trial feud between Leibowitz and Knight culminated toward the end of the hearings when Arthur Woodall, a state witness, during cross-examination by Leibowitz, said he took a knife from one of the negroes, that it was the same one identified as hers by Victoria Price, and that the negro told him he had taken it from Victoria.

Knight jumped up in great glee, clapped his hands and ⌐

dashed for the door. Leibowitz stopped short and stared after him.

"I move for a mistrial," he shouted. "This is something I haven't seen in fifteen years' experience at the bar. The chief prosecuting officer of the state of Alabama conducting himself in that fashion—and he has told me he wants to give these negroes a fair trial—jumping up and clapping his hands and dashing out with a smile and a laugh."

KNIGHT: That remark was not true, but, Your Honor, I am sorry I went out.

LEIBOWITZ: You clapped your hands.

KNIGHT: I did hit my hands and I am sorry I did that and I hope the jury won't consider it.

LEIBOWITZ: I never expected a display of that kind. I am mortified.

JUDGE HORTON: I accept the apology.

KNIGHT: I should not have done it.

JUDGE HORTON: The attorney general regrets it.

KNIGHT: I do and apologize to the court and to the jury and to opposing counsel.

JUDGE HORTON: The court did hear a sound. I wasn't looking at it; there doesn't seem to be any dispute in regard to the fact.

LEIBOWITZ: I never saw anything like this in my life.

JUDGE HORTON: Gentlemen of the jury, don't consider that at all. It is not proper for you to consider. Do not let it influence you whatever.

KNIGHT: I hope it won't influence them.

JUDGE HORTON: I overrule the motion for a mistrial.

But a clash of a more serious sort came when Wade Wright summed up the case for the state.

"Show them," he yelled in a voice well conditioned from practice with the All Day Singers, pointing at counsel table and specifically at Leibowitz, "that Alabama justice cannot be bought and sold with Jew money from New York."

It was the most direct plea yet made to the Thirteenth Juror.

Leibowitz jumped to his feet:

"I submit, Your Honor, that conviction now, after what he has said, will not be worth a pinch of snuff. I move for a mistrial.

"Motion denied."

The psalm chanter ranted on:

"That man Carter is a new kind of man to me. Did you watch his hands? If he had been with Brodsky another two weeks he would have been down here with a pack on his back atrying to sell you goods. Are you going to countenance that sort of thing?"

A wave of noes rose in fervent whisper from the front rows.

"Don't you know these people, these defense witnesses, are bought and paid for? May the Lord have mercy on the soul of Ruby Bates!"

"Amen," was the answering chorus.

"And those fancy city clothes of Ruby Bates. Where did they come from? Brodsky put fancy new clothes on Lester Carter, or maybe it should be Carterinsky, now."

He finished and Leibowitz arose to survey the hostile courtroom before beginning his summation. Looking past the jury he caught here and there a face he recognized as one of the whisperers. In this room were men who had threatened to ride him out of town on a rail, to string him up to a tree, to burn him on a fiery cross. He was a Jew, he was from the big city, he was defending "niggers," and defending them only too well.

Leibowitz began slowly, in even conversational tones. Not once did he raise his voice. He spoke with a grave eloquence that made his words animate to those whose ears were not closed.

"I shall appeal to your reason as logical, intelligent human beings," he said, "determined to give even this poor scrap of colored humanity a fair, square deal.

"What is the argument of the learned solicitor? What is it but an appeal to prejudice, to sectionalism, to bigotry? What he is saying is, 'Come on, boys; we can lick this Jew from New York. Stick it to him. We're among home folks.' It's the speech of a man taking unfair advantage, a hangman's speech.

"I am proud of my state. We have decent people in New York as you have in Alabama. Perhaps some of us are crowded into tenements like sardines in a can. But the soul of a man is the same. A decent man is a decent man in New York or Alabama.

"Mobs mean nothing to me. Let them hang me. I don't care. Life is only an incident in the Creator's scheme of things."

Logically, convincingly, he pointed out the discrepancies in the state's case. He demanded to know why Orville Gilley had not been called as a witness.

"If Ruby Bates had been subjected to the sort of treatment described by the state," he told the jury, "she would be howling for this negro's blood—not pleading for his life."

A recitation of the Lord's prayer and a plea for acquittal or death closed his argument.

Knight in rebuttal denied the prosecution had "framed" its case. It was "a framed defense." Describing Patterson in well chosen words, he referred to him as "that thing."

THE hearings were over. There was a visible let-down in the strained courtroom as Judge Horton gave the case to the jury with a warning against bigotry and race prejudice. He told them to bear in mind that Ruby Bates had contradicted her previous testimony on the stand and that other evidence as well tended to show that Victoria Price had testified falsely about her movements in Chattanooga.

"If in your minds," he said, "the conviction of this defendant depends on the testimony of Victoria Price, and you are convinced she has not sworn truly about any material point, you could not convict the defendant.

"Sift the evidence—find the truths and untruths—it will not be easy to keep your minds solely on the evidence. Much prejudice has crept into it. It has come not only from far away but from here at home as well.

"I have done what I thought to be right as the judge in this court no matter what the personal cost may be."

The jury deliberated for twenty-one hours. It was Palm Sunday when the verdict was announced. Judge Horton was summoned from his home in Athens, and a group of about one hundred white men gathered in the courthouse. There was not a black face within pistol shot save Patterson's. Alabama National Guardsmen armed with riot guns surrounded the defendant. No one thought to tell him to stand when court was convened. The jury filed in laughing, as over a private joke. Leibowitz was heartened. The verdict was handed up to Judge Horton.

"We find the defendant guilty as charged," he read, "and we fix his punishment as death in the electric chair."

Leibowitz had known that bigotry and race prejudice were his real obstacles. He had realized it was going to be hard to win over those twelve men reared in the isolated Southern hill country, as long as their minds were dominated by the Thirteenth Juror—prejudice.

Knowing the strength of his case he had built it up logically to what seemed its inevitable conclusion. These men were not to be won with tricks. If he could prove his case without a doubt they could not help but acquit. He had so proven it and the verdict was guilty.

How did it happen?

"If you ever saw those creatures," he said after his return, and the words came from his mouth like an Old Testament curse, "those bigots, whose mouths are slits in their faces, whose eyes pop out at you like a frog, whose chins drip tobacco juice, bewhiskered and filthy, you would not ask how they could do it."

It turned out to be a double edged curse. It reached Alabama and caused Judge Horton to delay the other trials indefinitely. It brought forth speeches of Alabama patriotism from Knight and others of the prosecution.

THOUSANDS of negroes and communists greeted Leibowitz upon his return to New York, carried him on their shoulders through the Penn Station to a waiting taxi, and paraded down Seventh Avenue to riot at Times Square, and again at 59th Street and yet again at 86th Street en route to Harlem. Scores were injured as police battled with the crowds.

Leibowitz was invited to speak at a Harlem mass meeting, where he was greeted as the new Moses.

"I promise you that with every drop of blood in my body—" He got no further. The crowd went mad.

"Yes, Lord, you are our leader."

"Yea, brother."

"Amen."

It was a stampede of sound. Leibowitz seized his coat and darted from the platform. Mobs closed around him, kissing his clothes, blessing him, grabbing his hand.

Bewildered, he looked down at his red and swollen hand with a naïve wonder.

"What did I say to start all that?" he asked of no one in particular.

It was the first time in Leibowitz' life that he had been on the popular side of a cause.

CHAPTER SIXTEEN

ALABAMA JUSTICE

VICTOR ELWOOD walked down Decatur's main street. He was selling mops, first class mops, if you were interested that-a-way. He started off down Melton street, stopping at Fourth Avenue, to chat with Mr. and Mrs. Lovett and perchance to sell a mop. He didn't sell the mop.

Undaunted he went on. Jones' lunchroom near Second Avenue caught his eye. It looked like a good bet. He talked to Wood, the owner. No sale.

Warren, the Second Avenue barber, was good for a lot of conversation, too, but wasn't in the market for mops. It was getting plenty warm. Elwood knocked off for that day. But the next and the next—and the next—were busy for him. He stayed nigh on to three weeks and only sold five mops. Not so good for a crack mop salesman. But Elwood wasn't a crack mop salesman. He was after conversation, and conversation he got aplenty.

There were the Lovetts—Mr. Lovett is a bookkeeper. They thought "the niggers ought to burn—if the state doesn't do it the people ought to take them down and lynch them. And the damn Jew lawyer, too."

Mr. Wood was even more heated:

"There shouldn't be any trial for them damn niggers—thirty cents' worth of rope would do the work. If the state don't kill them then the people here will—if they only bring them back. Those Goddarned New York Jews will be killed, too, if they try to come down here and clear those black bastards."

"The niggers and those damned New York Jews," opined Warren, the barber, who shared his shop with a Decatur jury member, "will be lynched if they ever come to Decatur again. The jury didn't pay any mind to what the defense said because they had their minds made up before they ever went into the jurors' room."

Altogether sixty-eight conversations of like tenor were recorded by Mr. Elwood whose deposition laid basis for a plea for a second change of venue, although Alabama law provides for only one.

LEIBOWITZ had met the Thirteenth Juror. He was both sadder and wiser as the Messers. Brodsky and Patterson had predicted, but he wasn't handing out any Stetson hats—yet.

Up to now he had won the majority of his cases by his ability to convince the jury of his client's innocence. Often, true, he had won a verdict on a technicality or on an appeal to a higher court by his knowledge of the law. This time he told it to the judge. He proved his case to the satisfaction of a Southerner, a man whose judicial qualities were hailed from one end of the country to the other.

Leibowitz never varied in his feeling of respect and admiration for the Morgan county circuit judge, even when Horton announced from the bench that the remain-

ing trials would be postponed indefinitely because of
Leibowitz' characterization of Morgan county jurors.

After the jury returned its verdict and Judge Horton
passed sentence, bitter criticism replaced the wholesale
praise that was his during the trial. Left wingers, in particular, censored his manner of conducting the trial, his
refusal to grant a mistrial on several different occasions.

They should have waited. Judge Horton was the only
one, save Leibowitz, in the whole welter of self-appointed
defenders and accusers of the nine negroes who kept to
the law and the evidence, who remembered that this was
a case of nine boys accused of a crime and likely to die
for it.

Men were fighting passionately for their principles;
radicals and conservatives; Southerners and Northerners;
the prejudiced and the supposedly unprejudiced: all were
enjoying the fight for the sake of the fight. They had
lost sight of first causes in the spurs to their localism,
their patriotism, their prejudice, their liberalism, or some
equally alien cause.

Leibowitz had a job to do. What acquittal might mean
to one group or the martyrdom of conviction to another
was nothing to him. These, his clients, were innocent and
they must be acquitted. He was not sorry that there were
strong humanitarian angles to the case. He was not sorry
that handling the case would bring him international fame.
It did not disturb him that he would be associated with
communists; he was not being paid by them. Nor was he
perturbed over the number of enemies he was bound to
make in the South.

Once he had taken the case the sweat of the artist was
upon him. Were he able to sort the pieces he had in hand

to form the balanced and perfect pattern necessary, he would achieve his masterpiece.

The pattern included no far-sweeping indictment of Alabama or its jury system, no plea for racial tolerance save as these were vitally related to his central motif. Great principles might be established, far-sweeping changes might come as the result of his work on this case; that was aside from the point; it was the case itself that was important.

No more did Horton let extraneous principles affect his view of the case. He was a Southerner, a resident of Alabama. He knew that many would turn on him, respected though he was and clothed with the authority of justice, should he appear to them to be favoring the negroes. He recognized Leibowitz' right to build a case for appeal for his clients, but he refused to stop the trial even when Leibowitz had proved his point. These details were for the higher courts should the case have to go there. No one scrutinizing his actions during the trial could help but feel that he hoped this case would be tried on the evidence.

But the jury did not try the case on the evidence. All the testimony at the trial was incompetent, immaterial and irrelevant from the point of view of those twelve men once they had heard Victoria Price make her accusation. The point at stake was not the guilt or innocence of the nine colored boys. They were guilty—guilty of being accused of rape by a white woman.

This is a point of view not readily understood by a Northerner, although in rape cases in any section there is a tendency to consider an accusation as tantamount to proof of guilt.

Morgan county's point of view as regards negroes is

not so much one of hatred as of fear. While a great deal of talk is heard about the inviolability of white women, the basic reason for lynching, judicial as well as actual, is less idealistic and much more deeply rooted than that. Your Southerner is fond of negroes, singly and specifically, but fears them in the mass. He feels that without the shadow of the speedily erected gallows, there will be no control of them.

"If we let these niggers go, whether they're guilty or innocent, it won't be safe for a white woman to walk the streets."

It would have been much more to the point as far as that Decatur jury was concerned to show evidence that acquittal of these boys, since they were falsely accused, might tend to improve the conduct of other negroes. But such evidence would not have been allowed under the law.

There was only one other answer in Decatur. Judge Horton could set aside the verdict. That he would was not even considered in Morgan county and hardly hoped for by the defense. So his announcement, made two months after the trials ended, came as a surprise to every one.

Leibowitz' every point was vindicated by Judge Horton in his seven thousand word opinion. The reversal was granted on grounds of insufficient evidence.

"In order to convict the defendant," he wrote, "Victoria Price must have sworn truly to the fact of being raped. The state relies on the evidence of the prosecutrix, as to the fact of the crime itself, necessarily claiming that her relation is true. The defense insists that her evidence is a fabrication, fabricated for the purpose of saving herself from a prosecution for vagrancy or some other charge.

"With seven boys present at the beginning of this trouble, with one seeing the entire affair, with some fifty or sixty persons meeting them at Paint Rock and taking the women, the white boy, Gilley, and the nine negroes in charge, with two physicians examining the women within one to one and one-half hours, according to the tendency of all the evidence, after the occurrence of the alleged rape, and with all the acts charged committed in broad daylight, we should expect from all this cloud of witnesses or from the mute and telling physical condition of the women or their clothes, some one fact in corroboration of this story.

"And yet, none of the seven white boys, or Orville Gilley, who remained on the train, was put on the stand, except Lester Carter.

"Neither Dr. Bridges nor Dr. Lynch, who aided him in examining the girls, saw the wound inflicted on the head by the pistol, the lacerated or bleeding back which lay on jagged rocks. The semen found in the vagina of Victoria Price was of small amount and the spermatozoa were non-motile or dead. They saw no blood flowing from the vagina. They did not testify as to seeing the semen all spattered over the coat or blood and semen on the clothes; or any torn garments or clothes. These doctors testified that when brought to the office that day neither woman was hysterical nor nervous about it all. Their respiration and pulse were normal.

"The conclusion becomes clearer and clearer that this woman was not forced into intercourse with all of these negroes upon that train, but that her condition was clearly due to the intercourse that she had had on the nights previous to this time."

Another point that Judge Horton felt was sufficient in

itself for a reversal was the fact that Victoria had washed the garments that might have proven—or disproven—her claims.

Improbability of the evidence he summed up as follows:

"Rape is a crime usually committed in secrecy. A secluded place or a place where one ordinarily would not be observed is the natural selection for the scene of such a crime. The time and place and stage of this alleged act are such as to make one wonder and question did such an act occur under such circumstances.

"The day is a sunshiny day the latter part of March; the time of day is shortly after the noon hour. The place is upon a gondola or car without a top. The gondola, according to the evidence of the conductor, was filled to within six inches to twelve or fourteen inches of the top. The whole performance necessarily was in plain view of any one observing the train as it passed. Open gondolas on each side. On top of this chert twelve negroes rape two white women. They undress them while they are standing up on the chert. This continues without intermission although that freight train travels for some forty miles through the heart of Jackson County, through Fackler, Hollywood, Scottsboro, Larkinsville, Lin Rock and Woodville, slowing up at several of these places until it is halted at Paint Rock.

"Gilley, a white boy, pulled back on the train by the negroes, according to Victoria Price, sitting off in one end of the gondola, is a witness to the whole scene; and yet he stays on the train, does not attempt to get help although no compulsion is being exercised on him. And in the end by a fortuitous circumstance just before the train pulls into Paint Rock, the rapists cease, and just in the nick of time the overalls are drawn up and fastened and the women appear clothed as the posse sighted them. The natural inclination of the mind is to doubt and to cease further search.

"The testimony of the prosecutrix was contradictory, often evasive, and time and again she refused to answer pertinent questions. The gravity of the offense and the importance of her testimony demanded candor and sincerity. In addition to this, the proof tends strongly to show that she knowingly testified falsely in many material aspects of the case."

Full credence was given to Lester Carter's evidence showing that Victoria had spent the night with Jack Tiller before going to Chattanooga, and had slept side by side with Orville Gilley in the Chattanooga hobo jungles.

Due note was taken of the condition of the negroes who were put on the stand by Leibowitz, of the variety of testimony regarding which car the fight occurred in, and the conflicting statements as to where the boys were taken from the train.

In a final indictment Judge Horton stated:

"History, sacred and profane, and the common experience of mankind, teach us that women of the character shown in this case are prone for selfish reasons to make false accusations both of rape and of insult upon the slightest provocation, or even without provocation for ulterior purposes. These women are shown by the very great weight of evidence, on this very day, before leaving Chattanooga, to have falsely accused two negroes of insulting them and of almost precipitating a fight between one of the white boys they were in company with and these two negroes. This tendency on the part of the women shows that they are predisposed to make false accusations upon any occasion where their selfish ends may be gained.

"The testimony of the prosecutrix in this case is not only uncorroborated, but it also bears on its face indications of improbability, and is contradicted by other evidence, and in addition thereto the evidence greatly preponderates in favor of the defendant.

"It is therefore ordered and adjudged by the court that the motion be granted that the verdict of the jury in this case and the judgment of the court sentencing this defendant to death be and the same is hereby set aside, and that a new trial be and the same is hereby ordered."

JUDGE HORTON's decision was a major victory for the defense. The colored boys were still in jail, all of them now waiting to be tried. Back where they were in 1931, except that now they had able counsel, counsel that had secured for them finally a judicial opinion on the evidence that should make further railroading difficult.

And the Messers. Brodsky and Patterson are ordering their own Stetson hats.

CHAPTER SEVENTEEN

TWO LITTLE WORDS

SCOTTSBORO was but a vacation interlude in the Leibowitz career, an excursion into the larger domain of law and issues, allowing him untrammeled emotional and experimental elbow room. It introduced him to the world as a humanitarian, a champion of the cause of the underdog. But he is first and foremost a criminal lawyer, and it was as such that he achieved his notable victory with Judge Horton.

The case was significant as indicating his progression. Scarcely more than a decade after he had represented a pickpocket in an obscure police court, he was appearing as chief advocate in a *cause célèbre,* in which the learned justices of the United States Supreme Court clashed with their brothers of the robe in Alabama. The case lifted Leibowitz out of the local milieu of New York and definitely established him as a national figure, with something of a foreshadowing of the legal stature of his illustrious predecessor, Clarence Darrow.

Biographies generally are written when their subjects are either deceased or in the sere and yellow. Leibowitz is still in the making. His future is in the lap of the gods. Only forty, he is just rounding into his full stride.

The distinguishing trait that has carried him on and up is a terrific inner compulsion, sending him into action with a thrust and a drive akin to a steam battering ram. His mind is omnivorous, his concentrative energy boundless, and his lust for the courtroom fray unappeasable. He sniffs it from afar, as he did Scottsboro.

The force of his aplomb and his deadly earnestness of purpose always make him a storm center. Opposing counsel frequently regard him aghast. Judges have repeatedly admonished him. It is not that Leibowitz doesn't know the law; it is that in the fury of the strife he is pressing every advantage for his client. His forte is preparation. No minute detail escapes him. He goes into court fortified for any eventuality. He has caused more men and women charged with crime to be turned loose than any other living member of the bar, but:

"I have merely given the defendant the full measure of his constitutional rights before the law."

It has been said he holds the world's record for snatching men from the electric chair, yet:

"I have only performed my professional duty as a lawyer in defending them. I have been accused of making murder safe in New York. It has been said that I take up the cudgels for the guilty, and defend menaces to society.

"That is not accurately put. My clients do not tell me they are guilty, nor are they, before the law, until their guilt is established. I have never defended a man who told me he was guilty as charged. When a man tells me he is not guilty, I may believe him to be guilty, and I have tried some cases of that kind. But what I think personally is beside the point."

Leibowitz is both a symbol of melting pot opportunity

—an immigrant boy who made good—and a symptom of what is wrong with the American system of jurisprudence —the need for reforms in procedure, and the revision of antiquated statutes to cope with the lawless element in this era of highly organized crime.

The Leibowitzes and the Darrows are not to blame for the technicalities that now handicap prosecutors. It is, in fact, their bounden duty to advantage themselves of the law's defects in the interest of their clients.

"And I get a thrill out of it," says Leibowitz, "because all the magic in the dictionary is summed up for me in two little words:

"Not Guilty."

THE END

Lightning Source UK Ltd.
Milton Keynes UK
174832UK00001B/111/A